Christopher Walsh

"Who are they that they should
beat a Michigan team?"
—FIELDING H. YOST

TRIUMPH
BOOKS

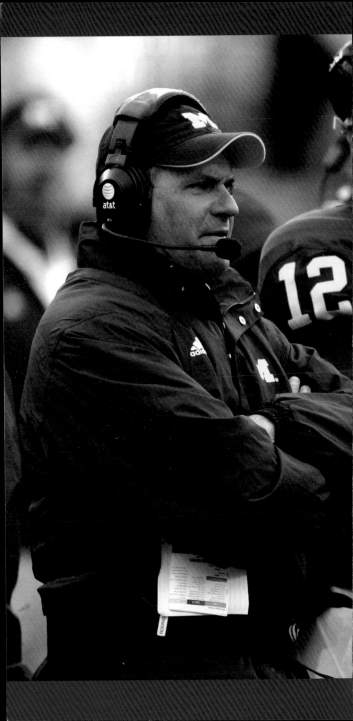

Table of Contents

Introduction

It was 1903, two years after the son of a Confederate soldier from West Virginia had arrived in Ann Arbor and pronounced the school name as "Meeshegan." Fielding H. Yost, one of the game's great innovators, seemingly always did things a little differently, much to the delight of the first and original fans of University of Michigan football.

In Yost's first 28 games no opponent defeated Michigan, including Stanford in the first Tournament of Roses Game, and only two had managed to score any points at all. His "point-a-minute" teams outscored the opposition 1,636–12, making it an early dynasty and the envy of every school in the nation.

After rolling into Minneapolis for a Halloween showdown with Minnesota, Yost, fearful that the home fans might contaminate his team's water supply (which at the time wasn't as far-fetched an idea as one might think), told Thomas B. Roberts to purchase a large container to ease his angst. The student manager secured a bland looking five-gallon jug for 30 cents from a local store.

Eager to prove its worth, Minnesota yielded only one touchdown and with roughly two minutes remaining reached the end zone to tie the game 6–6 at jam-packed Northrop Field. Fans stormed the field in celebration, and with an impending storm looming the game was called a tie (both teams would finish the season unbeaten).

In the middle of the chaos, the discarded jug was left behind and eventually brought by custodian Oscar Munson to L.J. Cooke, the head of the Minnesota athletics department. It was painted brown, and someone wrote on it: "Michigan Jug—Captured by Oscar, October 31, 1903" with the score "Michigan 6, Minnesota 6."

When Yost wrote asking for the jug back, Cooke wasn't ready to give up the makeshift trophy and responded: "We have your little brown jug; if you want it, you'll have to win it."

Michigan did in 1909, and that's how college football's oldest trophy-game tradition began, fittingly with one of the most decorated programs.

Some of the names now synonymous with the Wolverines include Bo Schembechler, Tom Harmon, Desmond Howard, Charles Woodson, Anthony Carter, Tom Brady, Benny Friedman, Rick Leach, and Bennie Oosterbaan.

Its traditions include the winged helmet, maize and blue, "The Victors," the "Big House," the "Go Blue" banner, "The 10-Year War," and lots and lots of trophies.

Michigan has the most victories in Division I-A (or Bowl Subdivision) history, has been ranked in season-ending Associated Press polls more than any other school, and can claim nine national titles and 42 conference championships.

It's left a lot more in its wake than a water jug. ∎

SEASON PREVIEW

When the University of Michigan hired Rich Rodriguez to replace Lloyd Carr as head football coach, the assumption was that his first season would be a rebuilding one while installing schemes he developed at his alma mater, West Virginia.

No one dared envision what occurred in 2008: the worst season in the 129-year history of Michigan football.

The Wolverines finished with a school-record nine losses, had the first losing season in 41 years, and missed a bowl game for the first time since 1967.

It dropped a record fifth straight to archrival Ohio State, allowed a school-record 347 points, and lost to rivals Ohio State, Notre Dame, and Michigan State in the same season for the first time since 1987.

It definitely took a toll on the first-year coach.

After losing the school's first-ever meeting against Toledo, marking Michigan's first defeat at the hands of the Mid-American Conference after 24 victories, Rodriguez said, "I'm just extremely disappointed and embarrassed."

When Michigan was a 20½-point underdog to Ohio State, the largest spread in the history of the series, and lost by 35, he snapped about the losing streak, "I've been here for one of them. So that's the only one I can really comment on. They've got one in a row on us, from what I've seen."

When later asked about what he learned from the difficult season, he responded, "Probably being quieter is better. Coach (Jim) Tressel and I talked about that before the (Ohio State) game. I said, 'Coach Tress, the quieter I am, the less drama I have to deal with.'"

With that the coach spoke volumes, especially following the rocky start that included numerous off-field distractions like Rodriguez suing his previous employer regarding his contract and bucking some of Michigan's longstanding traditions.

Yet none of those things had anywhere near the same impact as the inexperience, lack of depth at numerous spots, and offensive struggles.

"Transitions are hard," school president Mary Sue Coleman said. "We're in it for the long run."

That had better begin in 2009, with Rodriguez bringing in his first complete class of recruits and those already on the team having a better grasp of the schemes, especially the spread-option offense.

The coach also has a history of turning things around during his second year: West Virginia went 9–4 after the initial 3–8 campaign, Clemson went 9–3 in Rodriguez's second season as offensive coordinator, and Tulane went 12–0 in his second season there.

The Wolverines may not challenge for the Big Ten title, but the goal is to eventually end up back where Michigan has frequently been, on top.

"Coach (Bo) Schembechler, Coach (Gary) Moeller, Coach Carr had built the program to the point where playing at home in that Big House and that winged helmet comes out, there was a certain feeling that, 'Boy, it's going to be a tough game,'" Rodriguez said. "It's worth 10 to 14 points right there. That ain't the case anymore. That's obvious. Now I'd like to build it up to that point, and that's part of our challenge and our goal, but we're not there anymore where just putting on the winged helmet means something. We've got to deserve that.

"Everybody wants to know when we're going to win more games. When we deserve to win more games. It's as simple as that. When we deserve to win more games, we'll win more games. That's our challenge as coaches and certainly our challenge in our program in our players to get to that point. We'll get there. It's taken longer than I want, but we'll get there." ∎

Offense

Offense

The questions arose long before the University of Michigan offense led the Big Ten with 30 turnovers or failed to score more than once after having seven possessions in Ohio State territory.

Missed opportunities, lack of big plays despite having some prized young players, and not having an experienced quarterback familiar with Rich Rodriguez's spread-option attack took their toll in 2008, when the Wolverines offense ranked 109th in the nation (290.8 yards per game).

"The missed opportunities are a big thing we've dealt with all year," Rodriguez said. "We are not good enough to win ball games without taking advantage of those opportunities."

Actually, the questions started with the previous recruiting class, when top-rated prospect Terrelle Pryor opted to attend rival Ohio State, in part because he felt playing the spread wouldn't prepare him enough for the NFL. The quarterback helped lead the Buckeyes to the Fiesta Bowl.

Meanwhile, Michigan reached 25 points in just three games.

"I saw Michigan faking a play and having all 11 players look to the sideline and trying to come up with a different way to trick Miami of Ohio," television announcer Gary Danielson said. "They used to break the huddle and say, 'you can't stop us,' and they were pretty good on offense before. That was the day I said, 'That's it for me.'"

That will be the task of the 2009 season, to prove that not only is it not time to panic but also that the spread option can work at a major power like Michigan.

The tricky part will be to develop and improve while simultaneously featuring a number of young players—although the running game should be paced by an established veteran.

"You can't really blame Rich Rodriguez because everybody on the team did not buy in like they're supposed to," tailback Brandon Minor said. "We have a couple of guys not going hard. We'll correct that most definitely. That ain't going to happen on my watch as a senior."

Minor emerged his junior year to lead the team with 533 rushing yards and nine touchdowns, including an impressive performance against Penn State with 117 yards and two touchdowns. Sam McGuffie, who was supposed to be the featured back and had 486 yards and three touchdowns as a freshman, transferred.

"I'm going to prepare myself so that this doesn't happen again," Minor said. "I'm going to bust my tail and hope that others follow.

"I promise it won't be like this next year."

Two others to keep an eye on in 2009 are offensive lineman David Molk and wide receiver Martavious Odoms, both named to the Big Ten's All-Freshman team. They, along with whoever might emerge among the incoming recruits, could be heavily leaned upon as the coaches look to begin the turnaround.

"As far as buying in, I think the majority of them have," Rodrgiuez said. "But there is a handful who still maybe question things themselves, maybe their confidence, their role, how they can contribute, and I think that's typical everywhere in a transition year. But it wasn't as much as maybe I thought. But, again, until it's a hundred percent, then you don't know what you have.

"Everybody, as we move forward, will be guys who play for Michigan first and foremost and believe in this program and this university and if not, then they won't be playing for Michigan. It's as simple as that." ■

Defense

Defense

When defensive end Brandon Graham was named the 2008 winner of the Bo Schembechler Award, as the University of Michigan football team's MVP, he seemed genuinely surprised.

"I didn't see this one coming," Graham said after the team's season-ending banquet. "I didn't think I would be up here 'til next year."

Perhaps he should have looked closer at the team statistics, because no one on the roster stood out more in 2008. With 10 sacks and 20 tackles for a loss, he was one of the few bright spots during a dismal season in which the Wolverines gave up more points, 28.9 per game, than any Michigan team since statistics have been kept.

Graham's numbers were enough to finish second nationally in tackles for a loss, and third in Big Ten sacks, which was somewhat alarming because he was the lone non-senior starter on the line.

With experience up front and in the secondary, the defense carried the team through the first four games— or rather kept Michigan in the first four games—when it went 2–2 and pulled off a 27–25 upset of No. 9 Wisconsin.

Illinois, with Juice Williams tallying 431 yards of total offense, the most ever for an opposing player at the Big House, signaled the unit's regression. Notre Dame had already scored 35 points, and Illinois 45, but that was followed by 46 from Penn State, 35 by Michigan State, and 48 at Purdue.

Season Preview

"I'm going to keep going back to work. What do you want me to say?" Coach Rich Rodriguez said after the Purdue loss. "We're going to get up, go through the same routine. We're going to get up, work tomorrow, try to get better."

Actually, the Wolverines didn't just go through the same routine, and along the way the coaches made the surprise move of switching from a 4-3 base to a 3-3-5. For whatever reason, the results were nothing to boast about: big plays (like in the 42–7 loss to Ohio State), blown assignments, miscommunication, and a whole lot of confusion.

"It was just us, things that were going on on the sidelines," freshman defensive lineman Mike Martin told the *Ann Arbor News* after the Ohio State loss. "Guys who needed to be out weren't out. They were behind everybody (on the sideline). It was hard for them to get out."

Michigan finished ninth in the Big Ten with 366.9 yards per game and was 68th nationally in total defense. To put that into perspective, the previous year the Wolverines ranked second in the Big Ten in pass defense.

Consequently, at season's end defensive coordinator Scott Shafer, one of the few outsiders Rodriguez brought in for his staff (most of the other assistants followed him from West Virginia), stepped down. His replacement was none other than Greg Robinson, the former defensive coordinator of the Kansas City Chiefs, New York Jets, and Denver Broncos, and co-defensive coordinator and linebackers coach at Texas in 2004 when the Longhorns beat Michigan in the Rose Bowl.

"Greg's a high energy, creative, hard-working guy who has had success at both the NFL and collegiate levels," Texas Coach Mack Brown said in a statement. "He's a veteran coach with a wealth of knowledge who the players really respond to. His season here in 2004 produced one of the best defenses in Texas history and helped set the stage for our national championship season in 2005." ■

Player to Watch: Tate Forcier

In a perfect world—well, perfect for University of Michigan football—Pat White would have been able to follow his coach from West Virginia to Ann Arbor.

Instead, there were a lot of growing pains during Rich Rodriguez's first season leading the Wolverines, especially at quarterback. Between unproven Steven Threet, Nick Sheridan, and Justin Feagin, he hoped one would take to his spread-option attack and control of the offense.

Although they all played well in stretches, it didn't happen.

"They really tried hard," Rodriguez said. "Now, they're going to have to compete. But they're going to have to compete with everybody else that comes in."

That competitor is likely Tate Forcier, a 6-foot-1, 190-pound product of San Diego (Calif.) Scripps Ranch, who hails from a quarterback family. His brother Jason played at Michigan before transferring to Stanford because his skills didn't fit then-coach Lloyd Carr's pro-style offense and brother Chris is on the roster at UCLA.

Forcier and six of his new teammates enrolled early in January to get a head start on preparing for the 2009 season. One of the players he'll likely be throwing to is Feagin, who moved to slot receiver.

Actually, for much of the recruiting season it appeared that Forcier would have immediate com-

Coach Rich Rodriguez and Michigan's fortunes will be tied in part to how well highly regarded Tate Forcier plays at quarterback in 2009.

petition from another top-notch recruit, but Kevin Newsome reopened his recruitment in August and eventually signed with Penn State, and Texas native Shavodrick Beaver surprised Michigan fans by dropping the Wolverines to stay closer to home with Tulsa.

However, of the three, Forcier appeared to be the best fit for Rodriguez's system. "The 6-foot-1, 190-pound Forcier runs 40 yards in 4.55 seconds and has completed better than 69 percent of his passes each of the last three seasons," Josh Helmholdt wrote in the *Detroit Free Press*. "Because Forcier is further along in his development than Beaver, he was the odds-on favorite between the two to make an impact at quarterback next fall for the Wolverines."

Rodriguez wasn't afraid to start Pat White as a freshman at West Virginia, although he was a costarter with Adam Bednarek until the seventh game of the season. West Virginia went on to play Georgia in the Sugar Bowl and won 38–35. White passed for 6,049 yards over his career, with his 4,480 rushing yards a Bowl Subdivision quarterback record.

With Michigan making a big push to reclaim its own state, while at the same time continuing to look nationwide, the Wolverines added one of the top recruiting classes in the nation, of which many could make immediate contributions.

However, quarterback is obviously the key for Rodriguez and one of the reasons why former Michigan standout Rick Leach decided to spice up the offseason with the following comment at a team banquet: "I'll make you a promise before I go. My promise to you is, I know that day's coming. Maybe you had your fun and got your pound of flesh out of Michigan after 33 years. I don't care if it's Mark Dantonio, Charlie Weis, or—you better believe it—Jim Tressel. Your freakin' day is coming." ■

Tate Forcier fires downfield during the 2009 spring game. One of the men who will be trusted to carry the Wolverines into the future, Forcier is a highly touted recruit who will have to prove that he is the man to quarterback the team in 2009.

The Wolverine defense tries to chase down Tate Forcier during the 2009 spring game. Forcier may be at the head of his class, but there are several big-name recruits coming to UM.

2009 National Signing Day Class

Isaiah Bell	LB	6-0	209	Youngstown, Ohio
William Campbell	DT	6-5	317	Detroit, Mich.
Vladimir Emilien	DB	6-0	186	Lauderhill, Fla.
Tate Forcier	QB	6-0	184	San Diego, Calif.
Jeremy Gallon	ATH	5-8	165	Apopka, Fla.
Brendan Gibbons	K	6-0	202	West Palm Beach, Fla.
Cameron Gordon	WR	6-2	211	Inkster, Mich.
Thomas Gordon	ATH	5-10	199	Detroit, Mich.
Brandin Hawthorne	LB	6-0	181	Pahokee, Fla.
Mike Jones	DB	6-2	200	Orlando, Fla.
Teric Jones	RB	5-8	186	Detroit, Mich.
Anthony LaLota	DE	6-6	260	Princeton, N.J.
Taylor Lewan	OL	6-7	272	Scottsdale, Ariz.
Denard Robinson	ATH	6-0	179	Deerfield Beach, Fla.
Craig Roh	DE	6-5	230	Scottsdale, Ariz.
Michael Schofield	OL	6-6	272	Orland Park, Ill.
Vincent Smith	RB	5-6	159	Pahokee, Fla.
Je'Ron Stokes	WR	6-1	178	Philadelphia, Penn.
Fitzgerald Toussaint	RB	5-10	185	Youngstown, Ohio
Justin Turner	DB	6-2	186	Massillon, Ohio
Quinton Washington	OL	6-3	315	St. Stephen, S.C.
Adrian Witty	DB	5-9	175	Deerfield Beach, Fla.

The University of Michigan

Location: Ann Arbor, Michigan

Founded: 1917

Enrollment: 41,042

Nickname: Wolverines

Colors: Maize and blue

Mascot: The original live wolverine was named "Biff."

Stadium: Michigan Stadium (107,501, with ongoing renovations scheduled to be completed in 2010), nicknamed the "Big House"

Tickets: (734) 764-0247 or (866) 296-MTIX (6849)

Website: www.mgoblue.com

Consensus National Championships (3): 1947, 1948, 1997

Other National Championships (8): 1901, 1902, 1903, 1904, 1918, 1923, 1932, 1933

Big Ten Championships (42): 1898, 1901, 1902, 1903, 1904, 1906, 1918, 1922, 1923, 1925, 1926, 1930, 1931, 1932, 1933, 1943, 1947, 1948, 1949, 1950, 1964, 1969, 1971, 1972, 1973, 1974, 1976, 1977, 1978, 1980, 1982, 1986, 1988, 1989, 1990, 1991, 1992, 1997, 1998, 2000, 2003, 2004

Bowl Appearances: 39 (19–20)

First Season: 1879

2008 SEASON REVIEW

J.B. Fitzgerald drops Utah's David Reed in the second half of the 2008 season opener. The loss to Utah stung, but the Utes proved to be a strong team, going undefeated and finishing with a win over Alabama in the Sugar Bowl.

Game 1: Utah 25, Michigan 23

ANN ARBOR | Utah spoiled Rick Rodriguez's debut, and for the second straight year Michigan opened the season with a loss to a non-Bowl Championship Series school.

"They deserved to win," Rodriguez said.

Utah dominated most of the game, but a blocked punt and a fumble in the fourth quarter led to two Michigan touchdowns.

The last time the Wolverines lost consecutive openers (Appalachian State in 2007) was 1989–90, with both games against Notre Dame.

	1st Qtr	2nd Qtr	3rd Qtr	4th Qtr	Final
UTAH	6	16	3	0	**25**
MICHIGAN	10	0	0	13	**23**

SCORING PLAYS

MICHIGAN–TD, M Shaw 8 YD PASS FROM N Sheridan (K Lopata KICK) 3:40 1st Qtr

UTAH–TD, C Louks 8 YD RUN (PAT FAILED) 7:22 1st Qtr

MICHIGAN–FG, 50 YD 9:42 1st Qtr

UTAH–FG, L Sakoda 28 YD 0:56 2nd Qtr

UTAH–FG, L Sakoda 43 YD 5:12 2nd Qtr

UTAH–FG, L Sakoda 41 YD 11:45 2nd Qtr

UTAH–TD, B Godfrey 19 YD PASS FROM B Johnson (L Sakoda KICK) 14:47 2nd Qtr

UTAH–FG, L Sakoda 53 YD 7:23 3rd Qtr

MICHIGAN–TD, J Hemingway 33 YD PASS FROM S Threet (K Lopata KICK) 6:18 4th Qtr

MICHIGAN–TD, S McGuffie 3 YD RUN (TWO-POINT CONVERSION FAILED) 8:34 4th Qtr

GAME STATISTICS

	UTAH	MICHIGAN
First Downs	16	11
Yards Rushing	43–36	25–36
Yards Passing	305	167
Sacks – Yards Lost	6–39	3–7
Passing Efficiency	21–34–1	19–38–1
Punts	7–40.3	8–37.4
Fumbles–Lost	4–2	3–2
Penalties–Yards	15–137	8–53
Time of Possession	35:54	24:06

INDIVIDUAL STATISTICS – RUSHING
UTAH–Matt Asiata 13–77, Darrell Mack 8–17, Corbin Louks 1–8, Brent Casteel 1–0, Brian Johnson 20–MINUS 66. MICHIGAN–Brandon Minor 4–21, Sam McGuffie 8–8, Carlos Brown 1–4, Nick Sheridan 5–2, Michael Shaw 2–1, Steven Threet 5–0.

INDIVIDUAL STATISTICS – PASSING
UTAH–Brian Johnson 21–33–305–1. Team 0–1–0–0. MICHIGAN–Nick Sheridan 11–19–98–1. Steven Threet 8–19–69–0.

INDIVIDUAL STATISTICS – RECEIVING
UTAH–Bradon Godfrey 7–84, Freddie Brown 5–59, Jereme Brooks 1–55, Brent Casteel 5–49, Matt Asiata 1–39, David Reed 2–19. MICHIGAN–Greg Mathews 3–54, Junior Hemingway 2–41, Sam McGuffie 2–22, Carson Butler 2–17, Michael Shaw 3–17, Martavious Odoms 5–7, Darryl Stonum 1–5, Brandon Minor 1–4.

ATTENDANCE: 108,421

Game 2: Michigan 16, Miami (Ohio) 6

ANN ARBOR | Brandon Minor's 15-yard touchdown with 8:12 remaining helped Michigan improve to 24–0 against the Mid-American Conference.

"I'd rather win ugly than lose pretty," said Rodriguez, who also described his emotions at the start to the season as "Very frustrated. Exasperated. But we're not going to quit grinding away."

Looking for a quarterback to become the undisputed starter, Rodriguez twice inserted Nick Sheridan into the game.

"It's like a Clint Eastwood movie, *The Good, the Bad and the Ugly*," Rodriguez said. "I was hoping one of them would play so well we wouldn't have to [rotate]. But it's not just them."

	1st Qtr	2nd Qtr	3rd Qtr	4th Qtr	Final
MIAMI (OH)	0	3	3	0	**6**
MICHIGAN	10	0	0	6	**16**

SCORING PLAYS

MICHIGAN–TD, S Threet 12 YD RUN (K Lopata KICK) 4:12 1st Qtr

MICHIGAN–FG, K Lopata 47 YD 6:06 1st Qtr

MIAMI OH–FG, N Parseghian 26 YD 11:01 2nd Qtr

MIAMI OH–FG, N Parseghian 26 YD 8:22 3rd Qtr

MICHIGAN–TD, B Minor 15 YD RUN (PAT FAILED) 6:48 4th Qtr

GAME STATISTICS

	MIAMI OH	MICHIGAN
First Downs	16	15
Yards Rushing	32–47	35–178

2008 Review

Brandon Minor leaps over the Miami defense to score a touchdown in the Wolverines' 16–6 victory. The 15-yard scamper provided the final margin of victory in Michigan's first win of the year.

Yards Passing	205	103
Sacks – Yards Lost	3–30	0–0
Passing Efficiency	23–40–0	10–18–0
Punts	7–377	7–318
Fumbles–Lost	2–1	0–0
Penalties–Yards	4–30	2–15
Time of Possession	35:13	24:47

2008 Review

INDIVIDUAL STATISTICS – RUSHING

MIAMI OH–Thomas Merriweather 21–77, Andre Bratton 1–MINUS 1, Daniel Raudabaugh 7–MINUS 3, Jamal Rogers 1–MINUS 5, Clay Belton 2–MINUS 21. MICHIGAN–Sam McGuffie 17–74, Michael Shaw 2–45, Steven Threet 5–26, Brandon Minor 1–15, Nick Sheridan 2–10, Mark Moundros 1–7, Kevin Grady 3–6, Martavious Odoms 1–1, Team 3–MINUS 6.

INDIVIDUAL STATISTICS – PASSING

MIAMI OH–Daniel Raudabaugh 20–33–191–0, Clay Belton 3–7–14–0. MICHIGAN–Steven Threet 6–13–63–0, Nick Sheridan 4–5–40–0.

INDIVIDUAL STATISTICS – RECEIVING

MIAMI OH–Jamal Rogers 9–78, Dustin Woods 4–63, Eugene Harris 3–26, Chris Givens 2–19, Donovan Potter 1–6, Thomas Merriweather 1–6, Jake O'Connell 1–3, Jamel Miller 1–3, Andre Bratton 1–1. MICHIGAN–Martavious Odoms 3–57, Sam McGuffie 3–32, Darryl Stonum 1–8, Toney Clemons 2–3, Michael Shaw 1–3.

ATTENDANCE: 106,724

Game 3: Notre Dame 35, Michigan 17

SOUTH BEND | Although Notre Dame Coach Charlie Weis tore ligaments in his right knee after being hit along the sideline during the second quarter, the Fighting Irish took advantage of six turnovers, including four fumbles.

Jimmy Clausen, who was sacked eight times in the 2007 meeting, had two touchdown passes and two interceptions and wasn't sacked. Michigan had won the two previous meetings 38–0 and 47–21.

Rich Rodriguez became the first Michigan coach to start 1–2 or worse since Bump Elliot was 1–2 in 1959.

	1st Qtr	2nd Qtr	3rd Qtr	4th Qtr	Final
MICHIGAN	7	10	0	0	**17**
NOTRE DAME	21	7	0	7	**35**

SCORING PLAYS

NOTRE DAME–TD, R Hughes 2 YD RUN (B Walker KICK) 3:08 1st Qtr

NOTRE DAME–TD, D Kamara 10 YD PASS FROM J Clausen (B Walker KICK) 4:00 1st Qtr

NOTRE DAME–TD, G Tate 48 YD PASS FROM J Clausen (B Walker KICK) 10:09 1st Qtr

MICHIGAN–TD, S McGuffie 40 YD PASS FROM S Threet (K Lopata KICK) 13:04 1st Qtr

MICHIGAN–FG, K Lopata 23 YD 3:07 2nd Qtr

NOTRE DAME–TD, R Hughes 1 YD RUN (B Walker KICK) 6:13 2nd Qtr

MICHIGAN–TD, K Grady 7 YD RUN (K Lopata KICK) 9:19 2nd Qtr

NOTRE DAME–TD, B Smith 35 YD FUMBLE RETURN (B Walker KICK) 0:10 4th Qtr

MICHIGAN FOOTBALL

GAME STATISTICS

	MICHIGAN	NOTRE DAME
First Downs	21	14
Yards Rushing	42–159	34–113
Yards Passing	229	147
Sacks – Yards Lost	0–0	0–0
Passing Efficiency	19–28–2	10–21–2
Punts	4–52.8	6–43.8
Fumbles–Lost	7–4	3–0
Penalties–Yards	7–79	3–38
Time of Possession	32:12	27:48

INDIVIDUAL STATISTICS – RUSHING
MICHIGAN–Sam McGuffie 25–131, Zoltan Mesko 1–13, Steven Threet 5–8, Michael Shaw 2–5, Kevin Grady 4–4, Brandon Minor 3–1, Carlos Brown 1–0, Team 1–MINUS 3. NOTRE DAME–Robert Hughes 19–79, James Aldridge 9–28, Jimmy Clausen 2–5, Armando Allen 2–4, Team 2–MINUS 3.

INDIVIDUAL STATISTICS – PASSING
MICHIGAN–Steven Threet 16–23–175–0, Nick Sheridan 3–5–54–2. NOTRE DAME–Jimmy Clausen 10–21–147–2.

INDIVIDUAL STATISTICS – RECEIVING
MICHIGAN–Martavious Odoms 6–56, Sam McGuffie 4–47, Greg Mathews 4–46, Zion Babb 2–45, Darryl Stonum 3–35. NOTRE DAME–Golden Tate 4–127, Duval Kamara 1–10, Michael Floyd 2–10, David Grimes 1–3, Robby Parris 1–0, Robert Hughes 1–MINUS 3.

ATTENDANCE: 80,795

Sam McGuffie celebrates after scoring a key touchdown in the fourth quarter against Wisconsin. The victory was a major upset against the country's ninth-ranked team and gave the Wolverines a win in their Big Ten opener.

Game 4: Michigan 27, No. 9 Wisconsin 25

ANN ARBOR | After giving up five turnovers and 19 points during the first half, leading to boos from the sellout crowd on hand for the 500th game played at the Big House, Michigan pulled off the biggest comeback in stadium history.

"Never had a doubt," Coach Rich Rodriguez joked.

Michigan took its first lead on John Thompson's 25-yard interception return for a touchdown with 10:27 remaining, just seconds after Brandon Minor's 34-yard touchdown run. However, the game wasn't decided until Wisconsin's incomplete pass on a game-tying 2-point conversion with just 13 seconds remaining.

	1st Qtr	2nd Qtr	3rd Qtr	4th Qtr	Final
WISCONSIN (9)	6	13	0	6	**25**
MICHIGAN	0	0	7	20	**27**

SCORING PLAYS

WISCONSIN–FG, P Welch 21 YD 5:57 1st Qtr

WISCONSIN–FG, P Welch 42 YD 13:42 1st Qtr

WISCONSIN–TD, J Clay 5 YD RUN (P Welch KICK) 9:14 2nd Qtr

WISCONSIN–FG, P Welch 41 YD 10:13 2nd Qtr

WISCONSIN–FG, P Welch 52 YD 14:50 2nd Qtr

MICHIGAN–TD, K Koger 26 YD PASS FROM S Threet (K Lopata KICK) 12:38 3rd Qtr

MICHIGAN–TD, B Minor 34 YD RUN (K Lopata KICK) 4:33 4th Qtr

MICHIGAN–TD, J Thompson 25 YD INTERCEPTION RETURN 4:36 4th Qtr

MICHIGAN–TD, S McGuffie 3 YD RUN (K Lopata KICK) 9:49 4th Qtr

WISCONSIN–TD, D Gilreath 22 YD PASS FROM A Evridge 14:47 4th Qtr

GAME STATISTICS

	WISCONSIN (9)	MICHIGAN
First Downs	18	14
Yards Rushing	44–158	34–172
Yards Passing	226	96
Sacks – Yards Lost	4–20	0–0
Passing Efficiency	20–37–2	12–31–2
Punts	6–39.8	8–43.5
Fumbles–Lost	3–2	4–3
Penalties–Yards	5–45	4–30
Time of Possession	36:04	23:56

INDIVIDUAL STATISTICS – RUSHING
WISCONSIN–P.J. Hill 22–70, John Clay 3–52, Zach Brown 8–46, Bill Rentmeester 1–9, Isaac Anderson 1–3, Allan Evridge 9–MINUS 22. MICHIGAN–Steven Threet 9–89, Sam McGuffie 15–36, Brandon Minor 2–35, Kevin Grady 5–17, Carlos Brown 1–0, Team 1–MINUS 2, Martavious Odoms 1–MINUS 3.

INDIVIDUAL STATISTICS – PASSING
WISCONSIN–Allan Evridge 20–37–226–2. MICHIGAN–Steven Threet 12–31–96–2.

INDIVIDUAL STATISTICS – RECEIVING
WISCONSIN–David Gilreath 5–65, P.J. Hill 3–38, Lance Kendricks 1–29, Kyle Jefferson 4–24, Mickey Turner 1–22, Nick Toon 1–18, Travis Beckum 2–17, Isaac Anderson 2–16, Elijah Theus 1–MINUS 3. MICHIGAN–Greg Mathews 4–48, Kevin Koger 1–26, Brandon Minor 1–11, Carlos Brown 3–10, Martavious Odoms 2–4, Sam McGuffie 1–MINUS 3.

ATTENDANCE: 109,833

Game 5: Illinois 45, Michigan 20

ANN ARBOR | Although Michigan got off to a good start with 14 points in the first quarter, Illinois scored 28 unanswered points for its first victory in the Big House since 1999.

It was the most points the Illini have ever scored against the Wolverines and matched the famed Red Grange game of 1924 as the Illinois program's most lopsided victory over Michigan.

Illinois quarterback Juice Williams set a Michigan Stadium record with 431 yards of total offense (310 passing yards, two touchdowns; 121 rushing yards, two touchdowns) and tied the record for most offense ever by a Michigan opponent.

	1st Qtr	2nd Qtr	3rd Qtr	4th Qtr	Final
ILLINOIS	3	14	7	21	**45**
MICHIGAN	14	0	0	6	**20**

SCORING PLAYS

MICHIGAN–TD, S McGuffie 4 YD RUN (K Lopata KICK) 6:31 1st Qtr

ILLINOIS–FG, M Eller 48 YD 9:39 1st Qtr

MICHIGAN–TD, G Mathews 11 YD PASS FROM S Threet (K Lopata KICK) 14:11 1st Qtr

ILLINOIS–TD, J Williams 6 YD RUN (M Eller KICK) 0:05 2nd Qtr

ILLINOIS–TD, D Dufrene 57 YD PASS FROM J Williams (M Eller KICK) 4:11 2nd Qtr

ILLINOIS–TD, J Cumberland 77 YD PASS FROM J Williams (M Eller KICK) 1:26 3rd Qtr

ILLINOIS–TD, J Ford 2 YD RUN (M Eller KICK) 0:37 4th Qtr

MICHIGAN–TD, M Moundros 2 YD PASS FROM S Threet (PAT FAILED) 3:06 4th Qtr

ILLINOIS–TD, M LeShoure 1 YD RUN (M Eller KICK)
7:35 4th Qtr

ILLINOIS–TD, J Williams 2 YD RUN (M Eller KICK) 8:59
4th Qtr

GAME STATISTICS

	ILLINOIS	MICHIGAN
First Downs	19	17
Yards Rushing	47–191	35–69
Yards Passing	310	250
Sacks – Yards Lost	0–0	4–33
Passing Efficiency	13–26–0	18–35–0
Punts	6–39	8–46.9
Fumbles–Lost	0–0	5–2
Penalties–Yards	4–45	6–49
Time of Possession	33:06	26:54

INDIVIDUAL STATISTICS – RUSHING
ILLINOIS–Juice Williams 19–121, Daniel Dufrene 15–46, Arrelious Benn 3–20, Jason Ford 5–9, Mikel LeShoure 4–2, Troy Pollard 1–MINUS 7. MICHIGAN–Sam McGuffie 19–70, Brandon Minor 3–14, Michael Shaw 1–6, Martavious Odoms 1–3, Steven Threet 11–MINUS 24.

INDIVIDUAL STATISTICS – PASSING
ILLINOIS–Juice Williams 13–26–310–0. MICHIGAN–Steven Threet 18–35–250–0.

INDIVIDUAL STATISTICS – RECEIVING
ILLINOIS–Arrelious Benn 6–122, Jeff Cumberland 1–77, Daniel Dufrene 2–66, Fred Sykes 2–25, William Judson 1–14, A.J. Jenkins 1–6. MICHIGAN–Martavious Odoms 7–129, Greg Mathews 4–73, James Rogers 1–24, Toney Clemons 1–9, LaTerryal Savoy 1–7, Michael Shaw 1–7, Mark Moundros 1–2, Sam McGuffie 2–MINUS 1.

ATTENDANCE: 109,750

Boubacar Cissoko wasn't able to stop the Illini's A.J. Jenkins from hauling in a pass from Juice Williams, but Cissoko did bring him down.

Game 6: Toledo 13, Michigan 10

ANN ARBOR | Nick Moore caught 20 passes, a record against Michigan, for 162 yards, and Tyrrell Herbert returned one of his two interceptions 100 yards for a touchdown as Toledo pulled off the stunning upset in the first meeting between schools separated by just 45 miles.

Michigan quarterbacks had three interceptions, and K.C. Lopata missed a game-tying 26-yard field goal with 4 seconds remaining.

It was Michigan's first loss ever to a Mid-American Conference School (24–1).

	1st Qtr	2nd Qtr	3rd Qtr	4th Qtr	Final
TOLEDO	7	0	3	3	**13**
MICHIGAN	7	3	0	0	**10**

SCORING PLAYS

TOLEDO–TD, T Herbert 100 YD INTERCEPTION RETURN (A Steigerwald KICK) 8:55 1st Qtr

MICHIGAN–TD, B Minor 27 YD PASS FROM S Threet (K Lopata KICK) 14:37 1st Qtr

MICHIGAN–FG, K Lopata 26 YD 4:38 2nd Qtr

TOLEDO–FG, A Steigerwald 29 YD 6:03 3rd Qtr

TOLEDO–FG, A Steigerwald 48 YD 3:14 4th Qtr

GAME STATISTICS

	TOLEDO	MICHIGAN
First Downs	17	19
Yards Rushing	22–70	39–170
Yards Passing	257	120
Sacks – Yards Lost	1–8	1–6
Passing Efficiency	33–50–0	15–27–3
Punts	5–41.6	5–49.6
Fumbles–Lost	1–1	0–0
Penalties–Yards	7–74	5–60
Time of Possession	33:08	26:52

INDIVIDUAL STATISTICS – RUSHING
TOLEDO–DaJuane Collins 10–65, Jake Walker 4–17, Morgan Williams 4–14, Team 1–MINUS 2, Aaron Opelt 2–MINUS 8, Barry Church 1–MINUS 16. MICHIGAN–Sam McGuffie 25–105, Nick Sheridan 5–21, Michael Shaw 4–19, Steven Threet 2–15, Kevin Grady 2–6, Mark Moundros 1–4.

INDIVIDUAL STATISTICS – PASSING
TOLEDO–Aaron Opelt 33–50–257–0. MICHIGAN–Nick Sheridan 8–16–65–2, Steven Threet 7–11–55–1.

INDIVIDUAL STATISTICS – RECEIVING
TOLEDO–Nick Moore 20–162, Stephen Williams 6–67, Robin Bailey 1–9, Jake Walker 1–9, DaJuane Collins 1–5, Tom Burzine 1–4, John Allen 3–1. MICHIGAN–Sam McGuffie 5–44, Toney Clemons 4–30, Brandon Minor 1–27, Greg Mathews 5–19.

ATTENDANCE: 107,267

Game 7: Penn State 46, Michigan 17

STATE COLLEGE | Penn State snapped its nine-game losing streak to Michigan as Joe Paterno enjoyed his 380th victory while in the press box, where he coached for the third straight week due to a sore hip and leg.

After trailing 17–7 in the first half, Penn State scored 39 unanswered points. Previously, its largest win over Michigan was just 12 points. The Wolverines had 185 offensive yards during the first quarter but just 106 the rest of the game.

Michigan came in as 23½-point underdogs, the program's largest odds disadvantage ever.

	1st Qtr	2nd Qtr	3rd Qtr	4th Qtr	Final
MICHIGAN	10	7	0	0	**17**
PENN ST (3)	7	7	12	20	**46**

SCORING PLAYS

MICHIGAN–TD, B Minor 5 YD RUN (K Lopata KICK) 8:09 1st Qtr

MICHIGAN–FG, K Lopata 27 YD 11:21 1st Qtr

PENN ST–TD, E Royster 44 YD RUN (K Kelly KICK) 12:03 1st Qtr

MICHIGAN–TD, B Minor 1 YD RUN (K Lopata KICK) 1:47 2nd Qtr

PENN ST–TD, J Norwood 3 YD PASS FROM D Clark (K Kelly KICK) 14:37 2nd Qtr

PENN ST–FG, K Kelly 42 YD 8:14 3rd Qtr

PENN ST–SAFETY, J Odrick TACKLED IN END ZONE 10:21 3rd Qtr

PENN ST–TD, D Clark 1 YD RUN (K Kelly KICK) 11:56 3rd Qtr

PENN ST–FG, K Kelly 32 YD 0:04 4th Qtr

PENN ST–TD, D Clark 1 YD RUN (K Kelly KICK) 2:41 4th Qtr

PENN ST–FG, K Kelly 20 YD 9:40 4th Qtr

PENN ST–TD, S Green 80 YD PASS FROM P Devlin (K Kelly KICK) 12:55 4th Qtr

GAME STATISTICS

	MICHIGAN	PENN ST (3)
First Downs	15	22
Yards Rushing	46–202	38–231
Yards Passing	89	251
Sacks – Yards Lost	3–17	0–0
Passing Efficiency	12–22–0	19–33–0
Punts	7–37.4	3–44.7
Fumbles–Lost	5–1	3–1
Penalties–Yards	3–27	3–20
Time of Possession	29:41	30:19

2008 Review

INDIVIDUAL STATISTICS - RUSHING
MICHIGAN–Brandon Minor 23–117, Steven Threet 14–50, Sam McGuffie 4–36, Nick Sheridan 4–1, Team 1–MINUS 2. PENN ST–Evan Royster 18–174, Daryll Clark 9–45, Stephfon Green 10–28, Team 1–MINUS 16.

INDIVIDUAL STATISTICS - PASSING
MICHIGAN–Steven Threet 9–13–84–0, Nick Sheridan 3–9–5–0. PENN ST–Daryll Clark 18–31–171–0, Pat Devlin 1–1–80–0, Derrick Williams 0–1–0–0.

INDIVIDUAL STATISTICS - RECEIVING
MICHIGAN–Martavious Odoms 3–34, Kevin Koger 3–26, James Rogers 1–21, Darryl Stonum 2–9, Greg Mathews 1–6, Brandon Minor 1–MINUS 2, Sam McGuffie 1–MINUS 5. PENN ST–Deon Butler 8–105, Stephfon Green 1–80, Jordan Norwood 4–28, Derrick Williams 2–16, Evan Royster 3–13, Mickey Shuler 1–9.

ATTENDANCE: 110,017

Game 8: Michigan State 35, Michigan 21

ANN ARBOR | A year after Mike Hart referred to Michigan State as like a "little brother" Spartans fans chanted "Little Sis-ter!" while enjoying their first victory in the Big House since 1990.

Javon Ringer ran for 194 yards and two touch-

Steven Threet shows off his scrambling skills against
Penn State. The Wolverines lost to the top dogs in the Big
Ten, but Threet rushed for 50 yards on 14 carries.

downs, his nation-leading 15th and 16th of the season. The Spartans outgained Michigan 473–252 in recording their most lopsided victory in the rivalry since 1967.

Michigan lost four home games for the first time in four decades and four in a row overall for the first time since 1967.

	1st Qtr	2nd Qtr	3rd Qtr	4th Qtr	Final
MICHIGAN ST	7	7	7	14	**35**
MICHIGAN	7	7	7	0	**21**

SCORING PLAYS

MICHIGAN ST–TD, B White 61 YD PASS FROM B Hoyer (B Swenson KICK) 3:04 1st Qtr

MICHIGAN–TD, B Minor 19 YD PASS FROM S Threet (K Lopata KICK) 13:10 1st Qtr

MICHIGAN ST–TD, J Ringer 64 YD RUN (B Swenson KICK) 13:58 2nd Qtr

MICHIGAN–TD, B Minor 2 YD RUN (K Lopata KICK) 14:40 2nd Qtr

MICHIGAN–TD, S Threet 2 YD RUN (K Lopata KICK) 5:11 3rd Qtr

MICHIGAN ST–TD, C Gantt 4 YD PASS FROM B Hoyer (B Swenson KICK) 12:23 3rd Qtr

MICHIGAN ST–TD, J Ringer 3 YD RUN (B Swenson KICK) 8:01 4th Qtr

MICHIGAN ST–TD, J Rouse 7 YD PASS FROM B Hoyer (B Swenson KICK) 11:54 4th Qtr

GAME STATISTICS

	MICHIGAN ST	MICHIGAN
First Downs	22	13
Yards Rushing	48–167	31–84

Yards Passing	306	168
Sacks – Yards Lost	5–45	4–29
Passing Efficiency	18–30–0	13–27–3
Punts	4–42.8	8–44
Fumbles–Lost	4–3	2–1
Penalties–Yards	7–52	7–70
Time of Possession	35:18	24:42

INDIVIDUAL STATISTICS – RUSHING
MICHIGAN ST–Javon Ringer 37–194, Keyshawn Martin 1–25, Andre Anderson 1–1, Team 4–MINUS 8, Brian Hoyer 5–MINUS 45. MICHIGAN–Brandon Minor 15–55, Steven Threet 14–19, Sam McGuffie 2–10.

INDIVIDUAL STATISTICS – PASSING
MICHIGAN ST–Brian Hoyer 17–29–282–0, Keyshawn Martin 1–1–24–0. MICHIGAN–Steven Threet 13–27–168–3.

INDIVIDUAL STATISTICS – RECEIVING
MICHIGAN ST–Blair White 4–143, Mark Dell 3–72, Javon Ringer 2–25, Brian Hoyer 1–24, B.J. Cunningham 1–12, Andrew Hawken 2–10, Keyshawn Martin 2–10, Josh Rouse 1–7, Charlie Gantt 1–4, Jeff McPherson 1–MINUS 1. MICHIGAN–Martavious Odoms 6–42, Kevin Koger 2–41, Toney Clemons 1–29, Brandon Minor 1–19, James Rogers 1–19, Greg Mathews 1–13, Darryl Stonum 1–5.

ATTENDANCE: 110,146

Game 9: Purdue 48, Michigan 42

WEST LAFAYETTE | Greg Orton lateraled to Desmond Tardy after a catch to set up the game-winning touchdown with 26 seconds remaining as Michigan endured its seventh defeat, guaranteeing a losing season.

Also snapped was Michigan's string of 33 consecutive bowl appearances, which was the nation's longest active streak.

The win was Purdue's first against Michigan since 2000, and the Boilermakers had never scored more

Steven Threet chugs forward for yardage against Purdue. The offense put up a prodigious 42 points, but the Boilermakers were able to get past the Wolverines thanks to a 48-point performance.

than 37 points in the series.

"I'm going to keep going back to work," Coach Rich Rodriguez said after the game. "What do you want me to say?"

	1st Qtr	2nd Qtr	3rd Qtr	4th Qtr	Final
MICHIGAN	14	14	0	14	**42**
PURDUE	14	7	14	13	**48**

SCORING PLAYS

MICHIGAN–TD, B Minor 45 YD RUN (K Lopata KICK) 2:47 1st Qtr

MICHIGAN–TD, M Odoms 73 YD PUNT RETURN (K Lopata KICK) 5:04 1st Qtr

PURDUE–TD, K Sheets 2 YD RUN (C Wiggs KICK) 9:18 1st Qtr

PURDUE–TD, J Siller 10 YD RUN (C Wiggs KICK) 13:54 1st Qtr

MICHIGAN–TD, L Savoy 11 YD PASS FROM S Threet (K Lopata KICK) 2:32 2nd Qtr

MICHIGAN–TD, D Stonum 51 YD PASS FROM S Threet (K Lopata KICK) 9:31 2nd Qtr

PURDUE–TD, K Sheets 3 YD RUN (C Wiggs KICK) 14:25 2nd Qtr

PURDUE–TD, K Sheets 7 YD PASS FROM J Siller (C wigs KICK) 4:39 3rd Qtr

PURDUE–TD, K Sheets 5 YD RUN (C Wiggs KICK) 14:56 3rd Qtr

MICHIGAN–TD, B Minor 12 YD RUN (K Lopata KICK) 2:41 4th Qtr

PURDUE–TD, G Orton 5 YD PASS FROM J Siller (C wigs KICK) 7:46 4th Qtr

MICHIGAN–TD, B Minor 1 YD RUN (K Lopata KICK) 13:40 4th Qtr

PURDUE–TD, G Orton 25 YARD LATERAL FROM D Tardy (PAT BLOCKED) 14:35 4th Qtr

GAME STATISTICS

	MICHIGAN	PURDUE
First Downs	15	25
Yards Rushing	37–177	46–256
Yards Passing	123	266
Sacks – Yards Lost	3–21	0–0
Passing Efficiency	9–21–0	21–34–0
Punts	6–48.7	6–34.5
Fumbles–Lost	3–1	1–1
Penalties–Yards	5–40	6–48
Time of Possession	22:18	37:42

INDIVIDUAL STATISTICS – RUSHING
MICHIGAN–Brandon Minor 24–155, Michael Shaw 4–10, Toney Clemons 2–6, Steven Threet 7–6. PURDUE–Kory Sheets 30–118, Justin Siller 15–77, Anthony Heygood 1–61.

INDIVIDUAL STATISTICS – PASSING
MICHIGAN–Steven Threet 9–21–123–0.
PURDUE–Justin Siller 21–34–266–0.

INDIVIDUAL STATISTICS – RECEIVING
MICHIGAN–Darryl Stonum 2–61, Martavious Odoms 4–26, Greg Mathews 2–25, LaTerryal Savoy 1–11. PURDUE–Greg Orton 8–89, Desmond Tardy 1–48, Kory Sheets 3–43, Joe Whitest 2–29, Jerry Wasikowski 3–28, Keith Smith 3–22, Brandon Whittington 1–7.

ATTENDANCE: 59,135

Game 10: Michigan 29, Minnesota 6

MINNEAPOLIS | Despite ranking last in Big Ten scoring and passing defense, Michigan snapped a five-game losing streak by winning its 12th straight game at the Metrodome to keep the Little Brown Jug.

Minnesota was outgained 435–188 and managed only one first down during the first half. Meanwhile, K.C. Lopata kicked five field goals, and the running game tallied 232 yards.

Although the Little Brown Jug is college football's oldest rivalry trophy, the Gophers have only won it twice since 1977.

	1st Qtr	2nd Qtr	3rd Qtr	4th Qtr	Final
MICHIGAN	6	10	6	7	29
MINNESOTA	0	0	3	3	6

SCORING PLAYS

MICHIGAN–FG, K Lopata 44 YD 3:57 1st Qtr

MICHIGAN–FG, K Lopata 34 YD 14:29 1st Qtr

MICHIGAN–FG, K Lopata 26 YD 6:37 2nd Qtr

MICHIGAN–TD, G Mathews 8 YD PASS FROM N Sheridan (K Lopata KICK) 13:11 2nd Qtr

MICHIGAN–FG, K Lopata 48 YD 2:40 3rd Qtr

MINNESOTA–FG, J Monroe 28 YD 7:33 3rd Qtr

MICHIGAN–FG, K Lopata 23 YD 12:45 3rd Qtr

MINNESOTA–FG, J Monroe 32 YD 3:18 4th Qtr

MICHIGAN–TD, M Moundros 3 YD RUN (K Lopata KICK) 14:26 4th Qtr

Brandon Graham does his part on defense, breaking up this Minnesota pass. The Wolverines defense had one of its best games of the season and held the Golden Gophers to just nine points.

GAME STATISTICS

	MICHIGAN	MINNESOTA
First Downs	20	8
Yards Rushing	42–232	28–83
Yards Passing	203	105
Sacks – Yards Lost	0–0	4–22
Passing Efficiency	18–30–0	13–24–1
Punts	3–36	7–41.9
Fumbles–Lost	3–1	3–0
Penalties–Yards	2–10	7–51
Time of Possession	34:13	25:47

INDIVIDUAL STATISTICS – RUSHING

MICHIGAN–Michael Shaw 8–71, Brandon Minor 14–53, Justin Feagin 7–49, Nick Sheridan 8–33, Sam McGuffie 3–16, Zoltan Mesko 1–7, Mark Moundros 1–3. MINNESOTA–DeLeon Eskridge 11–80, Shady Salamon 2–6, Troy Stoudermire 1–2, Team 1–MINUS 2, Adam Weber 13–MINUS 3.

INDIVIDUAL STATISTICS – PASSING

MICHIGAN–Nick Sheridan 18–30–203–0. MINNESOTA–Adam Weber 13–24–105–1.

INDIVIDUAL STATISTICS – RECEIVING

MICHIGAN–Greg Mathews 6–79, Martavious Odoms 7–43, Sam McGuffie 1–39, Toney Clemons 2–27, Darryl Stonum 1–10, Michael Shaw 1–5. MINNESOTA–Brandon Green 2–36, Nick Tow–Arnett 1–30, Jack Simmons 3–20, DeLeon Eskridge 2–14, Shady Salamon 1–9, Ben Kuznia 1–3, Troy Stoudermire 1–0, Eric Decker 1–MINUS 3, Brodrick Smith 1–MINUS 4.

ATTENDANCE: 55,040

Game 11: Northwestern 21, Michigan 14

ANN ARBOR | The loss was Michigan's eighth overall and fifth at home, both the most in program history.

"I'm sick to my stomach right now," senior safety Brandon Harrison said.

Michigan led 14–7 midway through the second quarter but never scored again.

Despite cold, wet, and windy conditions, C.J. Bacher threw touchdown passes on Northwestern's first two possessions of the second half, as the Wildcats won at the Big House for just the second time since 1960 (1995 the other).

	1st Qtr	2nd Qtr	3rd Qtr	4th Qtr	Final
NORTHWESTERN	7	0	14	0	**21**
MICHIGAN	7	7	0	0	**14**

SCORING PLAYS

NORTHWESTERN–TD, S Simmons 21 YD RUN (A Villarreal KICK) 5:20 1st Qtr

MICHIGAN–TD, N Sheridan 3 YD RUN (K Lopata KICK) 14:37 1st Qtr

MICHIGAN–TD, R Reyes 3 YD BLOCKED PUNT RETURN (K Lopata KICK) 8:30 2nd Qtr

NORTHWESTERN–TD, R Lane 17 YD PASS FROM C Bacher (A Villarreal KICK) 3:24 3rd Qtr

NORTHWESTERN–TD, E Peterman 53 YD PASS FROM C Bacher (A Villarreal KICK) 5:36 3rd Qtr

GAME STATISTICS

	NORTHWESTERN	MICHIGAN
First Downs	14	15
Yards Rushing	37–59	46–181
Yards Passing	198	83
Sacks – Yards Lost	3–22	1–1
Passing Efficiency	17–29–2	12–36–1
Punts	9–33.1	7–34.1
Fumbles–Lost	0–0	3–1
Penalties–Yards	2–10	5–52
Time of Possession	27:19	32:41

INDIVIDUAL STATISTICS – RUSHING
NORTHWESTERN–Stephen Simmons 22–56, Mike Kafka 3–20, Andrew Brewer 1–0, Team 2–MINUS 2, C.J. Bacher 9–MINUS 15. MICHIGAN–Carlos Brown 23–115, Nick Sheridan 10–35, Michael Shaw 7–17, Steven Threet 4–12, Justin Feagin 1–1, Martavious Odoms 1–1.

INDIVIDUAL STATISTICS – PASSING
NORTHWESTERN–C.J. Bacher 17–29–198–2. MICHIGAN–Nick Sheridan 8–29–61–0, Steven Threet 4–7–22–1.

INDIVIDUAL STATISTICS – RECEIVING
NORTHWESTERN–Eric Peterman 5–79, Ross Lane 7–77, Rasheed Ward 2–22, Sidney Stewart 1–8, Josh Rooks 1–7, Kevin Mitchell 1–5. MICHIGAN–Greg Mathews 5–46, Carlos Brown 2–10, Darryl Stonum 2–10, Martavious Odoms 1–8, LaTerryal Savoy 1–6, Toney Clemons 1–3.

ATTENDANCE: 107,856

Game 12: No. 10 Ohio State 42, Michigan 7

COLUMBUS | Chris "Beanie" Wells had 134 rushing yards and two touchdowns to lead Ohio State to its fifth straight victory over Michigan in the rivalry's most lop-sided result since 1968 (50–14).

Terrelle Pryor, who had two touchdown passes, became the Buckeyes' first freshman quarterback to beat Michigan. The Wolverines managed just 198 yards and punted 12 times.

"As we get older, we'll look back on our career and realize to be a part of the first team to win five times in a row is something that is very special," Ohio State line-backer James Laurinaitis said after the game. "To be able to say that you're a part of this team is something that I'll remember for the rest of my life."

	1st Qtr	2nd Qtr	3rd Qtr	4th Qtr	Final
MICHIGAN	0	7	0	0	**7**
OHIO ST (10)	7	7	14	14	**42**

SCORING PLAYS

OHIO ST–TD, C Wells 59 YD RUN (R Pretorius KICK)
11:03 1st Qtr

OHIO ST–TD, B Hartline 53 YD PASS FROM T Pryor (R Pretorius KICK) 1:50 2nd Qtr

MICHIGAN–TD, B Minor 1 YD RUN (K Lopata KICK)
12:09 2nd Qtr

OHIO ST–TD, D Herron 49 YD RUN (R Pretorius KICK)
3:56 3rd Qtr

OHIO ST–TD, B Robiskie 8 YD PASS FROM T Pryor (R Pretorius KICK) 11:06 3rd Qtr

OHIO ST–TD, D Herron 2 YD RUN (R Pretorius KICK)

0:08 4th Qtr

OHIO ST–TD, B Hartline 18 YD PASS FROM T Boeckman
(R Pretorius KICK) 1:44 4th Qtr

GAME STATISTICS

	MICHIGAN	OHIO ST (10)
First Downs	11	13
Yards Rushing	41–111	43–232
Yards Passing	87	184
Sacks – Yards Lost	3–22	3–25
Passing Efficiency	8–25–0	8–16–1
Punts	12–36.5	7–34.7
Fumbles–Lost	2–2	0–0
Penalties–Yards	3–15	2–20
Time of Possession	29:25	30:35

INDIVIDUAL STATISTICS – RUSHING
MICHIGAN–Brandon Minor 14–67, Michael Shaw 12–
41, Martavious Odoms 1–8, Carlos Brown 3–3, Justin
Feagin 3–2, Nick Sheridan 8–MINUS 10. OHIO ST–Chris
Wells 15–134, Daniel Herron 8–80, Marcus Williams
2–11, Maurice Wells 6–8, Joe Gantz 1–3, Brandon
Saine 3–3, Terrelle Pryor 8–MINUS 7.

INDIVIDUAL STATISTICS – PASSING
MICHIGAN–Nick Sheridan 8–24–87–0, Team 0–1–0–0.
OHIO ST–Terrelle Pryor 5–13–120–1, Todd Boeckman
3–3–64–0.

INDIVIDUAL STATISTICS – RECEIVING
MICHIGAN–Martavious Odoms 5–37, Darryl Stonum
1–33, LaTerryal Savoy 1–14, Carlos Brown 1–3. OHIO
ST–Brian Hartline 2–71, Brian Robiskie 2–54, Dane San-
zenbacher 2–49, Jake Ballard 1–10, Maurice Wells 1–0.

ATTENDANCE: 105,564

Brandon Minor powers through Ohio State's James Laurinaitis during the second quarter of the Michigan-Ohio State game in 2008. The touchdown halved the Buckeye lead, but the Wolverines could not muster enough offense or defense against the nation's tenth-ranked team.

Trying to escape the tackle of Notre Dame's Maurice Crum, Brandon Minor goes down by his shoestrings. A pleasant surprise in 2008, Minor shouldered the bulk of the rushing load when Sam McGuffie went down with an injury.

FINAL STATISTICS

TEAM STATISTICS	MICH	OPP
SCORING	243	347
Points Per Game	20.2	28.9
FIRST DOWNS	186	204
Rushing	98	81
Passing	70	105
Penalties	18	18
RUSHING YARDAGE	1,771	1,643
Yards Gained Rushing	2,104	2,071
Yards Lost Rushing	333	428
Rushing Attempts	453	462
Average Per Rush	3.9	3.6
Average Per Game	147.6	136.9
TDs Rushing	17	21
PASSING YARDAGE	1,718	2,760
Att–Comp–Int	338–165–12	374–216–9
Average Per Pass	5.1	7.4
Average Per Catch	10.4	12.8
Average Per Game	143.2	230.0
TDs Passing	11	19
TOTAL OFFENSE	3,489	4,403
Total Plays	791	836
Average Per Play	4.4	5.3
Average Per Game	290.8	366.9
KICK RETURNS: #–Yards	64–1,372	48–982
PUNT RETURNS: #–Yards	26–224	21–165
INT RETURNS: #–Yards	9–119	12–269
KICK RETURN AVERAGE	21.4	20.5
PUNT RETURN AVERAGE	8.6	7.9
INT RETURN AVERAGE	13.2	22.4
FUMBLES–LOST	38–18	24–11
PENALTIES–Yards	57–500	65–570
Average Per Game	41.7	47.5
PUNTS–Yards	83–3,490	73–2,949

Average Per Punt	42.0	40.4
Net Punt Average	39.3	36.0
TIME OF POSSESSION/Game	27:39	32:21
3rd-Down Conversions	48/176	76/196
3rd–Down Pct	27%	39%
4TH–Down Conversions	14/20	4/12
4th–Down Pct	70%	33%
SACKS BY–Yards	29–211	22–136
MISC YARDS	20	14
TOUCHDOWNS SCORED	31	42
FIELD GOALS–ATTEMPTS	10–15	18–25
ON-SIDE KICKS	0–0	0–0
RED ZONE SCORES	27–35 77%	36–45 80%
RED ZONE TOUCHDOWNS	21–35 60%	27–45 60%
PAT–ATTEMPTS	27–29 93%	39–41 95%
ATTENDANCE	759,997	410,551
Games/Avg Per Game	7/108,571	5/82,110
Neutral Site Games	0/0	

SCORE BY QUARTERS

	1st	2nd	3rd	4th	Total
Michigan	92	65	20	66	243
Opponents	85	81	80	101	347

One of the bright spots of the 2008 season was the improved consistency of punter Zoltan Mesko, shown holding, and kicker K.C. Lopata. Both are veterans who had struggled to find their niche at Michigan, but both had excellent seasons.

INDIVIDUAL STATISTICS
RUSHING

	GP	Att	Gain	Loss	Net	Avg	TD	Long	Avg/G
Minor, Brandon	11	103	563	30	533	5.2	9	45	48.5
McGuffie, Sam	10	118	535	49	486	4.1	3	29	48.6
Shaw, Michael	10	42	230	15	215	5.1	0	48	21.5
Threet, Steven	11	76	358	157	201	2.6	2	58	18.3
Brown, Carlos	5	29	128	6	122	4.2	0	17	24.4
Sheridan, Nick	8	42	142	50	92	2.2	1	12	11.5
Feagin, Justin	4	11	56	4	52	4.7	0	34	13.0
Grady, Kevin	10	14	37	4	33	2.4	1	7	3.3
Mesko, Zoltan	12	2	20	0	20	10.0	0	13	1.7
Moundros, Mark	11	3	14	0	14	4.7	1	7	1.3
Odoms, M.	11	5	13	3	10	2.0	0	8	0.9
Clemons, Toney	9	2	8	2	6	3.0	0	8	0.7
TEAM	9	6	0	13	-13	-2.2	0	0	-1.4
Total	12	453	2,104	333	1,771	3.9	17	58	147.6
Opponents	12	462	2,071	428	1,643	3.6	21	64	136.9

PASSING

	GP	Effic	Cmp–Att–Int	Pct	Yds	TD	Lng	Avg/G
Threet, Steven	11	105.26	102–200–7	51.0	1,105	9	51	100.5

Sheridan, Nick							
8	81.09	63–137–5	46.0	613	2	45	76.6
TEAM							
9	0.00	0–1–0	0.0	0	0	0	.0.0
Feagin, Justin							
4	0.00	0–0–0	0.0	0	0	0	0.0
Total							
12	95.15	165–338–12	48.8	1,718	11	51	143.2
Opponents							
12	131.70	216–374–9	57.8	2,760	19	80	230.0

RECEIVING

GP	No.	Yds	Avg	TD		Lg	Avg/G
Odoms, M.							
11	49	443	9.0	0		50	40.3
Mathews, Greg							
11	35	409	11.7	2		35	37.2
McGuffie, Sam							
10	19	175	9.2	1		40	17.5
Stonum, Darryl							
11	14	176	12.6	1		51	16.0
Clemons, Toney							
9	11	101	9.2	0		29	11.2
Koger, Kevin							
8	6	93	15.5	1		35	11.6
Shaw, Michael							
10	6	32	5.3	1		8	3.2
Brown, Carlos							
5	6	23	3.8	0		11	4.6
Minor, Brandon							
11	5	59	11.8	2		27	5.4
Savoy, L.							
11	4	38	9.5	1		14	3.5
Rogers, James							
9	3	64	21.3	0		24	7.1

Greg Matthews reaches out to make a fingertip catch in the Metrodome against Minnesota. In addition to grabbing passes, Matthews also returned six punts.

Name						
Babb, Zion						
6	2	45	22.5	0	45	7.5
Hemingway, J						
4	2	41	20.5	1	33	10.2
Butler, Carson						
10	2	17	8.5	0	15	1.7
Moundros, Mark						
11	1	2	2.0	1	2	0.2
Total						
12	165	1,718	10.4	11	51	143.2
Opponents						
12	216	2,760	12.8	19	80	230.0

PUNT RETURNS

	No.	Yds	Avg	TD	Lg
Odoms, M.					
	10	126	12.6	1	73
Warren, Donovan					
	9	24	2.7	0	13
Mathews, Greg					
	6	54	9.0	0	32
Williams, M.					
	1	17	17.0	0	0
Reyes, Ricky					
	0	3	0.0	1	3
Total					
	26	224	8.6	2	73
Opponents					
	21	165	7.9	0	80

INTERCEPTIONS

	No.	Yds	Avg	TD	Lg
Trent, Morgan					
	3	0	0.0	0	0
Brown, Stevie					
	2	59	29.5	0	34
Warren, Donovan					
	1	15	15.0	0	15
Stewart, C.					
	1	2	2.0	0	2

Ezeh, Obi				
1	18	18.0	0	18
Thompson, John				
1	25	25.0	1	25
Total				
9	119	13.2	1	34
Opponents				
12	269	22.4	1	100

KICK RETURNS

	No.	Yds	Avg	TD	Lg
Cissoko, B.	20	467	23.4	0	53
Odoms, M.	20	461	23.0	0	45
McGuffie, Sam	7	148	21.1	0	35
Harrison, B.	6	111	18.5	0	35
Horn, Avery	5	104	20.8	0	33
Shaw, Michael	2	11	5.5	0	12
Moundros, Mark	1	1	1.0	0	1
Rogers, James	1	24	24.0	0	24
Stonum, Darryl	1	24	24.0	0	24
Trent, Morgan	1	21	21.0	0	21
Total	64	1,372	21.4	0	53
Opponents	48	982	20.5	0	55

FUMBLE RETURNS

	No.	Yds	Avg	TD	Lg
Brown, Stevie	1	7	7.0	0	7
Total	1	7	7.0	0	7
Opponents	2	45	22.5	1	35

SCORING

	TD	FGs	PATs	Rush	Rcv	Pass	Saf	Pts
Minor, Brandon								
	11	0–0	0–0	0–0	0	0–0	0	66
Lopata, K.C.								
	0	10–15	27–29	0–0	0	0–0	0	57
McGuffie, Sam								

4	0–0	0–0	0–0	0	0–0	0	24

Threet, Steven

| 2 | 0–0 | 0–0 | 0–1 | 0 | 0–1 | 0 | 12 |

Moundros, Mark

| 2 | 0–0 | 0–0 | 0–0 | 0 | 0–0 | 0 | 12 |

Mathews, Greg

| 2 | 0–0 | 0–0 | 0–0 | 0 | 0–0 | 0 | 12 |

Sheridan, Nick

| 1 | 0–0 | 0–0 | 0–0 | 0 | 0–0 | 0 | 6 |

Stonum, Darryl

| 1 | 0–0 | 0–0 | 0–0 | 0 | 0–0 | 0 | 6 |

Grady, Kevin

| 1 | 0–0 | 0–0 | 0–0 | 0 | 0–0 | 0 | 6 |

Odoms, M.

| 1 | 0–0 | 0–0 | 0–0 | 0 | 0–0 | 0 | 6 |

Savoy, L.

| 1 | 0–0 | 0–0 | 0–0 | 0 | 0–0 | 0 | 6 |

Hemingway, J.

| 1 | 0–0 | 0–0 | 0–0 | 0 | 0–0 | 0 | 6 |

Shaw, Michael

| 1 | 0–0 | 0–0 | 0–0 | 0 | 0–0 | 0 | 6 |

Koger, Kevin

| 1 | 0–0 | 0–0 | 0–0 | 0 | 0–0 | 0 | 6 |

Thompson, John

| 1 | 0–0 | 0–0 | 0–0 | 0 | 0–0 | 0 | 6 |

Reyes, Ricky

| 1 | 0–0 | 0–0 | 0–0 | 0 | 0–0 | 0 | 6 |

Total

| 31 | 10–15 | 27–29 | 0–1 | 0 | 0–1 | 0 | 243 |

Opponents

| 42 | 18–25 | 39–41 | 0–0 | 0 | 0–1 | 1 | 347 |

TOTAL OFFENSE

	GP	Plays	Rush	Pass	Total	Avg/G
Threet, Steven						
	11	276	201	1,105	1,306	118.7
Sheridan, Nick						
	8	179	92	613	705	88.1
Minor, Brandon						
	11	103	533	0	533	48.5
McGuffie, Sam						
	10	118	486	0	486	48.6
Shaw, Michael						
	10	42	215	0	215	21.5
Brown, Carlos						
	5	29	122	0	122	24.4
Feagin, Justin						
	4	11	52	0	52	13.0
Grady, Kevin						
	10	14	33	0	33	3.3
Mesko, Zoltan						
	12	2	20	0	20	1.7
Moundros, Mark						
	11	3	14	0	14	1.3
Odoms, M.						
	11	5	10	0	10	0.9
Clemons, Toney						
	9	2	6	0	6	0.7
TEAM						
	9	7	−13	0	−13	−1.4
Total						
	12	791	1,771	1,718	3,489	290.8
Opponents						
	12	836	1,643	2,760	4,403	366.9

Michael Shaw dances around Miami defenders in 2008. Shaw finished fifth on the Wolverines in total offense by racking up 215 total yards on the ground and 258 on kick returns.

FIELD GOALS

FGM–FGA	Pct	01–19	20–29	30–39	40–49	50–99	Lg	Blk
Lopata, K.C.								
10–15	66.7	0–0	5–7	1–2	3–4	1–2	50	1

PUNTING

	No.	Yds	Avg	Lg	TB	Fc	I20	Blk
Mesko, Zoltan								
	80	3,436	43.0	63	3	21	24	0
TEAM								
	2	19	9.5	12	0	0	0	1
Sheridan, Nick								
	1	35	35.0	35	0	0	1	0
Total								
	83	3,490	42.0	63	3	21	25	1
Opponents								
	73	2,949	40.4	74	5	12	27	2

KICKOFFS

	No.	Yds	Avg	TB	OB	Retn	Net	Ydln
Gingell, Jason								
	39	2,394	61.4	4	1			
Wright, Bryan								
	9	562	62.4	0	0			
TEAM								
	5	314	62.8	0	0			
Mesko, Zoltan								
	1	35	35.0	0	1			
Total								
	54	3,305	61.2	4	2	982	41.5	28
Opponents								
	72	4,489	62.3	5	3	1,372	41.9	28

ALL-PURPOSE

	GP	Rush	Rcv	PR	KR	IR	Total	Avg/G
Odoms, M.								
	11	10	443	126	461	0	1,040	94.5
McGuffie, Sam								
	10	486	175	0	148	0	809	80.9
Minor, Brandon								
	11	533	59	0	0	0	592	53.8

MICHIGAN FOOTBALL

Player								
Cissoko, B.	12	0	0	0	467	0	467	38.9
Mathews, Greg	11	0	409	54	0	0	463	42.1
Shaw, Michael	10	215	32	0	11	0	258	25.8
Threet, Steven	11	201	0	0	0	0	201	18.3
Stonum, Darryl	11	0	176	0	24	0	200	18.2
Brown, Carlos	5	122	23	0	0	0	145	29.0
Harrison, B.	12	0	0	0	111	0	111	9.2
Clemons, Toney	9	6	101	0	0	0	107	11.9
Horn, Avery	7	0	0	0	104	0	104	14.9
Koger, Kevin	8	0	93	0	0	0	93	11.6
Sheridan, Nick	8	92	0	0	0	0	92	11.5
Rogers, James	9	0	64	0	24	0	88	9.8
Brown, Stevie	12	0	0	0	0	59	59	4.9
Feagin, Justin	4	52	0	0	0	0	52	13.0
Babb, Zion	6	0	45	0	0	0	45	7.5
Hemingway, J.	4	0	41	0	0	0	41	10.2
Warren, Donovan	11	0	0	24	0	15	39	3.5
Savoy, L	11	0	38	0	0	0	38	3.5
Grady, Kevin	10	33	0	0	0	0	33	3.3
Thompson, John	11	0	0	0	0	25	25	2.3
Trent, Morgan	12	0	0	0	21	0	21	1.8

2008 Review

Player								
Mesko, Zoltan	12	20	0	0	0	0	20	1.7
Ezeh, Obi	12	0	0	0	0	18	18	1.5
Butler, Carson	10	0	17	0	0	0	17	1.7
Williams, M.	11	0	0	17	0	0	17	1.5
Moundros, Mark	11	14	2	0	1	0	17	1.5
Reyes, Ricky	2	0	0	3	0	0	3	1.5
Stewart, C.	11	0	0	0	0	2	2	0.2
TEAM	9	-13	0	0	0	0	-13	-1.4
Total	12	1,771	1,718	224	1,372	119	5,204	433.7
Opponents	12	1,643	2,760	165	982	269	5,819	484.9

DEFENSIVE STATISTICS

		Tackles					Sacks	
Player	GP-GS	Solo	Ast	Total	TFL	-Yds	No	-Yds
45 Ezeh, Obi	12	59	39	98	7.0	-27	1.0	-7
8A Mouton, Jonas	12	36	40	76	6.5	-16	1.0	-7
27 Harrison, B	12	42	27	69	7.0	-35	3.0	-22
3 Brown, Stevie	12	40	24	64	1.5	-17	1.0	-17
49 Thompson, John	11	30	23	53	2.5	-7	1	-25
6 Warren, Donovan	11	36	16	52	3.5	-9	1	-15
90 Jamison, Tim	12	30	20	50	10.5	-47	5.5	-39
55 Graham, Brandon	11	29	17	46	20.0	-97	10.0	-64
14 Trent, Morgan	12	28	13	41	2.5	-9	3	-0
5A Stewart, C	11	24	14	38	0	0	1	-2
67 Taylor, T	12	16	19	35	4.0	-19	1.5	-13
97 Johnson, Will	12	12	17	29	3.0	-15	2.0	-14
68 Martin, Mike	12	9	11	20	4.5	-19	2.0	-15
40 Williams, M	11	14	4	18	2.0	-14	1.0	-8
33 Cissoko, B	12	11	4	15	1.0	-2	0	0
53 Van Bergen, R	12	8	5	13	0	0	0	0
29 Woolfolk, Troy	10	7	2	9	0	0	0	0

MICHIGAN FOOTBALL

5 Butler, Carson	10	6	2	8	0	0	0	0
54 Panter, Austin	6	3	5	8	0.5	-3	0.5	-3
19 Johnson, Zach	12	6	2	8	0	0	0	0
42 Fitzgerald, J.B	12	3	5	8	0	0	0	0
58 Herron, Brandon	11	4	3	7	0	0	0	
TM TEAM	9	7	0	7	0	0	0	0
92 Banks, Greg	7	2	4	6	0.5	-1	0	0
38 Chambers, Artis	9	2	2	4	0	0	0	0
9A Evans, Marell	7	1	3	4	0.5	-2	0.5	-2
95 Sagesse, R	8	1	2	3	0	0	0	0
44 Moundros, Mark	11	2	1	3	0	0	0	
59 Griffin, Sean	11	1	1	2	0	0	0	0
18 Rogers, James	9	2	0	2	0	0	0	0
5B Leach, Kevin	5	0	2	2	0	0	0	0
17 Clemons, Toney	9	2	0	2	0	0	0	0
8I North, Tim	11	2	0	2	0	0	0	0
9 Odoms, M	11	2	0	2	0	0	0	0
88 Criswell, Andre	10	0	1	1	0	0	0	0
22 Stonum, Darryl	11	1	0	1	0	0	0	0
50 Molk, David	12	1	0	1	0	0	0	0
3E Potempa, Jimmy	1	1	0	1	0	0	0	0
34 Horn, Avery	7	1	0	1	0	0	0	0
89 Conover, Jon	11	1	0	1	0	0	0	0
57 Mealer, Elliott	1	1	0	1	0	0	0	0
60 Moosman, David	12	1	0	1	0	0	0	0
13 Mathews, Greg	11	1	0	1	0	0	0	0
99 Patterson, Adam	1	1	0	1	0	0	0	0
41 Mesko, Zoltan	12	0	1	1	0	0	0	0
25 Demens, Kenny	3	0	1	1	0	0	0	0
26 Babb, Zion	6	1	0	1	0	0	0	0
8 Sheridan, Nick	8	1	0	1	0	0	0	0
Total	12	488	330	818	77	-339	29	-211
Opponents	12	488	306	794	93	-308	22	-136

STARTING LINEUPS

Opener (Utah)	Last Game (Ohio State)
Offense	
WR 13 Greg Mathews	WR 13 Greg Mathews
T 71 Mark Ortmann	T 71 Mark Ortmann
G 62 Tim McAvoy	G 62 John Ferrara
C 50 David Molk	C 50 David Molk
G 60 David Moosman	G 60 David Moosman
T 52 Stephen Schilling	T 79 Perry Dorrestein
TE 5 Carson Butler	TE 83 Mike Massey
WR 22 Darryl Stonum	WR 22 Darryl Stonum
QB 8 Nick Sheridan	QB 8 Nick Sheridan
WR 9 Martavious Odoms	WR 9 Martavious Odoms
RB 23 Sean McGuffie	RB 23 Carlos Brown

Defense

DE 55 Brandon Graham	DE 55 Brandon Graham
DT 97 Will Johnson	DT 97 Will Johnson
NG 67 Terrance Taylor	NG 67 Terrance Taylor
DE 90 Tim Jamison	DE 90 Tim Jamison
SLB 54 Austin Panter	SLB 49 John Thompson
MLB 45 Obi Ezeh	MLB 45 Obi Ezeh
WLB 9 Marell Evans	WLB 8 Jonas Mouton
CB 14 Morgan Trent	CB 14 Morgan Trent
SS 27 Brandon Harrison	SS 27 Brandon Harrison
FS 3 Stevie Brown	FS 3 Stevie Brown
CB 6 Donovan Warren	CB 6 Donovan Warren

BIG TEN STANDINGS

	Conference			Overall		
	W-L	PF	PA	W-L	PF	PA
Penn State	7-1	271	109	11-1	482	149
Ohio State	7-1	238	98	10-2	338	157
Michigan State	6-2	201	208	9-3	314	263
Northwestern	5-3	191	187	9-3	294	232
Iowa	5-3	238	130	8-4	363	159
Minnesota	3-5	136	210	7-5	281	280
Wisconsin	3-5	206	227	7-6	357	345
Illinois	3-5	218	206	5-7	344	319
Purdue	2-6	175	196	4-8	296	301
Michigan	2-6	177	268	3-9	243	347
Indiana	1-7	116	328	3-9	246	423

2008 Review

FUTURE SCHEDULES

(Partial, subject to change)

2009

Sept. 5 Western Michigan

Sept. 12 Notre Dame

Sept. 19 Eastern Michigan

Sept. 26 Indiana

Oct. 3 at Michigan State

Oct. 10 at Iowa

Oct. 17 Delaware State

Oct. 24 Penn State

Oct. 31 at Illinois

Nov. 7 Purdue

Nov. 14 at Wisconsin

Nov. 21 Ohio State

2010

Sept. 4 TBA

Sept. 11 at Notre Dame

Sept. 18 Massachusetts

Sept. 25 Bowling Green

Oct. 2 at Indiana

Oct. 9 Michigan State

Oct. 16 Iowa

Oct. 30 at Penn State

Nov. 6 Illinois

Nov. 13 at Purdue

Nov. 20 Wisconsin

Nov. 27 at Ohio State

2011

Oct. 8 at Wisconsin

Oct. 15 Indiana

Oct. 22 at Michigan State

Oct. 29 at Iowa

Nov. 5 Minnesota

Nov. 12 Illinois

Nov. 19 at Northwestern

Nov. 26 Ohio State

2012

Oct. 6 Wisconsin

Oct .13 at Indiana

Oct. 20 Michigan State

Oct. 27 Iowa

Nov. 3 at Minnesota

Nov. 10 at Illinois

Nov. 17 Northwestern

Nov. 24 at Ohio State

Braylon Edwards reaches out for a pass against North-western in 2004. Following two years off the schedule, the Wolverines will play the Wildcats late in both the 2011 and 2012. seasons

THROUGH THE YEARS

1879
1-0-1

May 30	Racine	Chicago	W	1-0
Nov. 1	Toronto	Detroit	T	0-0
Coach: None				1-0
Captain: David N. Detar				

Michigan's first game was against Racine College and played at White Stockings Park in Chicago. Scoring was very different, thus the 1-0 final score. Michigan's first starting lineup was as follows: Rushers—Dave DeTarr, John Chase, Irving Pond, Jack Green, William Hannan, Frank Reid, Richard DePuy, Tom Edwards; Halfbacks—Charles Campbell, Edmund Barmore; Goalkeeper—Charles Mitchell. ... Football had been an organized sport on campus since 1873, with informal student games going back to as early as 1862. ... Maize and blue had already been selected as the school colors by a committee of students in 1867.

1880
1-0

Nov. 5	Toronto	Toronto	W	13-6
Coach: None		·		13-6
Captain: John Chase				

Toronto's six points came on three safety "touchdowns."

1881
0-3

Oct. 31	Harvard	Boston	L	4-0
Nov. 2	Yale	New Haven	L	11-0
Nov. 4	Princeton	Princeton	L	13-4
Coach: None				4-28
Captain: Walter Horton				

Attendance at Yale was 600.

1883
2-3

March 12	Detroit Independents	Ann Arbor	W	40-5
Nov. 19	Wesleyan	Middletown (Conn.)	L	14-6
Nov. 21	Yale	New Haven	L	64-0
Nov. 22	Harvard	Cambridge	L	3-0
Nov. 27	Stevens Institute	Hoboken (N.J.)	W	17-5
Coach: None				63-91
Captain: William J. Olcott				

No games were scheduled in 1882, the year Michigan played its first intercollegiate baseball game against Wisconsin on May 20. ... The Detroit Independents were mostly made up of former Michigan players. ... At the time, a touchdown was worth four points, a field goal five, and a point-after-touchdown four points. That lasted until 1888.

1884
2-0

Nov. 15	Albion	Ann Arbor	W	18-0
Nov. 22	Chicago U. Club	Ann Arbor	W	18-10
Coach: None				36-10
Captain: Horace Prettyman				

1885
3-0

Nov. 7	Windsor Club	Windsor, Ontario	W	10-0
Nov. 14	Windsor Club	Ann Arbor	W	30-0
Nov. 26	Peninsular Club	Detroit	W	42-0
Coach: None				82-0
Captain: Horace Prettyman				

1886
2-0

Oct. 16	Albion	Albion	W	50-0
Oct. 30	Albion	Ann Arbor	W	24-0
Coach: None				74-0
Captain: Horace Prettyman				

Albion claims scores of 18–0 and 50–0. ... Horace Prettyman was team captain for the third consecutive season.

1887
3-0

Nov. 12	Albion	Ann Arbor	W	32-0
Nov. 23	Notre Dame	South Bend	W	8-0
Nov. 24	Harvard Club (Chic)	Chicago	W	26-0
Coach: None				66-0
Captain: John Duffy				

Michigan played Notre Dame after teaching ND students how to play the game.

1888
4-1

April 20	Notre Dame	South Bend	W	26-6
April 21	Notre Dame	South Bend	W	10-4
Nov. 17	Detroit A.C.	Detroit	W	14-6
Nov. 24	Albion	Ann Arbor	W	76-4
Nov. 29	Chicago U. Club	Chicago	L	26-4
Coach: None				130-46
Captain: John Duffy				

Notre Dame reported the attendance of the April 20 game at 400.

1889
1–2

Nov. 9	Albion	Ann Arbor	W	33–4
Nov. 23	Cornell	Buffalo	L	56–0
Nov. 28	Chicago A.A.	Chicago	L	20–0
Coach: None				33–80
Captain: Edgar McPherran				

Charles Mills Gayley wrote the words to "The Yellow and Blue."

1890
4–1

Oct. 11	Albion	Ann Arbor	W	56–10
Oct. 18	Detroit A.C.	Detroit	W	18–0
Oct. 25	Albion	Ann Arbor	W	16–0
Nov. 1	Purdue	Ann Arbor	W	34–6
Nov. 15	Cornell	Detroit	L	20–5
Coach: None				129–36
Captain: William Malley				

George Jewett became Michigan's first black football player. ... The University of Michigan Athletic Association was formed.

George Jewett broke the color barrier at a pair of Big Ten schools. After a run-in with the dean of medicine inspired Jewett to transfer, he also became the first African American to play football at Northwestern.

Marquise Walker tries to break the grasp a Purdue tackler in 2001. The Boilermakers and Wolverines first met on the gridiron in 1890, which turned out to be the Wolverines' first game against an eventual Big Ten foe.

1891
4–5

Oct. 10	Ann Arbor H.S.	Ann Arbor	W	62–0
Oct. 17	Albion	Ann Arbor	L	10–4
Oct. 19	Olivet	Olivet	W	18–6
Oct. 24	Oberlin	Ann Arbor	W	26–6
Oct. 31	Butler	Ann Arbor	W	42–6
Nov. 14	Chicago A.C.	Chicago	L	10–0
Nov. 21	Cornell	Detroit	L	58–12
Nov. 26	Cleveland A.A.	Cleveland	L	8–4
Nov. 28	Cornell	Chicago	L	10–0
Coaches: Mike Murphy, Frank Crawford			168–114	
Captain: James Van Inwagen				

Mike Murphy and Frank Crawford became the program's first official coaches. By midseason Crawford was doing most of the coaching, and Murphy was essentially the head trainer. After his stint at Michigan, Crawford went on to coach Nebraska to a 9–4–1 record in 1893 and 1894 and Texas to a perfect 5–0 season in 1895. ... The Cornell game in Chicago drew only 300 fans.

1892
7–5

Oct. 8	Michigan A.A.	Ann Arbor	W	74–0
Oct. 12	Michigan A.A.	Detroit	W	68–0
Oct. 15	Wisconsin	Madison	W	10–6
Oct. 17	Minnesota	Minneapolis	L	14–6
Oct. 22	DePauw	Indianapolis	W	18–0
Oct. 24	Purdue	West Lafayette	L	24–0
Oct. 29	Northwestern	Chicago	L	10–8
Nov. 5	Albion	Ann Arbor	W	60–8
Nov. 8	Cornell	Ithaca	L	44–0
Nov. 12	Chicago	Toledo	W	18–10
Nov. 19	Oberlin	Ann Arbor	W	26–24
Nov. 22	Cornell	Detroit	L	30–10
Coach: Frank Barbour			298–170	
Captain: George B. Dygert				

Through the Years

Michigan's second head coach, Frank Barbour, was an 1892 graduate of Yale. ... The Northwestern game was played at the 25th Street Field in Chicago.

1893
7-3

Oct. 7	Detroit A.C.	Ann Arbor	W	6-0
Oct. 14	Detroit A.C.	Detroit	W	26-0
Oct. 21	Chicago	Chicago	L	10-6
Oct 28	Minnesota	Ann Arbor	L	34-20
Nov. 4	Wisconsin	Ann Arbor	L	34-18
Nov. 11	Purdue	West Lafayette	W	46-8
Nov. 13	DePauw	Greencastle	W	34-0
Nov. 18	Northwestern	Ann Arbor	W	72-6
Nov. 25	Kansas	Kansas City	W	22-0
Nov. 30	Chicago	Chicago	W	28-10
Coach: Frank Barbour			278-102	
Captain: George B. Dygert				

The athletic facility, which would later be known as Regents Field, opened with a capacity of 400.

1894
9-1-1

Oct. 6	Michigan Military Academy	Ann Arbor	T	12-12
Oct. 13	Albion	Ann Arbor	W	26-10
Oct. 17	Olivet	Ann Arbor	W	48-0
Oct. 21	Michigan Military Academy	Ann Arbor	W	40-6
Oct. 24	Adrian	Ann Arbor	W	46-0
Oct. 28	Case	Cleveland	W	18-8
Nov. 3	Cornell	Ithaca	L	22-0
Nov. 10	Kansas	Kansas City	W	22-12
Nov. 17	Oberlin	Ann Arbor	W	14-6
Nov. 24	Cornell	Detroit	W	12-4
Nov. 29	Chicago	Chicago	W	6-4
Coach: William McCauley			244-84	
Captain: James Baird				

Tom Harmon takes a sip of water during a break in the action during the Wolverines' 85–0 drubbing of Chicago in 1939. Chicago had been a power in the early days of the conference.

Attending Michigan as a medical student, William McCauley was named the program's third head coach. ... The players weighed an average of 170 pounds. ... Michigan's 12–4 victory over Cornell marked the first time a western team defeated an established football power from the East. ... The Cornell game was played at the Detroit Athletic Club Field.

1895
8–1

Oct. 5	Michigan Military Academy			
		Ann Arbor	W	34–0
Oct. 12	Detroit Athletic Club	Ann Arbor	W	42–0
Oct. 19	Adelbert	Ann Arbor	W	64–0
Oct. 26	Rush Lake Forest	Ann Arbor	W	40–0
Nov. 2	Oberlin	Ann Arbor	W	42–0
Nov. 9	Harvard	Cambridge	L	4–0
Nov. 16	Purdue	Ann Arbor	W	12–10
Nov. 23	Minnesota	Detroit	W	20–0
Nov. 28	Chicago	Chicago	W	12–0
Coach: William McCauley				266–14
Captain: Frederick Henninger				

The Chicago game attracted 10,000 fans, which was reflective of the growing rivalry between the schools. ... The Minnesota game was played at Baseball Park in Detroit. ... The original stands at Regents Field burned down.

1896
9–1

Oct. 3	Michigan Normal	Ann Arbor	W	18–0
Oct. 10	Grand Rapids (HS)	Ann Arbor	W	44–0
Oct. 15	P&S (Chicago)	Ann Arbor	W	28–0
Oct. 17	Rush Lake Forest	Ann Arbor	W	66–0
Oct. 24	Purdue	West Lafayette	W	16–0
Oct. 31	Lehigh	Detroit	W	40–0
Nov. 7	Minnesota	Minneapolis	W	6–4
Nov. 14	Oberlin	Ann Arbor	W	10–0
Nov. 21	Wittenberg	Ann Arbor	W	28–0
Nov. 26	Chicago	Chicago Coliseum	L	7–6
Coach: William Ward				262–11
Captain: Henry Senter				

Michigan was a charter member of the Western Conference, which eventually became the Big Ten. It went 2–1 in conference play. … P&S was short for Physicians and Surgeons, Chicago. … The Lehigh game was played at D.A.C. Park in Detroit. … The University of Michigan marching band was organized by a student director and began playing at football games.

1897
6–1–1

Oct. 2	Michigan Normal	Ann Arbor	W	24–0
Oct. 9	Ohio Wesleyan	Ann Arbor	T	0–0
Oct. 16	Ohio State	Ann Arbor	W	34–0
Oct. 23	Oberlin	Ann Arbor	W	16–6
Oct. 30	Alumni	Ann Arbor	E (L)	15–0
Nov. 6	Purdue	Ann Arbor	W	34–4
Nov. 13	Minnesota	Detroit	W	14–0
Nov. 20	Wittenberg	Ann Arbor	W	32–0
Nov. 25	Chicago	Chicago Stadium	L	21–12
Coach: Gustave Ferbert				166–31
Captain: James R. Hogg				

Michigan won the first game against Ohio State. … The Alumni game was considered an exhibition and is not included in season and all-time results.

... The Minnesota game was played at D.A.C. Park in Detroit.

1898

10–0, Big Ten champions

Oct. 1	Michigan Normal	Ann Arbor	W	21–0
Oct. 8	Kenyon	Ann Arbor	W	29–0
Oct. 12	Michigan Agricultural	Ann Arbor	W	39–0
Oct. 17	Western Reserve	Ann Arbor	W	18–0
Oct. 19	Case	Ann Arbor	W	23–5
Oct. 23	Notre Dame	Ann Arbor	W	23–0
Oct. 31	Alumni	Ann Arbor	E (W)	11–2
Nov. 5	Northwestern	Evanston	W	6–5
Nov. 12	Illinois	Detroit	W	12–5
Nov. 19	Beloit	Ann Arbor	W	22–0
Nov. 24	Chicago	Chicago	W	12–11
Coach: Gustave Ferbert				205–26
Captain: John Bennett				
All-American: William Cunningham				

Louis Elbel, a senior student, created the fight song "The Victors" after watching Michigan upset powerhouse Chicago in the season finale to win its first conference title. ... William Cunningham was Michigan's first All-American. ... The Alumni game was considered an exhibition. ... Michigan Agricultural College later became known as Michigan State.

"The Victors" was not immediately considered the fight song of the university when it was written. Instead, the classic tune "There'll Be a Hot Time in the Old Town Tonight" was favored.

1899
8–2

Sept. 30	Hillsdale	Ann Arbor	W	11–0
Oct. 7	Albion	Ann Arbor	W	26–0
Oct. 11	Western Reserve	Ann Arbor	W	17–0
Oct. 18	Notre Dame	Ann Arbor	W	12–0
Oct. 21	Alumni	Ann Arbor	E (T)	0–0
Oct. 28	Illinois	Champaign	W	5–0
Nov. 4	Virginia	Detroit	W	38–0
Nov. 11	Pennsylvania	Philadelphia	L	11–10
Nov. 18	Case	Ann Arbor	W	28–6
Nov. 25	Kalamazoo	Ann Arbor	W	24–9
Nov. 30	Wisconsin	Chicago	L	17–5
Coach: Gustave Ferbert				176–43
Captain: Allen Steckle				

The Alumni game was considered an exhibition. ... The neutral-site game against Wisconsin attracted 18,000 fans in Chicago. ... The nickname "Wolverines" was used in reference to the football team for the first time by the *Michigan Daily* on November 11.

1900
7–2–1

Sept. 29	Hillsdale	Ann Arbor	W	29–0
Oct. 6	Kalamazoo	Ann Arbor	W	11–0
Oct. 13	Case	Ann Arbor	W	24–6
Oct. 20	Purdue	Ann Arbor	W	11–6
Oct. 27	Illinois	Chicago	W	12–0
Nov. 3	Indiana	Bloomington	W	12–0
Nov. 10	Iowa	Detroit	L	28–5
Nov. 17	Notre Dame	Ann Arbor	W	7–0
Nov. 24	Ohio State	Ann Arbor	T	0–0
Nov. 29	Chicago	Chicago	L	15–6
Coach: Langdon "Biff" Lea				117–55
Captain: Neil Snow				

Langdon "Biff" Lea, a Princeton graduate, coached one season and then returned to assist his alma mater. Meanwhile, Fielding Yost coached a season at Stanford University before the school enacted a rule allowing only graduates to coach its football teams. He was subsequently hired by Michigan.

1901

11–0, National champions, Big Ten champions (tie)

Sept. 28	Albion	Ann Arbor	W	55–0
Oct. 5	Case	Ann Arbor	W	57–0
Oct. 12	Indiana	Ann Arbor	W	33–0
Oct. 19	Northwestern	Ann Arbor	W	29–0
Oct. 26	Buffalo	Ann Arbor	W	128–0
Nov. 2	Carlisle	Detroit	W	22–0
Nov. 9	Ohio State	Columbus	W	21–0
Nov. 16	Chicago	Ann Arbor	W	22–0
Nov. 23	Beloit	Ann Arbor	W	89–0
Nov. 28	Iowa	Chicago	W	55–0
Jan. 1,	Stanford	Rose Bowl	W	49–0
Coach: Fielding Yost				555–0
Captain: Hugh White				
All-American: Neil Snow				

In his first year Fielding Yost guided Michigan to the first Tournament of Roses Game, played at Tournament Park, where it crushed Stanford 49–0, with the losing team conceding with nine minutes remaining. Neil Snow scored five touchdowns on carries of 2, 4, 6, 8, and 17 yards. Touchdowns only counted for five points, but Snow's five touchdowns and 25 points are still Rose Bowl records. Willie Heston, a freshman, did not score a touchdown but gained 170 yards on 18 carries. The lopsided score helped convince organizers to try chariot races as the marquee event, with football not returning for 14 years. ... The Ohio State game drew 33,000 fans.

Fielding Yost takes a moment to pose during his coaching tenure at Michigan. Yost led the Wolverines to six of their 11 national championships, including four in a row from 1901 to 1904.

1902
11–0, Nation champions, Big Ten champions (tie)

Sept. 27	Albion	Ann Arbor	W	88–0
Oct. 4	Case	Ann Arbor	W	48–6
Oct. 8	Michigan Agricultural	Ann Arbor	W	119–0
Oct. 11	Indiana	Ann Arbor	W	60–0
Oct. 18	Notre Dame	Toledo	W	23–0
Oct. 25	Ohio State	Ann Arbor	W	86–0
Nov. 1	Wisconsin	Chicago	W	6–0
Nov. 8	Iowa	Ann Arbor	W	107–0
Nov. 15	Chicago	Chicago	W	21–0
Nov. 22	Oberlin	Ann Arbor	W	63–0
Nov. 27	Minnesota	Ann Arbor	W	23–6

Coach: Fielding Yost   644–12

Captain: Harrison "Boss" Weeks

All-Conference: Joseph Maddock, William Heston, Curtis Redden

Fielding Yost wasn't able to duplicate the 555–0 point differential from his first season, but the 644–12 differential was pretty close as Michigan won its second national championship. Incidentally, Yost was credited with creating the linebacker position and was the first to use offensive motion as a decoy.

1903
11–0–1, National champions, Big Ten champions

Oct. 3	Case	Ann Arbor	W	31–0
Oct. 8	Albion	Ann Arbor	W	76–0
Oct. 10	Beloit	Ann Arbor	W	79–0
Oct. 14	Ohio Northern	Ann Arbor	W	65–0
Oct. 17	Indiana	Ann Arbor	W	51–0
Oct. 21	Ferris State	Ann Arbor	W	88–0
Oct. 24	Drake	Ann Arbor	W	47–0
Oct. 31	Minnesota	Minneapolis	T	6–6
Nov. 7	Ohio State	Ann Arbor	W	36–0
Nov. 14	Wisconsin	Ann Arbor	W	16–0
Nov. 21	Oberlin	Ann Arbor	W	42–0

Nov. 26	Chicago	Chicago	W	28–0

Coach: Fielding Yost	565–6

Captain: Curtis Redden

All-American: William Heston

All-Conference: Joseph Maddock, William Heston, Curtis Redden

Because he feared water contamination, Fielding Yost ordered team manager Tommy Roberts to purchase a five-gallon jug from a Minneapolis store. However, after the Wolverines left it behind following the 6–6 tie—the first non-victory for Yost at Michigan—Minnesota athletics director L.J. Cooke told Yost, "If you want it, you'll have to come up and win it." Michigan did so in 1909, and the two teams have played for the Little Brown Jug every year since 1929.

1904
10–0, National champions,
Big Ten champions (tie)

Oct. 1	Case	Ann Arbor	W	33–0
Oct. 5	Ohio Northern	Ann Arbor	W	48–0
Oct. 8	Kalamazoo	Ann Arbor	W	95–0
Oct. 12	P&S (Chicago)	Ann Arbor	W	72–0
Oct. 15	Ohio State	Columbus	W	31–6
Oct. 19	American Med School	Ann Arbor	W	72–0
Oct. 22	West Virginia	Ann Arbor	W	130–0
Oct. 29	Wisconsin	Madison	W	28–0
Nov. 5	Drake	Ann Arbor	W	36–4
Nov. 12	Chicago	Ann Arbor	W	22–12

Coach: Fielding Yost	567–22

Captain: William Heston

All-American: William Heston

All-Conference: William Heston, Tom Hammond, Frank Longman, John Curtis

Willie Heston scored 21 touchdowns for a career total of 71. Fielding Yost had faced Heston, then at San Jose State, while at Stanford and encouraged him to join him at Michigan and study law. During Heston's four years the Wolverines went

43–0–1 (11–0, 11–0, 11–0–1, and 10–0), and outscored opponents 2,326–40 (550–0, 644–12, 565–6, and 577–22) on the "point-a-minute" teams. Heston was 5-foot-8, 190 pounds, and ran the 100-yard dash in 10-flat. ... P&S was the College of Physicians and Surgeons from Chicago. American Medical School was also located in Chicago.

1905
12–1

Sept. 30	Ohio Wesleyan	Ann Arbor	W	65–0
Oct. 4	Kalamazoo	Ann Arbor	W	44–0
Oct. 7	Case	Ann Arbor	W	36–0
Oct. 11	Ohio Northern	Ann Arbor	W	23–0
Oct. 14	Vanderbilt	Ann Arbor	W	18–0
Oct. 21	Nebraska	Ann Arbor	W	31–0
Oct. 25	Albion	Ann Arbor	W	70–0
Oct. 28	Drake	Ann Arbor	W	48–0
Nov. 4	Illinois	Champaign	W	33–0
Nov. 11	Ohio State	Ann Arbor	W	40–0
Nov. 18	Wisconsin	Ann Arbor	W	12–0
Nov. 25	Oberlin	Ann Arbor	W	75–0
Nov. 30	Chicago	Chicago	L	2–0
Coach: Fielding Yost				495–2
Captain: Fred S. Norcross				

All-Conference: Thom Hammond, Frank Longman, John Curtis, Henry Schulte

Chicago scored the only points against Michigan (two), which cost Michigan the conference title. The loss also snapped a 56-game unbeaten streak, during which the Wolverines outscored the opposition 2,821–40. Against everyone else the opposition had a winning percentage of .695, with 44 of the 56 teams having winning records.

Adolph "Germany" Schulz poses during his All-American 1907 season. He was considered the finest center of his day and is still considered one of the best to ever man the position.

1906
4–1

Oct. 6	Case	Ann Arbor	W	28–0
Oct. 20	Ohio State	Columbus	W	6–0
Oct. 27	Illinois	Ann Arbor	W	28–9
Nov. 3	Vanderbilt	Ann Arbor	W	10–4
Nov. 10	Alumni	Ann Arbor	E (T)	0–0
Nov. 17	Pennsylvania	Philadelphia	L	17–0
Coach: Fielding Yost				72–30
Captain: John Curtis				

All-Conference: John Curtis, John Garrels, Adolph "Germany" Schulz

Michigan was without future College Football Hall of Famer Adolph "Germany" Schulz, a massive center who was 6-foot-4, 245 pounds, after he dropped out of school due to lack of funds. He worked in a steel mill in Fort Wayne, Indiana, and earned the money to return to college, where he played two more seasons. ... The Alumni game was considered an exhibition.

1907
5–1

Oct. 5	Case	Ann Arbor	W	9–0
Oct. 12	Michigan Agricutural	Ann Arbor	W	46–0
Oct. 19	Wabash	Indianapolis	W	22–0
Oct. 26	Ohio State	Ann Arbor	W	22–0
Nov. 2	Vanderbilt	Nashville	W	8–0
Nov. 16	Pennsylvania	Ann Arbor	L	6–0
Coach: Fielding Yost				107–6
Captain: Paul Magoffin				

All-American: Adolph "Germany" Schulz

All-Conference: Walter Rheinschild, Adolph "Germany" Schulz, Harry Hammond

Due to a dispute over eligibility and training rules, Michigan left the Big Ten conference.

1908
5-2-1

Oct. 3	Case	Ann Arbor	W	16-6
Oct. 10	Michigan Agricultural	East Lansing	T	0-0
Oct. 17	Notre Dame	Ann Arbor	W	12-6
Oct. 24	Ohio State	Columbus	W	10-6
Oct. 31	Vanderbilt	Ann Arbor	W	24-6
Nov. 7	Kentucky	Ann Arbor	W	62-0
Nov. 14	Pennsylvania	Ann Arbor	L	29-0
Nov. 21	Syracuse	Syracuse	L	28-4
Coach: Fielding Yost				128-81
Captain: Adolph "Germany" Schulz				

Center Adolph "Germany" Schulz was responsible for two innovations during his career at Michigan. First, he invented the spiral snap, whereas previously centers sent the ball end-over-end. Also, he dropped back off the line to become a roving center in addition to being football's first linebacker. At the time, centers always played on the line on defense. Wrote Grantland Rice in 1928: "Schulz stands as the fastest giant who ever played football, a human bulwark fast enough to tackle at either end, as he brought down his man after the manner of a hawk snaring a quail."

1909
6-1

Oct. 9	Case	Ann Arbor	W	3-0
Oct. 16	Ohio State	Ann Arbor	W	33-6
Oct. 23	Marquette	Milwaukee	W	6-5
Oct. 30	Syracuse	Ann Arbor	W	43-0
Nov. 6	Notre Dame	Ann Arbor	L	11-3
Nov. 13	Pennsylvania	Philadelphia	W	12-6
Nov. 20	Minnesota	Minneapolis	W	15-6
Coach: Fielding Yost				115-34
Captain: Dave Allerdice				
All-American: Albert Benbrook				

Benbrook was named an All-American at a time when nearly all selections were East Coast players.

1910
3–0–3

Oct. 8	Case	Ann Arbor	T	3–3
Oct. 15	Michigan Agricultural	Ann Arbor	W	6–3
Oct. 22	Ohio State	Columbus	T	3–3
Oct. 29	Syracuse	Syracuse	W	11–0
Nov. 12	Pennsylvania	Philadelphia	T	0–0
Nov. 19	Minnesota	Ann Arbor	W	6–0
Coach: Fielding Yost				29–9
Captain: Albert Benbrook				
All-American: Albert Benbrook, Stanfield Wells				

Through the Years

Albert Benbrook was the first western lineman to become a two-time All-American. Weighing over 200 pounds, he was considered huge for his time. According to the College Football Hall of Fame, Benbrook's final game was memorable. Michigan made use of the liberalized forward passing rules implemented in 1906 to defeat Minnesota. A forward pass took Michigan to the Minnesota 3-yard line in the late stages of a scoreless contest. After two unsuccessful runs into the line, Benbrook ordered that the next play be run over his side. He opened the hole that led to a touchdown and a 6–0 victory.

One of the earliest uses of the forward pass was by Yale's Walter Camp in 1876. The play was considered illegal at the time and remained so for 30 more years.

1911
5-1-2

Oct. 7	Case	Ann Arbor	W	24-0
Oct. 14	Michigan Agricultural	East Lansing	W	15-3
Oct. 21	Ohio State	Ann Arbor	W	19-0
Oct. 28	Vanderbilt	Ann Arbor	W	9-8
Nov. 4	Syracuse	Ann Arbor	T	6-6
Nov. 11	Cornell	Ithaca	L	6-0
Nov. 18	Pennsylvania	Ann Arbor	W	11-9
Nov. 25	Nebraska	Lincoln	T	6-6
Coach: Fielding Yost				90-38
Captain: Fred Conklin				

The 1911 season was the last before major reforms were made to the game. For example, the forward pass was legal, but a pass could not be caught beyond the goal line, nor more than 20 yards beyond the line of scrimmage.

1912
5-2

Oct. 5	Case	Ann Arbor	W	34-0
Oct. 12	Michigan Agricultural	Ann Arbor	W	55-7
Oct. 19	Ohio State	Columbus	W	14-0
Oct. 26	Syracuse	Syracuse	L	18-7
Nov. 2	South Dakota	Ann Arbor	W	7-6
Nov. 9	Pennsylvania	Philadelphia	L	27-21
Nov. 16	Cornell	Ann Arbor	W	20-7
Coach: Fielding Yost				158-65
Captain: George Thomson				

The Athletic Administration Building, or "Club House" as it was known, became the center of campus athletics in 1912. It has been renamed the Marie D. Hartwig Building for the first director of women's athletics and now houses the ticket office, sports information office, and the athletic alumni and development offices.

The Ivy League Schools were powers throughout the first half of the 20th century, though their dominance waned as the years went by. Michigan lost to Penn in 1912 but was led by Heisman winner Tom Harmon when they faced off in 1940.

1913
6–1

Oct. 4	Case	Ann Arbor	W	48–0
Oct. 11	Mount Union	Ann Arbor	W	14–0
Oct. 18	Michigan Agricultural	Ann Arbor	L	12–7
Oct. 25	Vanderbilt	Nashville	W	33–2
Nov. 1	Syracuse	Ann Arbor	W	43–7
Nov. 8	Cornell	Ithaca	W	17–0
Nov. 15	Pennsylvania	Ann Arbor	W	13–0
Coach: Fielding Yost				175–21
Captain: George Paterson				
All–Americans: James Craig, Miller Pontius				

The 1913 season is the earliest for which
Michigan has complete attendance figures. Penn
attracted 19,687 fans, bringing the season total
up to 56,648.

1914
6–3

Sept. 30	DePauw	Ann Arbor	W	58–0
Oct. 3	Case	Ann Arbor	W	69–0
Oct. 7	Mount Union	Ann Arbor	W	27–7
Oct. 10	Vanderbilt	Ann Arbor	W	23–3
Oct. 17	Michigan Agricultural	East Lansing	W	3–0
Oct. 24	Syracuse	Syracuse	L	20–6
Oct. 31	Harvard	Cambridge	L	7–0
Nov. 7	Pennsylvania	Ann Arbor	W	34–3
Nov. 14	Cornell	Ann Arbor	L	28–13
Coach: Fielding Yost				233–68
Captain: James Raynsford				
All-American: John Maulbetsch				

John Maulbetsch, Michigan's 153-pound
"Featherweight Fullback" earned Walter Camp's
All-America recognition as a sophomore. He would
also be known as the "Human Bullet" because of
his unusually low, line-plunging style of play,

1915
4-3-1

Oct. 6	Lawrence	Ann Arbor	W	39-0
Oct. 9	Mount Union	Ann Arbor	W	35-0
Oct. 13	Marietta	Ann Arbor	W	28-6
Oct. 16	Case	Ann Arbor	W	14-3
Oct. 23	Michigan Agricultural	Ann Arbor	L	24-0
Oct. 30	Syracuse	Ann Arbor	L	14-7
Nov. 6	Cornell	Ann Arbor	L	34-7
Nov. 13	Pennsylvania	Philadelphia	T	0-0
Coach: Fielding Yost				130-81
Captain: William Cochran				

The three-game losing streak was the first for Fielding Yost in his 15th season at Michigan.

1916
7-2

Oct. 4	Marietta	Ann Arbor	W	38-0
Oct. 7	Case	Ann Arbor	W	19-3
Oct. 11	Carroll	Ann Arbor	W	54-0
Oct. 14	Mount Union	Ann Arbor	W	26-0
Oct. 21	Michigan Agricultural	Ann Arbor	W	9-0
Oct. 28	Syracuse	Ann Arbor	W	14-13
Nov. 4	Washington U.	Ann Arbor	W	66-7
Nov. 11	Cornell	Ithaca	L	23-20
Nov. 18	Pennsylvania	Ann Arbor	L	10-7
Coach: Fielding Yost				253-56
Captain: John Maulbetsch				

With its wide-open offense and dominating defense, Michigan won seven straight games before losing a close game on the road at Cornell. ... The John Maulbetsch Award is now presented after spring practice to the freshman candidate who best displays desire.

1917

8–2

Oct. 6	Case	Ann Arbor	W	41–0
Oct. 10	Western State	Ann Arbor	W	17–13
Oct. 13	Mount Union	Ann Arbor	W	69–0
Oct. 17	Detroit	Ann Arbor	W	14–3
Oct. 20	Michigan Agricultural	East Lansing	W	27–0
Oct. 27	Nebraska	Ann Arbor	W	20–0
Nov. 3	Kalamazoo	Ann Arbor	W	62–0
Nov. 10	Cornell	Ann Arbor	W	42–0
Nov. 17	Pennsylvania	Philadelphia	L	16–0
Nov. 24	Northwestern	Evanston	L	21–12
Coach: Fielding Yost				304–53
Captain: Cedric Smith				
All-American: Ernest Allmendinger, Cedric Smith, Frank Culver				

Michigan's season attendance was 68,238.

1918

5–0, National champions,
Big Ten champions (tie)

Oct. 5	Case	Ann Arbor	W	33–0
Oct. 9	Chicago	Chicago	W	13–0
Oct. 16	Syracuse	Ann Arbor	W	15–0
Oct. 23	Michigan Agricultural	Ann Arbor	W	21–6
Oct. 30	Ohio State	Columbus	W	14–0
Coach: Fielding Yost				96–6
Captain: Elton "Tad" Wieman				
All-American: Frank Steketee				
All-Conference: Ernie Vick, Angus Goetz				

Michigan returned to the Big Ten conference. ... Scheduled games with Camp Custer (Oct. 12), Michigan Agricultural (Oct. 19), Ohio State (Oct. 26 at Columbus), Northwestern (Nov. 2), Cornell (Nov. 16), Syracuse (Nov. 16 in place of Cornell), and Minnesota (Nov. 23) were all canceled due to the influenza epidemic and war-related travel restrictions. Only the Michigan Agricultural and Ohio State games were rescheduled.

1919
3–4

Oct. 4	Case	Ann Arbor	W	34–0
Oct. 18	Michigan Agricultural	Ann Arbor	W	26–0
Oct. 25	Ohio State	Ann Arbor	L	13–3
Nov. 1	Northwestern	Ann Arbor	W	16–13
Nov. 8	Chicago	Chicago	L	13–0
Nov. 15	Illinois	Champaign	L	29–7
Nov. 22	Minnesota	Ann Arbor	L	634–7
Coach: Fielding Yost				93–102
Captain: Angus Goetz				
All-Conference: Ernie Vick				

Coach Fielding Yost had his only losing season at Michigan.

1920
5–2

Oct. 9	Case	Ann Arbor	W	35–0
Oct. 16	Michigan Agricultural	Ann Arbor	W	35–0
Oct. 23	Illinois	Ann Arbor	L	7–6
Oct. 30	Tulane	Ann Arbor	W	21–10
Nov. 6	Ohio State	Columbus	L	14–7
Nov. 13	Chicago	Ann Arbor	W	14–0
Nov. 20	Minnesota	Minneapolis	W	3–0
Coach: Fielding Yost				121–21
Captain: Angus Goetz				
All-Conference: Ernie Vick				

Fielding Yost poses with the Michigan Field House in the background. The building was later renamed for Yost and today serves as the iconic home of Michigan's hockey program.

1921
5–1–1

Oct. 1	Mount Union	Ann Arbor	W	44–0
Oct. 8	Case	Ann Arbor	W	65–0
Oct. 15	Michigan Agricultural	Ann Arbor	W	30–0
Oct. 22	Ohio State	Ann Arbor	L	14–0
Oct. 29	Illinois	Illinois	W	3–0
Nov. 12	Wisconsin	Madison	T	7–7
Nov. 19	Minnesota	Ann Arbor	W	38–0
Coach: Fielding Yost				187–21
Captain: Robert Dunne				
All-American: Paul Goebel, Ernie Vick				
All-Conference: Ernie Vick, Robert Dunne				

Said Fielding Yost about center Ernie Vick: "He is the most accurate passer from center that has ever put a ball into play. Under pressure he was dependable at all times." Walter Camp echoed those comments when he selected Vick as an All-American: "He is the only man who has throughout the season added great power and aggressiveness to steadiness and consistency." … In addition to coaching, Yost also served as athletics director, a position he held until 1941.

Fielding Yost helped make college football the national passion that it is today. He was one of the first coaches to lobby for better salaries for coaches, which were paltry in his era. The professionalization of coaches helped improve the caliber of play and made the game more exciting.

1922
6–0–1, Big Ten champions (tie)

Oct. 7	Case	Ann Arbor	W	48–0
Oct. 14	Vanderbilt	Nashville	T	0–0
Oct. 21	Ohio State	Columbus	W	19–0
Oct. 28	Illinois	Ann Arbor	W	24–0
Nov. 4	Michigan Agricultural	Ann Arbor	W	63–0
Nov. 18	Wisconsin	Ann Arbor	W	13–6
Nov. 25	Minnesota	Minneapolis	W	16–7
Coach: Fielding Yost				183–13
Captain: Paul Goebel				
All-American: Harry Kipke				
All-Conference: Bernard Kirk, Harry Kipke				

Harry Kipke was named an All-American as a punter, but opposing coaches were more concerned with his offensive abilities as a ball carrier, passer, and blocker.

1923
8–0, National champions,
Big Ten champions (tie)

Oct. 6	Case	Ann Arbor	W	46–0
Oct. 13	Vanderbilt	Ann Arbor	W	3–0
Oct. 20	Ohio State	Ann Arbor	W	23–0
Oct. 27	Michigan Agricultural	Ann Arbor	W	37–0
Nov. 3	Iowa	Iowa City	W	9–3
Nov. 10	Quantico Marines	Ann Arbor	W	26–6
Nov. 17	Wisconsin	Madison	W	6–3
Nov. 24	Minnesota	Ann Arbor	W	10–0
Coach: Fielding Yost				150–12
Captain: Harry Kipke				
All-American: Jack Blott				
All-Conference: Harry Kipke, Jack Blott, Stanley Muirhead				

Although Michigan can claim the national title, most services preferred Big Ten rival Illinois (the two teams didn't play). Billingsley had Michigan No. 1, and the National Championship Foundation split its title. Board, Football Research, Helms,

and Parke Davis all preferred Illinois, while
California and Cornell also received consideration.

1924
6–2

Oct. 4	Miami (Ohio)	Ann Arbor	W	55–0
Oct. 11	Michigan Agricultural	East Lansing	W	7–0
Oct. 18	Illinois	Champaign	L	39–14
Oct. 25	Wisconsin	Ann Arbor	W	21–0
Nov. 1	Minnesota	Minneapolis	W	13–0
Nov. 8	Northwestern	Ann Arbor	W	27–0
Nov. 15	Ohio State	Columbus	W	16–6
Nov. 22	Iowa	Ann Arbor	L	9–2
Coach: George Little				155–54
Captain: Herb F. Steger				
All-American: Edliff R. Slaughter				

After serving primarily as Fielding Yost's top assistant for two seasons, George Little was named
head coach. However, after just one season he
left to accept the athletics director position at
Wisconsin. He later served as athletics director
at Rutgers and as the executive secretary of the
National Football Foundation and Hall of Fame. ...
Yost served on George Little's staff as an advisory
coach. ... 1924 was an unusual season in that
Michigan had as many road games (four) as home
games. ... Yost Field House was dedicated.

George Little left Michigan to accept the position
of head coach and athletics director at Wisconsin.
His 1925 team only lost one game: to Fielding
Yost's Michigan Wolverines.

1925

7–1, Big Ten champions

Oct. 3	Michigan State	Ann Arbor	W	39–0
Oct. 10	Indiana	Ann Arbor	W	63–0
Oct. 17	Wisconsin	Madison	W	21–0
Oct. 24	Illinois	Champaign	W	3–0
Oct. 31	Navy	Ann Arbor	W	54–0
Nov. 7	Northwestern	Soldier Field	L	3–2
Nov. 14	Ohio State	Ann Arbor	W	10–0
Nov. 21	Minnesota	Ann Arbor	W	35–0
Coach: Fielding Yost				227–3

Captain: Robert Brown

All-American: Robert Brown, Thomas Edwards, Harry Hawkins, Benny Friedman, Bennie G. Oosterbaan

All-Conference: Bennie G. Oosterbaan, Thomas Edwards, Benny Friedman, Harry Hawkins, Bob Brown

With George Little's departure, Fielding Yost returned as head coach. A field goal by Northwestern, the only points Michigan gave up all season, cost the Wolverines their claim on the national championship. ... Bennie Oosterbaan arrived on the Michigan campus and wound up being a student-athlete, assistant football coach (1928–47), head basketball coach (1938–46), head football coach (1948–58), and director of alumni relations (1959–72). In 1925 he led the conference in scoring with eight touchdowns.

4

Colleges that Fielding Yost coached before finding a home at Michigan. He spent only one year at each, manning the helm at Ohio Wesleyan, Nebraska, Kansas, and Stanford.

1926

7–1, Big Ten champions (tie)

Oct. 2	Oklahoma A&M	Ann Arbor	W	42–3
Oct. 9	Michigan State	Ann Arbor	W	55–3
Oct. 16	Minnesota	Ann Arbor	W	20–0
Oct. 23	Illinois	Ann Arbor	W	13–0
Oct. 30	Navy	Baltimore	L	10–0
Nov. 6	Wisconsin	Ann Arbor	W	37–0
Nov. 13	Ohio State	Columbus	W	17–16
Nov. 20	Minnesota	Minneapolis	W	7–6
Coach: Fielding Yost				191–38
Captain: Benny Friedman				
All-American: Benny Friedman, Bennie G. Oosterbaan				
All-Conference: Bennie G. Oosterbaan, Benny Friedman, William Flora				

Through the Years

After 25 years leading Michigan, Fielding Yost stepped down, this time for good, with a 165–29–10 record. ... Yost's final meeting with Ohio State was memorable. Down 10–0 early on, Michigan's air attack of quarterback Benny Friedman and end Bennie Oosterbaan led a 17–16 comeback victory. "He never makes a mistake," Yost said while watching Friedman capture All-America honors in both 1925 and 1926. ... Oosterbaan keyed a 7–6 victory against Minnesota with a 60-yard run and fumble recovery. ... The schedule was unusual in that Michigan played Minnesota twice, with each school hosting one, but the Wolverines won both games. ... The game against Navy at Baltimore Stadium attracted 80,000 fans.

1927

6–2

Oct. 1	Ohio Wesleyan	Ann Arbor	W	33–0
Oct. 8	Michigan State	Ann Arbor	W	21–0
Oct. 15	Wisconsin	Madison	W	14–0
Oct. 22	Ohio State	Ann Arbor	W	21–0
Oct. 29	Illinois	Champaign	L	14–0
Nov. 5	Chicago	Chicago	W	14–0
Nov. 12	Navy	Ann Arbor	W	27–12

Nov. 19	Minnesota	Ann Arbor	L	13–7
Coach: Elton E. "Tad" Wieman				137–39
Captain: Bennie G. Oosterbaan				
All-American: Bennie G. Oosterbaan				
All-Conference: Bennie G. Oosterbaan, Raymond Baer, Louis Gilbert				

Tad Wieman succeeded Fielding Yost as head coach. Led by Bennie Oosterbaan, Michigan outscored the competition 137–39. The Wolverines played their first game at Michigan Stadium on October 1, 1927, defeating Ohio Wesleyan, 33–0. Fashioned after the Yale Bowl, Michigan Stadium cost in excess of $950,000 and initially had a seating capacity of 72,000. Numerous renovations and additions over the years have dramatically increased the seating to 107,501.

1928
3–4–1

Oct. 6	Ohio Wesleyan	Ann Arbor	L	17–7
Oct. 13	Indiana	Ann Arbor	L	6–0
Oct. 20	Ohio State	Columbus	L	19–7
Oct. 27	Wisconsin	Ann Arbor	L	7–0
Nov. 3	Illinois	Ann Arbor	W	3–0
Nov. 10	Navy	Baltimore	T	6–6
Nov. 17	Michigan State	Ann Arbor	W	3–0
Nov. 24	Iowa	Ann Arbor	W	10–7
Coach: Elton E. "Tad" Wieman				36–62
Captain: George Rich				
All-American: Otto Pommerening				
All-Conference: Otto Pommerening				

The 36 points scored were the fewest since 1884, when Michigan played only two games. ... Bennie Oosterbaan became the first player in school history to earn All-America honors three times. Following graduation, he turned down contracts from professional baseball and football organizations to join the Michigan coaching staff. ... Tad Wieman, known as a student of line play, finished with a 9–6–1 record for his two campaigns at Michigan, then moved on to Princeton where in five years his combined mark was 20–18–3. His brightest accomplishment there was four victories in five meetings with rival Yale.

1929
5-3-1

Sept. 28	Albion	Ann Arbor	W	39-0
Sept. 28	Mount Union	Ann Arbor	W	16-6
Oct. 5	Michigan State	Ann Arbor	W	17-0
Oct. 12	Purdue	West Lafayette	L	30-16
Oct. 19	Ohio State	Ann Arbor	L	7-0
Oct. 26	Illinois	Champaign	L	14-0
Nov. 9	Harvard	Ann Arbor	W	14-12
Nov. 16	Minnesota	Minneapolis	W	7-6
Nov. 23	Iowa	Ann Arbor	T	0-0
Coach: Harry Kipke				109-75
Captain: Joe Truskowski				
All-Conference: Alan Boyard				

Harry Kipke, a former Michigan standout, was hired as head coach and through 1937 compiled a 46–26–4 record. His teams enjoyed a 20-game stretch in which the opposing team failed to score 15 times. "Perhaps it is elementary, but if they can't score, they can't beat you," Kipke said. "When the defense is strong and positive, there's an actual advantage in letting the other team strain and struggle. This permits you to conserve your own weapons." ... In an attempt to generate extra revenue, Michigan hosted Albion and Mount Union on the same day and won both games. However, it attracted only 16,412 fans. ... Both Ohio State and Harvard (for homecoming) drew more than 85,000 fans, but Iowa attracted only 50,619. ... Glenn Edward "Bo" Schembechler was born April 1, 1929, in Barberton, Ohio. The nickname "Bo" was given to him by his sister who was trying to say "brother."

1930

8–0–1, Big Ten champions (tie)

Sept. 27	Denison	Ann Arbor	W	33–0
Sept. 27	Michigan Normal	Ann Arbor	W	7–0
Oct. 4	Michigan State	Ann Arbor	T	0–0
Oct. 11	Purdue	Ann Arbor	W	14–13
Oct. 18	Ohio State	Columbus	W	13–0
Oct. 25	Illinois	Ann Arbor	W	15–7
Nov. 8	Harvard	Cambridge	W	6–3
Nov. 15	Minnesota	Ann Arbor	W	7–0
Nov. 22	Chicago	Ann Arbor	W	16–0
Coach: Harry Kipke				111–23
Captain: James Simrall				
All-Conference: Maynard Morrison, Harry Newman				

Michigan hosted both Denison and Michigan Normal on the same day but only squeaked by the latter 7–0. Again, the doubleheader failed to draw a large crowd, attracting only 12,760 fans.

1931

8–1–1, Big Ten champions (tie)

Oct. 3	Central St. Teachers	Ann Arbor	W	27–0
Oct. 3	Michigan Normal	Ann Arbor	W	34–0
Oct. 10	Chicago	Ann Arbor	W	13–7
Oct. 17	Ohio State	Ann Arbor	L	20–7
Oct. 24	Illinois	Champaign	W	35–0
Oct. 31	Princeton	Princeton	W	21–0
Nov. 7	Indiana	Ann Arbor	W	22–0
Nov. 14	Michigan State	Ann Arbor	T	0–0
Nov. 21	Minnesota	Ann Arbor	W	6–0
Nov. 28	Wisconsin	Ann Arbor	W	16–0
Coach: Harry Kipke				181–27
Captain: Roy Hudson				
All-American: Maynard Morrison				
All-Conference: Maynard Morrison, Harry Newman, Ivan Williamson, Bill Hewitt				

For the third straight year Michigan hosted two opponents on the same day to open the season and won both games. Again, it didn't draw a big crowd (13,169). ... Michigan benefited from having to play only two road games, at Illinois and Princeton, and won both.

1932

8–0, National champions,
Big Ten champions (tie)

Oct. 1	Michigan State	Ann Arbor	W	26–0
Oct. 8	Northwestern	Ann Arbor	W	15–6
Oct. 15	Ohio State	Columbus	W	14–0
Oct. 22	Illinois	Ann Arbor	W	32–0
Oct. 29	Princeton	Ann Arbor	W	14–7
Nov. 5	Indiana	Bloomington	W	7–0
Nov. 12	Chicago	Ann Arbor	W	12–0
Nov. 19	Minnesota	Minneapolis	W	3–0
Coach: Harry Kipke				123–13
Captain: Ivan Williamson				
All-American: Harry Newman, Charles Bernard, Ted Petoskey				
All-Conference: Harry Newman, Ivan Williamson, Francis Wistert, Charles Bernard				

Although Michigan was named national champions by more than one service, Southern California was considered the consensus choice. ... Harry Newman, who scored 31 of his team's 123 points, was a unanimous All-America selection and won the Helms Foundation Player of the Year Award. He guided three teams to a combined record of 24–1–2. ... Gerald R. Ford, who became the 38th President of the United States, was named best freshman during spring practice.

1933

**7–0–1, National champions,
Big Ten champions (tie)**

Oct. 7	Michigan State	Ann Arbor	W	20–6
Oct. 14	Cornell	Ann Arbor	W	40–0
Oct. 21	Ohio State	Ann Arbor	W	13–0
Oct. 28	Chicago	Chicago	W	28–0
Nov. 4	Illinois	Champaign	W	7–6
Nov. 11	Iowa	Ann Arbor	W	10–6
Nov. 18	Minnesota	Ann Arbor	T	0–0
Nov. 25	Northwestern	Evanston	W	13–0
Coach: Harry Kipke				131–18
Captain: Stanley Fay				
All-American: Charles Bernard, Francis "Whitey" Wistert, Ted Petoskey				
All-Conference: Francis "Whitey" Wistert, Charles Bernard, Ted Petoskey, Herman Everhardus				

Harry Kipke became one of only three Michigan
coaches to lead teams to four consecutive conference championships, along with Fielding Yost
and Bo Schembechler, during which his teams
went 34–1–3. ... Although he had no football background prior to attending Michigan, tackle Francis
"Whitey" Wistert would become the first of three
brothers to earn All-America recognition and be
enshrined in the National Football Foundation's
Hall of Fame.

9 **Varsity letters won by Harry
Kipke during his playing days at
Michigan. He lettered in football, basketball, and baseball
and was the captain of Michigan's 1923 national championship team.**

1934
1-7

Oct. 6	Michigan State	Ann Arbor	L	16-0
Oct. 13	Chicago	Chicago	L	27-0
Oct. 20	Georgia Tech	Ann Arbor	W	9-2
Oct. 27	Illinois	Ann Arbor	L	7-6
Nov. 3	Minnesota	Minneapolis	L	34-0
Nov. 10	Wisconsin	Ann Arbor	L	10-0
Nov. 17	Ohio State	Columbus	L	34-0
Nov. 24	Northwestern	Ann Arbor	L	13-6
Coach: Harry Kipke				21-143
Captain: Thomas Austin				

Center Gerald Ford was named the team's most valuable player. ... Georgia Tech refused to play if Willis Ward, the second black player to letter for Michigan, took the field. University officials agreed to not have him play. Ford reportedly threatened to quit the team in response to the university's decision. Michigan scored only 12 points the rest of the season, all by Ward.

1935
4-4

Oct. 5	Michigan State	Ann Arbor	L	25-6
Oct. 12	Indiana	Ann Arbor	W	7-0
Oct. 19	Wisconsin	Madison	W	20-12
Oct. 26	Columbia	New York	W	19-7
Nov. 2	Pennsylvania	Ann Arbor	W	16-6
Nov. 9	Illinois	Champaign	L	3-0
Nov. 16	Minnesota	Ann Arbor	L	40-0
Nov. 23	Ohio State	Ann Arbor	L	39-0
Coach: Harry Kipke				68-131
Captain: William Renner				
All-Conference: Matt Patanelli				

Ohio State became the signature game on the schedule when the annual showdown was moved to become the regular-season finale for both teams.

1936
1–7

Oct. 3	Michigan State	Ann Arbor	L	21–7
Oct. 10	Indiana	Ann Arbor	L	14–3
Oct. 17	Minnesota	Minneapolis	L	26–0
Oct. 24	Columbia	Ann Arbor	W	13–0
Oct. 31	Illinois	Ann Arbor	L	9–6
Nov. 7	Pennsylvania	Philadelphia	L	27–7
Nov. 14	Northwestern	Ann Arbor	L	9–0
Nov. 21	Ohio State	Columbus	L	21–0
Coach: Harry Kipke				36–127
Captain: Matt Patanelli				

The Associated Press poll was created, and the 1936 season was one of few times Michigan wasn't ranked at any point. However, the final three opponents on the schedule were ranked, including No. 1 Northwestern (although the Wildcats weren't able to win the national title).

1937
4–4

Oct. 2	Michigan State	Ann Arbor	L	19–14
Oct. 9	Northwestern	Evanston	L	7–0
Oct. 16	Minnesota	Ann Arbor	L	39–6
Oct. 23	Iowa	Iowa City	W	7–6
Oct. 30	Illinois	Champaign	W	7–6
Nov. 6	Chicago	Ann Arbor	W	13–12
Nov. 13	Pennsylvania	Philadelphia	W	7–0
Nov. 20	Ohio State	Ann Arbor	L	21–0
Coach: Harry Kipke				54–110
Captain: Joe Rinaldi				
All-Conference: Ralph Heikkinen				

Coach Harry Kipke experimented with special markings on the helmets. For three games Michigan's helmets featured white stripes, but the design was abandoned midway through the season.

1938
6-1-1

Oct. 1	Michigan State	Ann Arbor	W	14-0
Oct. 8	Chicago	Ann Arbor	W	45-7
Oct. 15	Minnesota	Minneapolis	L	7-6
Oct. 22	Yale	New Haven	W	15-13
Oct. 29	Illinois	Ann Arbor	W	14-0
Nov. 5	Pennsylvania	Ann Arbor	W	19-13
Nov. 12	Northwestern	Ann Arbor	T	0-0
Nov. 19	Ohio State	Columbus	W	18-0

Coach: Herbert O. "Fritz" Crisler   131-40

Captain: Fred Janke

Ranking (AP): First poll No. 12; Postseason No. 16

All-American: Ralph Heikkinen

All-Big Ten (first team): Ralph Heikkinen, Forest Evashevski, Tom Harmon

Leaders: Rushing—Tom Harmon (398 yards, 77 carries); Passing—Tom Harmon (21 of 45, 310 yards); Receiving—Paul Kromer (9 catches, 72 yards).

Michigan hired Fritz Crisler, considered the father of two-platoon football and known for his buck lateral and spinner offense. He also served as director of athletics (1941–68) and was on the football rules committee for 41 years, nine as its chairman. Crisler brought the famed winged helmet with him from Princeton and thought it would help his passers spot receivers downfield. "Michigan had a plain black helmet and we wanted to dress it up a little," Crisler said. "We added some color (maize and blue) and used the same basic helmet I had designed at Princeton." ... Prior to playing Yale, Michigan was ranked for the first time in the Associated Press poll at No. 12.

Michigan center Gerald Ford gets ready to snap in 1934. Voted the team's most valuable player that season, Ford went on to greatness when he became president of the United States.

1939
6–2

Oct. 7	Michigan State	Ann Arbor	W	26–13
Oct. 14	Iowa	Ann Arbor	W	27–7
Oct. 21	Chicago	Chicago	W	85–0
Oct. 28	Yale	Ann Arbor	W	27–7
Nov. 4	Illinois	Champaign	L	16–7
Nov. 11	Minnesota	Ann Arbor	L	20–7
Nov. 18	Pennsylvania	Philadelphia	W	19–17
Nov. 25	Ohio State	Ann Arbor	W	21–14

Coach: Herbert O. "Fritz" Crisler   219–94

Captain: Archie Kodros

Ranking (AP): First poll No. 6; Postseason No. 20

All-American: Tom Harmon

All-Big Ten (first team): Forest Evashevski, Tom Harmon

Leaders: Rushing—Tom Harmon (884 yards, 130 carries);
Passing—Tom Harmon (37 of 94, 488 yards); Receiving—Forest
Evashevski (14 catches, 134 yards).

**Tom Harmon, known as "Ol' 98," went 95 yards
on an interception return against Iowa, scored on
Penn with carries of 65 and 35 yards, and scored
all of his team's points in the 27–7 victory over
Yale. He led the nation in scoring. ... The rest of
the potent Michigan backfield featured Forest
Evashevski, Paul Kromer, and Bob Westfall.**

1940
7–1

Sept. 28	California	Berkley	W	41–0
Oct. 5	Michigan State	Ann Arbor	W	21–14
Oct. 12	Harvard	Cambridge	W	26–0
Oct. 19	Illinois	Ann Arbor	W	28–0
Oct. 26	Pennsylvania	Ann Arbor	W	14–0
Nov. 9	Minnesota	Minneapolis	L	7–6
Nov. 16	Northwestern	Ann Arbor	W	20–13
Nov. 23	Ohio State	Columbus	W	40–0

Coach: Herbert O. "Fritz" Crisler   196–34

Captain: Forest Evashevski

Ranking (AP): First poll No. 3; Postseason No. 3

Through the Years

Major Awards: Tom Harmon, Heisman Trophy, Maxwell Award

All-American: Tom Harmon, Edward Frutig

All-Big Ten (first team): Forest Evashevski, Edward Frutig, Ralph Fritz, Tom Harmon

Leaders: Rushing—Tom Harmon (852 yards, 191 carries); Passing—Tom Harmon (43 of 94, 506 yards); Receiving—Ed Frutig (12 catches, 181 yards).

Tom Harmon opened the season on his 21st birthday and scored on runs of 94 (opening kickoff), 86, 72 (punt return), and 65 yards at Cal. He even eluded a drunk fan on the 86-yard score. ... Harmon's final college game was Michigan's 40–0 victory at Ohio State. He ran for three touchdowns, passed for two, kicked four extra points, returned three kickoffs for 81 yards, intercepted three passes, and punted three times for an average of 50 yards. Consequently, the Columbus crowd gave him a standing ovation. Harmon led the nation in scoring for the second consecutive year, which had never been done before, and right before he won the Heisman Trophy was on the cover of *Life* magazine. ... For the first time, both Michigan and its opponent were ranked in the Associated Press poll when they played. No. 3 Michigan defeated No. 8 Penn, but the Wolverines failed to move up and subsequently lost to No. 2 Minnesota.

1941
6-1-1

Sept. 27	Michigan State	Ann Arbor	W	19–7
Oct. 4	Iowa	Ann Arbor	W	6–0
Oct. 11	Pittsburgh	Ann Arbor	W	40–0
Oct. 18	Northwestern	Evanston	W	14–7
Oct. 25	Minnesota	Ann Arbor	L	7–0
Nov. 1	Illinois	Champaign	W	20–0
Nov. 15	Columbia	New York	W	28–0
Nov. 22	Ohio State	Ann Arbor	T	20–20
Coach: Herbert O. "Fritz" Crisler				147–41
Captain: Bob Westfall				
Ranking (AP): First poll No. 6; Postseason No. 5				

All-American: Bob Westfall

All-Big Ten (first team): Bob Ingalls, Bob Westfall

Leaders: Rushing—Bob Westfall (688 yards, 156 carries); Passing—Tom Kuzma (26 of 59, 317 yards); Receiving—George Ceithaml (10 catches, 77 yards).

Sophomore linebacker and center Mervin Pregulman intercepted an Otto Graham pass and ran it back 65 yards for a touchdown during a 14-7 victory at Northwestern. ... Bob Westfall was sixth in the nation in rushing yards. During his three years, Westfall ran for 1,864 yards, a Michigan fullback record that stood for 30 years.

1942
7-3

Sept. 26	Great Lakes	Ann Arbor	W	9-0
Oct. 3	Michigan State	Ann Arbor	W	20-0
Oct. 10	Iowa Pre-Flight	Ann Arbor	L	26-14
Oct. 17	Northwestern	Ann Arbor	W	34-16
Oct. 24	Minnesota	Minneapolis	L	16-14
Oct. 31	Illinois	Ann Arbor	W	28-14
Nov. 7	Harvard	Ann Arbor	W	35-7
Nov. 14	Notre Dame	South Bend	W	32-20
Nov. 21	Ohio State	Columbus	L	21-7
Nov. 28	Iowa	Ann Arbor	W	28-14

Coach: Herbert O. "Fritz" Crisler — 221-134

Captain: George Ceithaml

Ranking (AP): First poll No. 3; Postseason No. 9

All-American: Albert Wistert, Julius Franks

All-Big Ten (first team): Albert Wistert, Julius Franks, George Ceithaml

Leaders: Rushing—Bob Wiese (466 yards, 133 carries); Passing—Bob Chappuis (28 of 64, 358 yards); Receiving—George Ceithaml (18 catches, 232 yards).

Following in the footsteps of his brother Whitey, Albert "Ox" Wistert was voted the team's Most Valuable Player and named All-American. He went on to serve as co-captain of the 1943 College All-Star team that defeated the pro champion Washington Redskins, 27-7, in Chicago. When

Wistert eventually quit the game in 1952, the Philadelphia Eagles retired his No. 70 jersey.

1943

8–1, Big Ten champions (tie)

Sept. 18	Camp Grant	Rockford (Ill.)	W	26–0
Sept. 25	Western Michigan	Ann Arbor	W	57–6
Oct. 2	Northwestern	Evanston	W	21–7
Oct. 9	Notre Dame	Ann Arbor	L	35–12
Oct. 23	Minnesota	Ann Arbor	W	49–6
Oct. 30	Illinois	Champaign	W	42–6
Nov. 6	Indiana	Ann Arbor	W	23–6
Nov. 13	Wisconsin	Ann Arbor	W	27–0
Nov. 20	Ohio State	Ann Arbor	W	45–7

Coach: Herbert O. "Fritz" Crisler   302–73

Captain: Paul White

Ranking (AP): First poll No. 2; Postseason No. 3

All-American: William Danley, Mervin Pregulman

All-Big Ten (first team): Fred Negus, Bill Daley, Bob Wiese

Leaders: Rushing—Bill Daley (817 yards, 120 carries); Passing—Elroy Hirsch (9 of 22, 213 yards); Receiving—Farnham Johnson (4 catches, 109 yards).

Michigan won its first Big Ten title in 10 years. ... After helping lead Wisconsin to an 8–1–1 record in 1942, Elroy "Crazy Legs" Hirsch was a marine trainee at Michigan. He lettered in football, baseball, basketball, and track, making him the first four-sport letterman in school history. ... Mervin Pregulman, one of the most versatile linemen who ever played the game and who moved from guard to tackle to center as necessary, was finally named an All-American.

1944

8–2

Sept. 16	Iowa Pre-Flight	Ann Arbor	W	12–7
Sept. 23	Marquette	Milwaukee	W	14–0
Sept. 30	Indiana	Ann Arbor	L	20–0
Oct. 7	Minnesota	Minneapolis	W	28–13
Oct. 14	Northwestern	Ann Arbor	W	27–0
Oct. 28	Purdue	Ann Arbor	W	40–14
Nov. 4	Pennsylvania	Philadelphia	W	41–19
Nov. 11	Illinois	Ann Arbor	W	14–0
Nov. 18	Wisconsin	Ann Arbor	W	14–0
Nov. 25	Ohio State	Columbus	L	18–14

Coach: Herbert O. "Fritz" Crisler   204–91

Captain: Bob Wiese

Ranking (AP): First poll No. 12; Postseason No. 8

All-Big Ten (first team): Bob Wiese, Milan Lazetich, Joe Ponsetto

Leaders: Rushing—Bob Nussbaumer (502 yards, 78 carries);
Passing—Bill Culligan (12 of 39, 245 yards); Receiving—Dick
Rifenburg (8 catches, 232 yards).

**Don Lund and Joe Ponsetto acted as co-captains
after Bob Wiese left for military service.**

1945

7–3

Sept. 15	Great Lakes	Ann Arbor	W	27–2
Sept. 22	Indiana	Ann Arbor	L	13–7
Sept. 29	Michigan State	Ann Arbor	W	40–0
Oct. 6	Northwestern	Evanston	W	20–7
Oct. 13	Army	Yankee Stadium	L	28–7
Oct. 27	Illinois	Champaign	W	19–0
Nov. 3	Minnesota	Ann Arbor	W	26–0
Nov. 10	Navy	Baltimore Stadium	L	33–7
Nov. 17	Purdue	Ann Arbor	W	27–13
Nov. 24	Ohio State	Ann Arbor	W	7–3

Coach: Herbert O. "Fritz" Crisler   187–99

Captain: Joe Ponsetto

Ranking (AP): First poll No. 9; Postseason No. 6

All-Big Ten (first team): Harold Watts

Leaders: Rushing—Wally Teninga (317 yards, 66 carries);

Fritz Crisler looks on with one of his players during the 1947 game against Ohio State. The Wolverines won 21-0 en route to the national championship. It was the perfect capstone to Crisler's career, as he stopped coaching the team after that season.

Passing—Pete Elliott (19 of 52, 393 yards); Receiving—Hank Fonde (11 catches, 148 yards).

Bruce Hilkene was initially named captain but missed the season due to wartime service in the U.S. Navy. He returned for the 1946 season and was team captain in 1947.

1946
6-2-1

Sept. 28	Indiana	Ann Arbor	W	21-0
Oct. 5	Iowa	Ann Arbor	W	14-7
Oct. 12	Army	Ann Arbor	L	20-13
Oct. 19	Northwestern	Ann Arbor	T	14-14
Oct. 26	Illinois	Ann Arbor	L	13-9
Nov. 2	Minnesota	Minneapolis	W	21-0
Nov. 9	Michigan State	Ann Arbor	W	55-7
Nov. 16	Wisconsin	Ann Arbor	W	28-6
Nov. 23	Ohio State	Columbus	W	58-6

Coach: Herbert O. "Fritz" Crisler — 233-73

Captain: Art Renner

Ranking (AP): First poll No. 4; Postseason No. 6

All-American: Elmer Madar

All-Big Ten (first team): Elmer Madar, Bob Chappuis

Leaders: Rushing—Bob Chappuis (502 yards, 116 carries); Passing—Bob Chappuis (52 of 92, 734 yards); Receiving—Bobby Mann (14 catches, 285 yards).

Chalmers "Bump" Elliott joined the marines in 1943 and was assigned to officer training at Purdue where he was a standout halfback. However, during the war he was a gunner on a B-25 bomber in the Army Air Corps. On February 13, 1945, his bomber was shot down behind German lines, and he parachuted into the Po Valley near Florence, Italy. An Italian family sympathetic to the Allies found him and hid him in the attic where he was never discovered, even after the German command moved its headquarters into the neighboring house. Eventually the Allied troops liberated the town. After World War II Elliott enrolled at Michigan and later made several

trips back to Italy to visit the family. ... The Big Ten lifted its postseason ban on September 1, and a five-year pact was signed between the conference and Pac-10.

1947

10–0, National champions,
Big Ten champions (tie)

Sept. 27	Michigan State	Ann Arbor	W	55–0
Oct. 4	Stanford	Ann Arbor	W	49–13
Oct. 11	Pittsburgh	Ann Arbor	W	69–0
Oct. 18	Northwestern	Evanston	W	49–21
Oct. 25	Minnesota	Ann Arbor	W	13–6
Nov. 1	Illinois	Champaign	W	14–7
Nov. 8	Indiana	Ann Arbor	W	35–0
Nov. 15	Wisconsin	Madison	W	40–6
Nov. 22	Ohio State	Ann Arbor	W	21–0
Jan. 1	Southern California	Rose Bowl	W	49–0

Coach: Herbert O. "Fritz" Crisler	394–53

Captain: Bruce Hilkene

Ranking (AP): First poll No. 2; Postseason No. 2

All-American: Robert Chappuis, Chalmers "Bump" Elliott

All-Big Ten (first team): Bob Mann, Howard Yerges, Bob Chappuis, Chalmers "Bump" Elliott

Leaders: Rushing—J. Weisenburger (773 yards, 121 carries); Passing—Bob Chappuis (62 of 110, 1,164 yards); Receiving—Chalmers "Bump" Elliott (18 catches, 318 yards).

Michigan and Notre Dame traded the top spot in the polls throughout much of the season. Notre Dame was No. 1 and Michigan No. 2 in the final regular-season Associated Press poll, but after the Wolverines crushed Southern California in the Rose Bowl the AP held an unprecedented postbowl poll, with voters reversing themselves. However, the final regular-season poll was considered binding, making it one of the most controversial championships in history. Nearly every other poll had Michigan ranked first. ... Led by All-Americans Bob Chappuis and Bump Elliott, Michigan led the nation in total offense (412.7 yards per game) and passing average (173.9).

In one game, Chappuis ran and passed for 307 yards, a school record that lasted 20 years. ... Elliott was named the Big Ten's most valuable player. He scored a conference-high eight touchdowns. ... Fullback Jack Weisenburger punched in three touchdowns against Southern California, which suffered its worst defeat in program history until 1966.

1948

9–0, National champions, Big Ten champions

Sept. 25	Michigan State	East Lansing	W	13-7
Oct. 2	Oregon	Ann Arbor	W	14-0
Oct. 9	Purdue	West Lafayette	W	40-0
Oct. 16	Northwestern	Ann Arbor	W	28-0
Oct. 23	Minnesota	Minneapolis	W	27-14
Oct. 30	Illinois	Ann Arbor	W	28-20
Nov. 6	Navy	Ann Arbor	W	35-0
Nov. 13	Indiana	Ann Arbor	W	54-0
Nov. 20	Ohio State	Columbus	W	13-3

Coach: Bennie G. Oosterbaan   252–44

Captain: Dominic Tomasi

Ranking (AP): First poll No. 7; Postseason No. 1

All-American: Richard Rifenburg, Pete Elliott, Alvin Wistert

All-Big Ten (first team): Dick Rifenburg, Alvin Wistert, Dominic Tomasi, Pete Elliott

Leaders: Rushing—Tom Peterson (330 yards, 109 carries); Passing—Chuck Ortmann (41 of 87, 856 yards); Receiving—Dick Rifenburg (22 catches, 508 yards).

Bennie G. Oosterbaan's first season as head coach was probably his best, and his peers named him national coach of the year. The Wolverines shut out five opponents, and the undefeated team was the unanimous choice as national champions. ... Pete Elliott earned 12 letters at Michigan and helped the football team to a 32–5–1 record over four years. He was an All-Big Ten guard in basketball (Michigan won the conference title in 1948), and runner-up at the conference golf championships. The brother of Chalmers "Bump" Elliott, he went on to become head coach at Nebraska,

California, Illinois, and Miami (Fla.), and executive director of the Pro Football Hall of Fame in Canton, Ohio.

1949
6-2-1, Big Ten champions (tie)

Sept. 24	Michigan State	Ann Arbor	W	7-3
Oct. 1	Stanford	Stanford	W	27-7
Oct. 8	Army	Ann Arbor	L	21-7
Oct. 15	Northwestern	Evanston	L	21-20
Oct. 22	Minnesota	Ann Arbor	W	44-7
Oct. 29	Illinois	Champaign	W	13-0
Nov. 5	Purdue	Ann Arbor	W	20-12
Nov. 12	Indiana	Ann Arbor	W	20-7
Nov. 19	Ohio State	Ann Arbor	T	7-7
Coach: Bennie G. Oosterbaan				135-85

Captain: Alvin Wistert

Ranking (AP): First poll No. 1; Postseason No. 7

All-American: Alvin Wistert, Allen Wahl

All-Big Ten (first team): Alvin Wistert, Lloyd Heneveld, Charles Ortmann

Leaders: Rushing—Don Dufek (392 yards, 122 carries); Passing—Chuck Ortmann (45 of 126, 627 yards); Receiving—Harry Allis (23 catches, 338 yards).

Alvin "Moose" Wistert was the last of three brothers to gain enshrinement into the College Football Hall of Fame, joining Francis "Whitey" and Albert. All three wore No. 11 for Michigan (since retired in their honor). Moose was a high-school dropout and spent six years with the Marine Corps during World War II before entering college. Not wishing to live in the shadow of his brothers, he enrolled at Boston University and lettered as a 30-year-old freshman before transferring to Michigan, where he became an All-American and team captain. In 1949, at age 33, he became the oldest player ever named All-American.

1950

6–3–1, Big Ten champions

Sept. 30	Michigan State	Ann Arbor	L	14–7
Oct. 7	Dartmouth	Ann Arbor	W	27–7
Oct. 14	Army	Yankee Stadium	L	27–6
Oct. 21	Wisconsin	Ann Arbor	W	26–13
Oct. 28	Minnesota	Minneapolis	T	7–7
Nov. 4	Illinois	Ann Arbor	L	7–0
Nov. 11	Indiana	Ann Arbor	W	20–7
Nov. 18	Northwestern	Ann Arbor	W	34–23
Nov. 25	Ohio State	Columbus	W	9–3
Jan. 1	California	Rose Bowl	W	14–6
Coach: Bennie G. Oosterbaan				150–114
Captain: Allen Wahl				
Ranking (AP): Preseason No. 3; Postseason No. 9				
All-American: Allen Wahl				
All-Big Ten (first team): Charles Ortmann, Allen Wahl, Don Dufek				
Leaders: Rushing—Don Dufek (702 yards, 174 carries); Passing—Chuck Ortmann (56 of 120, 736 yards); Receiving—Lowell Perry (24 catches, 374 yards).				

California was heavily favored and dominated early on, but scoreless Michigan turned the tables in the fourth quarter of the Rose Bowl. Team MVP Don Dufek ran four identical plays starting from the 4-yard line and finally scored on fourth-and-1 to take the lead. Dufek scored again from the 7. In the second half, Michigan had a 15–2 edge in first downs and a 226–52 total yardage advantage. ... The Associated Press held its first preseason poll. Previously the first poll was taken several weeks after the start of the season.

Michigan head coach Bennie Oosterbaan smiles as he looks out onto the practice field. A member of Alpha Sigma Phi and a two-sport All-American at UM, Oosterbaan did his alma mater proud by winning the national championship in his first season at the helm.

1951
4–5

Sept. 29	Michigan State	Ann Arbor	L	25–0
Oct. 6	Stanford	Ann Arbor	L	23–13
Oct. 13	Indiana	Ann Arbor	W	33–14
Oct. 20	Iowa	Iowa City	W	21–0
Oct. 27	Minnesota	Ann Arbor	W	54–27
Nov. 3	Illinois	Champaign	L	7–0
Nov. 10	Cornell	Ithaca	L	20–7
Nov. 17	Northwestern	Ann Arbor	L	6–0
Nov. 24	Ohio State	Ann Arbor	W	7–0

Coach: Bennie G. Oosterbaan   135–122

Captain: Bill Putich

Ranking (AP): Preseason No. 17; Postseason NR

All-American: Lowell Perry

All-Big Ten (first team): Lowell Perry, Tom Johnson

Leaders: Rushing—Don Peterson (549 yards, 152 carries);
Passing—Bill Putich (32 of 77, 380 yards); Receiving—Lowell
Perry (16 catches, 395 yards).

Rival Michigan State used the season-opening victory to launch its first of six national title bids, although Tennessee was considered the consensus national champion.

1952
5–4

Sept. 27	Michigan State	Ann Arbor	L	27–13
Oct. 4	Stanford	Stanford	L	14–7
Oct. 11	Indiana	Ann Arbor	W	28–13
Oct. 18	Northwestern	Evanston	W	48–14
Oct. 25	Minnesota	Ann Arbor	W	21–0
Nov. 1	Illinois	Ann Arbor	L	22–13
Nov. 8	Cornell	Ann Arbor	W	49–7
Nov. 15	Purdue	Ann Arbor	W	21–10
Nov. 22	Ohio State	Columbus	L	27–7

Coach: Bennie G. Oosterbaan   207–134

Captain: Merritt Green

All-Big Ten (first team): Roger Zatkoff, Arthur Walker, Bob Timm,
Dick O'Shaughnessy

Leaders: Rushing—Ted Kress (623 yards, 135 carries);
Passing—Ted Kress (45 of 85, 559 yards); Receiving—Lowell
Perry (31 catches, 492 yards).

1953
6-3

Sept. 26	Washington	Ann Arbor	W	50-0
Oct. 3	Tulane	Ann Arbor	W	26-7
Oct. 10	Iowa	Ann Arbor	W	14-13
Oct. 17	Northwestern	Ann Arbor	W	20-12
Oct. 24	Minnesota	Minneapolis	L	22-0
Oct. 31	Pennsylvania	Ann Arbor	W	24-14
Nov. 7	Illinois	Champaign	L	19-3
Nov. 14	Michigan State	East Lansing	L	14-6
Nov. 21	Ohio State	Ann Arbor	W	20-0
Coach: Bennie G. Oosterbaan				163-101

Captain: Dick O'Shaughnessy

Ranking (AP): Preseason NR; Postseason No. 20

All-Big Ten (first team): Arthur Walker, Ted Kress, Bob Topp

Leaders: Rushing—Tony Branoff (501 yards, 101 carries);
Passing—Lou Baldacci (21 of 51, 302 yards); Receiving—Bob
Topp (23 catches, 331 yards).

**Michigan and Michigan State started playing for
the Paul Bunyan Trophy, a four-foot wooden stat-
ute donated by Michigan Governor G. Mennen
Williams.**

1954
6-3

Sept. 25	Washington	Seattle	W	14-0
Oct. 2	Army	Ann Arbor	L	26-7
Oct. 9	Iowa	Ann Arbor	W	14-13
Oct. 16	Northwestern	Evanston	W	7-0
Oct. 23	Minnesota	Ann Arbor	W	34-0
Oct. 30	Indiana	Ann Arbor	L	13-9
Nov. 6	Illinois	Ann Arbor	W	14-7
Nov. 13	Michigan State	Ann Arbor	W	33-7
Nov. 20	Ohio State	Columbus	L	21-7
Coach: Bennie G. Oosterbaan				139-87

Captain: Ted Cachey

Ranking (AP): Preseason NR; Postseason No. 15

All-American: Arthur Walker

All-Big Ten (first team): Ron Kramer, Arthur Walker

Leaders: Rushing—Fred Baer (439 yards, 107 carries);
Passing—Jim Maddock (16 of 35, 293 yards); Receiving—Ron
Kramer (23 catches, 303 yards).

Ron Kramer was Michigan's leading receiver but also topped the Big Ten in punting.

1955
7-2

Sept. 24	Missouri	Ann Arbor	W	42-7
Oct. 1	Michigan State	Ann Arbor	W	14-7
Oct. 8	Army	Ann Arbor	W	26-2
Oct. 15	Northwestern	Ann Arbor	W	14-2
Oct. 22	Minnesota	Minneapolis	W	14-13
Oct. 29	Iowa	Ann Arbor	W	33-21
Nov. 5	Illinois	Champaign	L	25-6
Nov. 12	Indiana	Ann Arbor	W	30-0
Nov. 19	Ohio State	Ann Arbor	L	17-0

Coach: Bennie G. Oosterbaan   179-94

Captain: Ed Meads

Ranking (AP): Preseason No. 3; Postseason No. 12

All-American: Ron Kramer

All-Big Ten (first team): Ron Kramer, Tom Maentz

Leaders: Rushing—Tony Branoff (387 yards, 86 carries);
Passing—Jim Maddock (20 of 52, 343 yards); Receiving—Ron
Kramer (12 catches, 253 yards).

Against Missouri in the season opener, Ron Kramer hauled in seven passes, three of which went for touchdowns, and set the Michigan record for touchdown receptions in a single game.

1956
7-2

Sept. 29	UCLA	Ann Arbor	W	42-13
Oct. 6	Michigan State	Ann Arbor	L	9-0
Oct. 13	Army	Ann Arbor	W	48-14
Oct. 20	Northwestern	Ann Arbor	W	34-20
Oct. 27	Minnesota	Ann Arbor	L	20-7
Nov. 3	Iowa	Iowa City	W	17-14
Nov. 10	Illinois	Ann Arbor	W	17-7
Nov. 17	Indiana	Ann Arbor	W	49-26
Nov. 24	Ohio State	Columbus	W	19-0

Coach: Bennie G. Oosterbaan   233-123

Captain: Tom Maentz

Ranking (AP): Preseason No. 8; Postseason No. 7

All-American: Ron Kramer

All-Big Ten (first team): Ron Kramer

Leaders: Rushing—Jim Pace (498 yards, 103 carries);
Passing—Bob Ptacek (15 of 23, 245 yards); Receiving—Ron
Kramer (18 catches, 353 yards).

Ron Kramer was frequently injured but finished his career with 102 points, along with 54 passes for 888 yards. The 6-foot-3, 225-pound end became the No. 1 draft pick of the Green Bay Packers in 1957 and contributed to their championship teams in 1961 and 1962. ... Michigan Stadium hosted more than 100,000 fans for the first time, with 101,001 attending the Michigan State game.

1957
5-3-1

Sept. 28	Southern California	Los Angeles	W	16-6
Oct. 5	Georgia	Ann Arbor	W	26-0
Oct. 12	Michigan State	Ann Arbor	L	35-6
Oct. 19	Northwestern	Ann Arbor	W	34-14
Oct. 26	Minnesota	Minneapolis	W	24-7
Nov. 2	Iowa	Ann Arbor	T	21-21
Nov. 9	Illinois	Champaign	L	20-19
Nov. 16	Indiana	Ann Arbor	W	27-13

| Nov. 23 | Ohio State | Ann Arbor | L | 31–14 |

Coach: Bennie G. Oosterbaan — 187–147

Captain: Jim Orwig

Ranking (AP): Preseason No. 6; Postseason NR

All-American: Jim Pace

All-Big Ten (first team): Jim Pace

Leaders: Rushing—Jim Pace (664 yards, 123 carries);
Passing—Jim Van Pelt (42 of 80, 629 yards); Receiving—Gary
Prahst (15 catches, 233 yards).

With the victory against Michigan, Ohio State was able to claim a share of the national championship. Auburn, which had been placed on probation by the Southeastern Conference for paying two high-school players $500 apiece, was No. 1 in the Associated Press poll, while the coaches ranked the Buckeyes first.

1958
2–6–1

Sept. 27	Southern California	Ann Arbor	W	20–19
Oct. 4	Michigan State	East Lansing	T	12–12
Oct. 11	Navy	Ann Arbor	L	20–14
Oct. 18	Northwestern	Evanston	L	55–24
Oct. 25	Minnesota	Ann Arbor	W	20–19
Nov. 1	Iowa	Ann Arbor	L	37–14
Nov. 8	Illinois	Ann Arbor	L	21–8
Nov. 15	Indiana	Ann Arbor	L	8–6
Nov. 22	Ohio State	Columbus	L	20–14

Coach: Bennie G. Oosterbaan — 132–211

Captain: John Herrnstein

Leaders: Rushing—Darrell Harper (309 yards, 55 carries);
Passing—Bob Ptacek (65 of 115, 763 yards); Receiving—Gary
Prahst (22 catches, 313 yards).

Bennie Oosterbaan's last season resulted in a 2–6–1 finish. His record at Michigan was 63–33–4.

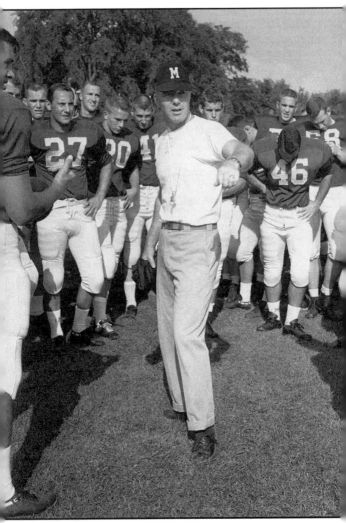

Bump Elliott gives instructions as he opens summer practice for the first time as head coach at Michigan in 1959.
Facing the camera and wearing number 27 is the man
who would lead the offense that year, Stan Noskin.

1959

4-5

Sept. 26	Missouri	Ann Arbor	L	20-15
Oct. 3	Michigan State	Ann Arbor	L	34-8
Oct. 10	Oregon State	Ann Arbor	W	18-7
Oct. 17	Northwestern	Ann Arbor	L	20-7
Oct. 24	Minnesota	Minneapolis	W	14-6
Oct. 31	Wisconsin	Ann Arbor	L	19-10
Nov. 7	Illinois	Champaign	W	20-15
Nov. 14	Indiana	Bloomington	L	26-7
Nov. 21	Ohio State	Ann Arbor	W	23-14

Coach: Chalmers "Bump" Elliott · 122-161

Captain: George Genyk

Leaders: Rushing—Fred Julian (289 yards, 72 carries); Passing—Stan Noskin (61 of 115, 747 yards); Receiving—Bob Johnson (20 catches, 264 yards).

Former Michigan standout Chalmers "Bump" Elliott was named head coach, a position he would hold for 10 years. One of his opposing coaches was his brother Pete, at Illinois.

Through the Years

1960
5–4

Sept. 24	Oregon	Ann Arbor	W	21–0
Oct. 1	Michigan State	East Lansing	L	24–17
Oct. 8	Duke	Ann Arbor	W	31–6
Oct. 15	Northwestern	Ann Arbor	W	14–7
Oct. 22	Minnesota	Ann Arbor	L	10–0
Oct. 29	Wisconsin	Madison	L	16–13
Nov. 5	Illinois	Ann Arbor	W	8–7
Nov. 12	Indiana	Ann Arbor	W	29–7
Nov. 19	Ohio State	Columbus	L	7–0
Coach: Chalmers "Bump" Elliott				133–84

Captain: Gerald Smith

Leaders: Rushing—Bennie McRae (352 yards, 80 carries); Passing—Dave Glinka (54 of 124, 755 yards); Receiving—Bob Johnson (15 catches, 230 yards).

Michigan began an impressive run against Northwestern and wouldn't lose to the Wildcats in the Big House until 1995.

1961
6–3

Sept. 30	UCLA	Ann Arbor	W	29–6
Oct. 7	Army	Ann Arbor	W	38–8
Oct. 14	Michigan State	Ann Arbor	L	28–0
Oct. 21	Purdue	Ann Arbor	W	16–14
Oct. 28	Minnesota	Minneapolis	L	23–20
Nov. 4	Duke	Ann Arbor	W	28–14
Nov. 11	Illinois	Champaign	W	38–6
Nov. 18	Iowa	Ann Arbor	W	23–14
Nov. 25	Ohio State	Ann Arbor	L	50–20
Coach: Chalmers "Bump" Elliott				212–163

Captain: George Mans

All-Big Ten (first team): Bennie McRae

Leaders: Rushing—Dave Raimey (496 yards, 99 carries); Passing—Dave Glinka (46 of 96, 588 yards); Receiving—George Mans (15 catches, 149 yards).

1962
2-7

Sept. 29	Nebraska	Ann Arbor	L	25-13
Oct. 6	Army	Ann Arbor	W	17-7
Oct. 13	Michigan State	East Lansing	L	28-0
Oct. 20	Purdue	West Lafayette	L	37-0
Oct. 27	Minnesota	Ann Arbor	L	17-0
Nov. 3	Wisconsin	Ann Arbor	L	34-12
Nov. 10	Illinois	Ann Arbor	W	14-10
Nov. 17	Iowa	Iowa City	L	28-14
Nov. 24	Ohio State	Columbus	L	28-0

Coach: Chalmers "Bump" Elliott — 70-214

Captain: Bob Brown

Leaders: Rushing—Dave Raimey (385 yards, 124 carries);
Passing—Bob Chandler (29 of 63, 401 yards); Receiving—
Harvey Chapman (11 catches, 223 yards).

The "Go Blue: M Club Supports You" banner made
its debut. Although the graduate "M" club made
the permanent banner, the undergraduate "M"
club started the tradition with a yellow block "M"
on a six-foot wide strip of fabric. The "Go Blue"
banner measures approximately 40 feet long by 4
feet wide. It's been twice stolen and once attacked
by the 1973 Ohio State team.

1963
3-4-2

Sept. 28	Southern Methodist	Ann Arbor	W	29-16
Oct. 5	Navy	Ann Arbor	L	26-13
Oct. 12	Michigan State	Ann Arbor	T	7-7
Oct. 19	Purdue	Ann Arbor	L	23-12
Oct. 26	Minnesota	Minneapolis	L	6-0
Nov. 2	Northwestern	Ann Arbor	W	27-6
Nov. 9	Illinois	Champaign	W	14-8
Nov. 16	Iowa	Ann Arbor	T	21-21
Nov. 30	Ohio State	Ann Arbor	L	14-10

Coach: Chalmers "Bump" Elliott — 131-127

Captain: Joe O'Donnell

All-Big Ten (first team): Tom Keating, Joe O'Donnell

Leaders: Rushing—Mel Anthony (394 yards, 103 carries); Passing—Robert Timberlake (47 of 98, 593 yards); Receiving—John Henderson (27 catches, 330 yards).

The Ohio State game was postponed one week from November 23 due to the assassination of President John F. Kennedy.

1964

9–1, Big Ten champions

Sept. 26	Air Force Academy	Ann Arbor	W	24–7
Oct. 3	Navy	Ann Arbor	W	21–0
Oct. 10	Michigan State	East Lansing	W	17–10
Oct. 17	Purdue	Ann Arbor	L	21–20
Oct. 24	Minnesota	Ann Arbor	W	19–12
Oct. 31	Northwestern	Ann Arbor	W	35–0
Nov. 7	Illinois	Ann Arbor	W	21–6
Nov. 14	Iowa	Iowa City	W	34–20
Nov. 21	Ohio State	Columbus	W	10–0
Jan. 1	Oregon State	Rose Bowl	W	34–7

Coach: Chalmers "Bump" Elliott — 235–83

Captain: Jim Conley

Ranking (AP): Preseason NR; Postseason No. 4

All-American: Robert Timberlake, William Yearby

All-Big Ten (first team): Robert Timberlake, Jim Conley, William Yearby, Tom Cecchini

Leaders: Rushing—Mel Anthony (702 yards, 145 carries); Passing—Robert Timberlake (70 of 137, 884 yards); Receiving—John Henderson (31 catches, 427 yards).

Despite a 21–20 loss to Purdue, Michigan won its first Big Ten title since 1950 after finishing no higher than fifth during the previous seven years. ... Against Oregon State in the Rose Bowl, Michigan took control in the second quarter on tailback Mel Anthony's 84-yard touchdown and on the subsequent possession, a 43-yard scoring run by Carl Ward. Paul Brothers completed his first six passes on the Beavers opening 84-yard drive, but the Wolverines came back to accumulate 415 yards.

1965
4–6

Sept. 18	North Carolina	Chapel Hill	W	31–24
Sept. 25	California	Ann Arbor	W	10–7
Oct. 2	Georgia	Ann Arbor	L	15–7
Oct. 9	Michigan State	Ann Arbor	L	24–7
Oct. 16	Purdue	Ann Arbor	L	17–15
Oct. 23	Minnesota	Minneapolis	L	14–13
Oct. 30	Wisconsin	Ann Arbor	W	50–14
Nov. 6	Illinois	Champaign	W	23–3
Nov. 13	Northwestern	Evanston	L	34–22
Nov. 20	Ohio State	Ann Arbor	L	9–7

Coach: Chalmers "Bump" Elliott   185–161

Captain: Tom Cecchini

Ranking (AP): Preseason No. 4; Postseason NR

All-American: William Yearby

All-Big Ten (first team): Tom Mack, Rich Volk, Carl Ward, William Yearby

Leaders: Rushing—Carl Ward (639 yards, 112 carries); Passing—Wally Gabler (58 of 125, 825 yards); Receiving—Jack Clancy (52 catches, 762 yards).

Bump Elliott was a standout player before his coaching days: he played three sports at Purdue and later set school records at Michigan. Had his football career not been interrupted by World War II, he could have been considered one of the sport's all-time greats.

1966
6–4

Sept. 17	Oregon State	Ann Arbor	W	41–0
Sept. 24	California	Berkley	W	17–7
Oct. 1	North Carolina	Ann Arbor	L	21–7
Oct. 8	Michigan State	East Lansing	L	20–7
Oct. 15	Purdue	Ann Arbor	L	22–21
Oct. 22	Minnesota	Ann Arbor	W	49–0
Oct. 29	Wisconsin	Madison	W	28–17
Nov. 5	Illinois	Ann Arbor	L	28–21
Nov. 12	Northwestern	Ann Arbor	W	28–20
Nov. 19	Ohio State	Columbus	W	17–3

Coach: Chalmers "Bump" Elliott   236–138

Captain: Jack Clancy

All-American: Jack Clancy, Richard Volk

All-Big Ten (first team): Don Bailey, Jack Clancy, Jim Detwiler, Dave Fisher, Frank Nunley, Rick Volk

Leaders: Rushing—Dave Fisher (637 yards, 131 carries); Passing—Dick Vidmer (117 of 226, 1,611 yards); Receiving—Jack Clancy (76 catches, 1,079 yards).

1967
4–6

Sept. 23	Duke	Ann Arbor	W	10–7
Sept. 30	California	Berkley	L	10–9
Oct. 7	Navy	Ann Arbor	L	26–21
Oct. 14	Michigan State	Ann Arbor	L	34–0
Oct. 21	Indiana	Ann Arbor	L	27–20
Oct. 28	Minnesota	Minneapolis	L	20–15
Nov. 4	Northwestern	Ann Arbor	W	7–3
Nov. 11	Illinois	Champaign	W	21–14
Nov. 18	Wisconsin	Madison	W	27–14
Nov. 25	Ohio State	Ann Arbor	L	24–14

Coach: Chalmers "Bump" Elliott   144–179

Captain: Joe Dayton

All-Big Ten (first team): Joe Dayton, Ron Johnson, Tom Stincic

Leaders: Rushing—Ron Johnson (1,005 yards, 220 carries); Passing—Dennis Brown (82 of 156, 913 yards); Receiving—Jim Berline (54 catches, 624 yards).

Ron Johnson was Michigan's first player to gain 1,000 rushing yards in a single season.

1968

8–2

Sept. 21	California	Ann Arbor	L	21–7
Sept. 28	Duke	Durham	W	31–10
Oct. 5	Navy	Ann Arbor	W	32–9
Oct. 12	Michigan State	Ann Arbor	W	28–14
Oct. 19	Indiana	Bloomington	W	27–22
Oct. 26	Minnesota	Ann Arbor	W	33–20
Nov. 2	Northwestern	Evanston	W	35–0
Nov. 9	Illinois	Ann Arbor	W	36–0
Nov. 16	Wisconsin	Ann Arbor	W	34–9
Nov. 23	Ohio State	Columbus	L	50–14

Coach: Chalmers "Bump" Elliott 277–155

Captain: Ron Johnson

Ranking (AP): Preseason NR; Postseason No. 12

All-American: Ron Johnson

All-Big Ten (first team): Ron Johnson, Tom Stincic, Jim Mandich, Dennis Brown, Phil Seymour, Tom Goss, Tom Curtis

Leaders: Rushing—Ron Johnson (1,391 yards, 255 carries); Passing—Dennis Brown (109 of 229, 1,562 yards); Receiving—Jim Mandich (43 catches, 576 yards).

Tom Curtis set a then-NCAA career record with 431 interception return yards and led the nation with 10 pickoffs. His 25 career interceptions set a school record and ranked second all time in the Big Ten and fourth in NCAA history. ... Ron Johnson was named the team's most valuable player for the second time and was also team captain, an All-American, and Big Ten MVP. In 10 games he scored 19 touchdowns, rushed for 1,391 yards, caught passes for 166 yards, and returned nine kickoffs for 150 yards. Against Wisconsin, his 347 rushing yards set an NCAA record that stood for three years.

1969

8–3, Big Ten champions (tie)

Sept. 20	Vanderbilt	Ann Arbor	W	42–14
Sept. 27	Washington	Ann Arbor	W	45–7
Oct. 4	Missouri	Ann Arbor	L	40–17
Oct. 11	Purdue	Ann Arbor	W	31–20
Oct. 18	Michigan State	East Lansing	L	23–12
Oct. 25	Minnesota	Minneapolis	W	35–9
Nov. 1	Wisconsin	Ann Arbor	W	35–7
Nov. 8	Illinois	Champaign	W	57–0
Nov. 15	Iowa	Iowa City	W	51–6
Nov. 22	Ohio State	Ann Arbor	W	24–12
Jan. 1	Southern California	Rose Bowl	L	10–3

Coach: Glenn E. "Bo" Schembechler   352–148

Captain: Jim Mandich

Ranking (AP): Preseason NR; Postseason No. 9

All-American: James Mandich, Tom Curtis

All-Big Ten (first team): James Mandich, Phil Seymour, Tom Curtis, Dan Dierdorf, Guy Murdock, Billy Taylor, Marty Huff

Leaders: Rushing—Bill Taylor (864 yards, 141 carries); Passing—Don Moorhead (103 of 210, 1,261 yards); Receiving—Jim Mandich (50 catches, 662 yards).

Michigan outrushed Vanderbilt 367–55 in Bo Schembechler's debut for a 42–14 victory. ... It accumulated 266 rushing yards and 108 passing yards while creating seven turnovers (including three interceptions by Bobby Pierson) to defeat Ohio State 24–12, ending the Buckeyes' 22-game winning streak. With the Wolverines losing 50–14 the year before, Schembechler made every player on the scout team wear No. 50 during practices. Glenn Doughty sustained a knee injury just before the Rose Bowl, and Schembechler suffered a heart attack. Defensive coordinator Jim Young coached the game, Michigan's first-ever bowl loss. ... James Mandich's 119 career receptions and 1,494 career yards ranked first all time among Michigan tight ends.

1970

9–1

Sept. 19	Arizona	Ann Arbor	W	20–9
Sept. 26	Washington	Seattle	W	17–3
Oct. 3	Texas A&M	Ann Arbor	W	14–10
Oct. 10	Purdue	West Lafayette	W	29–0
Oct. 17	Michigan State	Ann Arbor	W	34–20
Oct. 24	Minnesota	Ann Arbor	W	39–13
Oct. 31	Wisconsin	Madison	W	29–15
Nov. 7	Illinois	Ann Arbor	W	42–0
Nov. 14	Iowa	Ann Arbor	W	55–0
Nov. 21	Ohio State	Columbus	L	20–9

Coach: Glenn E. "Bo" Schembechler 288–90

Captains: Don Moorehead, Henry Hill

Ranking (AP): Preseason 8; Postseason 9

All-American: Dan Dierdorf, Marty Huff, Henry Hill

All-Big Ten (first team): Phil Seymour, Dan Dierdorf, Guy Murdock, Billy Taylor, Marty Huff, Paul Staroba, Reggie McKenzie, Don Moorhead, Pete Newell, Henry Hill, Thom Darden

Leaders: Rushing—Bill Taylor (911 yards, 197 carries); Passing—Don Moorhead (87 of 190, 1,167 yards); Receiving—Paul Staroba (35 catches, 519 yards).

All-American Dan Dierdorf went on to play 13 years with the St. Louis Cardinals in the NFL (1971–1983) and was named All-Pro five times and the league's best offensive lineman in 1976, 1977, and 1978. He was elected to the Pro Football Hall of Fame in 1996 and had a successful career as a broadcaster.

1971

11–1, Big Ten champions

Sept. 11	Northwestern	Evanston	W	21–6
Sept. 18	Virginia	Ann Arbor	W	56–0
Sept. 25	UCLA	Ann Arbor	W	38–0
Oct. 2	Navy	Ann Arbor	W	46–0
Oct. 9	Michigan State	East Lansing	W	24–13
Oct. 16	Illinois	Ann Arbor	W	35–6
Oct. 23	Minnesota	Minneapolis	W	35–7
Nov. 30	Indiana	Ann Arbor	W	61–7
Nov. 6	Iowa	Ann Arbor	W	63–7
Nov. 13	Purdue	West Lafayette	W	20–17
Nov. 20	Ohio State	Ann Arbor	W	10–7
Jan. 1	Stanford	Rose Bowl	L	13–12

Coach: Glenn E. "Bo" Schembechler   421–83

Captains: Frank Gusich, Guy Murdock

Ranking (AP): Preseason No. 4; Postseason No. 6

All-American: Thom Darden, Mike Taylor, Reggie McKenzie, Bill Taylor

All-Big Ten (first team): Reggie McKenzie, Thom Darden, Mike Taylor, Mike Keller

Leaders: Rushing—Bill Taylor (1,297 yards, 249 carries); Passing—Tom Slade (27 of 63, 364 yards); Receiving—Glenn Doughty (16 catches, 203 yards).

Guard Reggie McKenzie was a consensus All-American selection as Michigan had an undefeated regular season with no ties, its first since 1948. "Being called an All-American at Michigan and being selected to the College Football Hall of Fame are really huge," McKenzie said. "I feel truly blessed and honored." ... On the 70th anniversary of the first Rose Bowl game, Michigan and Stanford met again, with the Cardinal making a key goal-line stand and rallying to score a game-winning field goal in the final seconds.

1972

10–1, Big Ten champions

Sept. 16	Northwestern	Ann Arbor	W	7–0
Sept. 23	UCLA	Los Angeles	W	26–9
Sept. 30	Tulane	Ann Arbor	W	41–7
Oct. 7	Navy	Ann Arbor	W	35–7
Oct. 14	Michigan State	Ann Arbor	W	10–0
Oct. 21	Illinois	Champaign	W	31–7
Oct. 28	Minnesota	Ann Arbor	W	42–0
Nov. 4	Indiana	Bloomington	W	21–7
Nov. 11	Iowa	Iowa City	W	31–0
Nov. 18	Purdue	Ann Arbor	W	9–6
Nov. 25	Ohio State	Columbus	L	14–11

Coach: Glenn E. "Bo" Schembechler   264–57

Captains: Tom Coyle, Randy Logan

Ranking (AP): Preseason No. 10; Postseason No. 6

All-American: Randy Logan, Paul Seymour

All-Big Ten (first team): Paul Seymour, Tom Coyle, Clint Spearman, Fred Grambau, Randy Logan, Ed Shuttlesworth, Dave Brown

Leaders: Rushing—Ed Shuttlesworth (723 yards, 157 carries); Passing—Dennis Franklin (59 of 123, 818 yards); Receiving—Paul Seal (18 catches, 243 yards).

With No. 9 Ohio State knocking off undefeated No. 3 Michigan the rivalry was reaching an all-time high, with the 10-year period from 1969–78 that Bo Schembechler faced Woody Hayes later dubbed "The 10-Year War." ... Despite the impressive 10–1 record, Michigan didn't play in a postseason game.

1973

10–0–1, Big Ten champions (tie)

Sept. 15	Iowa	Iowa City	W	31–7
Sept. 22	Stanford	Ann Arbor	W	47–10
Sept. 29	Navy	Ann Arbor	W	14–0
Oct. 6	Oregon	Ann Arbor	W	24–0
Oct. 13	Michigan State	East Lansing	W	31–0
Oct. 20	Wisconsin	Ann Arbor	W	35–6

Oct. 27	Minnesota	Minneapolis	W	34–7
Nov. 3	Indiana	Ann Arbor	W	49–13
Nov. 10	Illinois	Ann Arbor	W	21–6
Nov. 17	Purdue	West Lafayette	W	34–9
Nov. 24	Ohio State	Ann Arbor	T	10–10

Coach: Glenn E. "Bo" Schembechler	330–68

Captains: Dave Gallagher, Paul Seal

Ranking (AP): Preseason No. 5; Postseason No. 6

All-American: Dave Brown, Dave Gallagher

All-Big Ten (first team): Ed Shuttlesworth, Dave Brown, Mike Hoban, Clint Haslerig, Dave Gallagher, Dennis Franklin

Leaders: Rushing—Ed Shuttlesworth (745 yards, 193 carries); Passing—Dennis Franklin (36 of 67, 534 yards); Receiving—Paul Seal (14 catches, 254 yards).

Although Michigan finished a three-year stretch in which it went 30–2–1, it again failed to play in a bowl despite not having a loss. After Mike Lantry missed field-goal attempts of 58 and 48 yards in the final 1:06, resulting in the 10–10 tie against Ohio State, Big Ten commissioner Wayne Duke polled the league's athletics directors to pick which team would represent the conference in the Rose Bowl. The deciding vote for Ohio State was cast by rival Michigan State's Burt Smith. "This is the lowest day of my career as a player and coach," Bo Schembechler said.

After the dust settled in the famous 10-Year War that had journalists calling the Big Ten the "Big Two, Little Eight," there was nothing small about the hatred in the Ohio State-Michigan rivalry. Bo Schembechler's Wolverines had a slight edge, posting a 5–4–1 record over Woody Hayes' Buckeyes during the span.

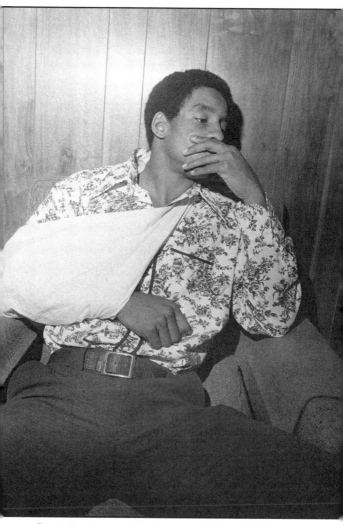

Dennis Franklin reacts to the news on TV that Ohio State had been selected to represent the Big Ten in the Rose Bowl. Franklin had tied the game with a touchdown but broke his collarbone in the effort.

1974

10–1, Big Ten champions (tie)

Sept. 14	Iowa	Ann Arbor	W	24–7
Sept. 21	Colorado	Ann Arbor	W	31–0
Sept. 28	Navy	Ann Arbor	W	52–0
Oct. 5	Stanford	Stanford	W	27–16
Oct. 12	Michigan State	Ann Arbor	W	21–7
Oct. 19	Wisconsin	Madison	W	24–20
Oct. 26	Minnesota	Ann Arbor	W	49–0
Nov. 2	Indiana	Bloomington	W	21–7
Nov. 9	Illinois	Champaign	W	14–6
Nov. 16	Purdue	Ann Arbor	W	51–0
Nov. 23	Ohio State	Columbus	L	12–10

Coach: Glenn E. "Bo" Schembechler	324–75

Captains: David Brown, Dennis Franklin

Ranking (AP): Preseason No. 6; Postseason No. 3

All-American: David Brown

All-Big Ten (first team): Dave Brown, Dennis Franks, Steve Strinko, Dan Jilek, Jeff Perlinger, Tim Davis, Don Dufek Jr.

Leaders: Rushing—Gordon Bell (1,048 yards, 174 carries); Passing—Dennis Franklin (58 of 104, 933 yards); Receiving—Gil Chapman (23 catches, 378 yards).

During 33 games, defensive back Dave Brown's teams surrendered more than 10 points only five times and registered 11 shutouts. After a 16-year pro career, Brown died at the age of 52 while an assistant coach at Texas Tech.

62

Professional career interceptions for Dave Brown. He carried his dominating defensive play over to the NFL, and when he retired he was seventh all time in career picks.

1975

8–2–2

Sept. 13	Wisconsin	Madison	W	23–6
Sept. 20	Stanford	Ann Arbor	T	19–19
Sept. 27	Baylor	Ann Arbor	T	14–14
Oct. 4	Missouri	Ann Arbor	W	31–7
Oct. 11	Michigan State	East Lansing	W	16–6
Oct. 18	Northwestern	Ann Arbor	W	69–0
Oct. 25	Indiana	Ann Arbor	W	55–7
Nov. 1	Minnesota	Minneapolis	W	28–21
Nov. 8	Purdue	Ann Arbor	W	28–0
Nov. 15	Illinois	Champaign	W	21–15
Nov. 22	Ohio State	Ann Arbor	L	21–14
Jan. 1	Oklahoma	Orange Bowl	L	14–6

Coach: Glenn E. "Bo" Schembechler — 324–130

Captains: Don Dufek Jr., Kirk Lewis

Ranking (AP): Preseason No. 3; Postseason No. 8

All-American: Don Dufek Jr.

All-Big Ten (first team): Dan Jilek, Tim Davis, Don Dufek Jr., Jim Smith, Jim Czirr, Gordon Bell, Greg Morton, Calvin O'Neal

Leaders: Rushing—Gordon Bell (1,388 yards, 273 carries); Passing—Rick Leach (32 of 100, 680 yards); Receiving—Jim Smith (24 catches, 553 yards).

Under pressure from its coaches, including Bo Schembechler, the Big Ten finally ended its policy of limiting postseason appearances to just the Rose Bowl. It led to an Orange Bowl matchup between No. 2 Oklahoma and No. 4 Michigan. Oklahoma was led by defensive standouts Leroy and Dewey Selmon (10 and 13 tackles, respectively), and with Ohio State's 23–10 loss in the Rose Bowl to UCLA the Sooners were consensus national champions. ... The last time Michigan failed to attract at least 100,000 fans for a home game was the Indiana game (93,857). However, Michigan also went over 1 million in total season attendance for the first time (1,006,519).

Rob Lytle celebrates in the California sunshine of the Rose Bowl after scoring in the first half. Lytle had a magical season, rushing for 1,469 yards for the Big Ten champions and finishing his stellar career with 3,317 total yards on the ground.

1976

10–2, Big Ten champions (tie)

Sept. 11	Wisconsin	Ann Arbor	W	40–27
Sept. 18	Stanford	Ann Arbor	W	51–0
Sept. 25	Navy	Ann Arbor	W	70–14
Oct. 2	Wake Forest	Ann Arbor	W	31–0
Oct. 9	Michigan State	Ann Arbor	W	42–10
Oct. 16	Northwestern	Evanston	W	38–7
Oct. 23	Indiana	Bloomington	W	35–0
Oct 30	Minnesota	Ann Arbor	W	45–0
Nov. 6	Purdue	West Lafayette	L	16–14
Nov. 13	Illinois	Ann Arbor	W	38–7
Nov. 20	Ohio State	Columbus	W	22–0
Jan. 1	Southern California	Rose Bowl	L	14–6

Coach: Glenn E. "Bo" Schembechler — 432–95

Captains: Kirk Lewis, Calvin O'Neal, Rob Lytle

Ranking (AP): Preseason No. 2; Postseason No. 3

All-American: Mark Donahue, Rob Lytle, Calvin O'Neal, Jim Smith

All-Big Ten (first team): Jim Smith, Greg Morton, Calvin O'Neal, Bill Dufek, Mark Donahue, Walt Downing, Rick Leach, Rob Lytle, John Anderson

Leaders: Rushing—Rob Lytle (1,469 yards, 221 carries); Passing—Rick Leach (50 of 105, 973 yards); Receiving—Jim Smith (26 catches, 714 yards).

The 22–0 victory against Ohio State was the series' largest margin of victory in 30 years and the first shutout recorded against the Buckeyes in 112 games (dating back to 1964). At the conclusion of the regular season, Michigan led the nation in total offense (448.1 yards per game), scoring offense (38.7 points), and scoring defense (7.2 points). ... Rob Lytle finished his career with a then school-record 3,317 yards. ... Michigan ranked third in the final Associated Press poll, its highest finish under Bo Schembechler at that point.

1977

10–2, Big Ten champions (tie)

Sept. 10	Illinois	Champaign	W	37–9
Sept. 17	Duke	Ann Arbor	W	21–9
Sept. 24	Navy	Ann Arbor	W	14–7
Oct. 1	Texas A&M	Ann Arbor	W	41–3
Oct. 8	Michigan State	East Lansing	W	24–14
Oct. 15	Wisconsin	Ann Arbor	W	56–0
Oct. 22	Minnesota	Minneapolis	L	16–0
Oct. 29	Iowa	Ann Arbor	W	23–6
Nov. 5	Northwestern	Ann Arbor	W	63–20
Nov. 12	Purdue	West Lafayette	W	40–7
Nov. 19	Ohio State	Ann Arbor	W	14–6
Jan. 2	Washington	Rose Bowl	L	27–20

Coach: Glenn E. "Bo" Schembechler   353–124

Captains: Walt Downing, Dwight Hicks

Ranking (AP): Preseason No. 2; Postseason No. 9

All-American: John Anderson, Mark Donahue, Walt Downing

All-Big Ten (first team): Mark Donahue, Walt Downing, Rick Leach, John Anderson, Mike Kenn, Dwight Hicks, Jim Pickens

Leaders: Rushing—Russell Davis (1,092 yards, 225 carries); Passing—Rick Leach (90 of 174, 1,348 yards); Receiving—Ralph Clayton (24 catches, 477 yards).

With a defense featuring defensive linemen Curtis Greer and Chris Godfrey, outside linebacker Mel Owens, and defensive backs Mike Harden and Dwight Hicks, Michigan held all but three opponents to fewer than 10 points. ... Despite the efforts of quarterback Rick Leach, who threw a Rose Bowl-record 76-yard touchdown pass to Curt Stephenson, Warren Moon was able to lead Washington, which only went 7–4 during the regular season, to a Rose Bowl victory. Interceptions by Michael Jackson and Nesby Glasgow ended Michigan's final efforts.

1978

10–2, Big Ten champions (tie)

Sept. 16	Illinois	Ann Arbor	W	31–0
Sept. 23	Notre Dame	South Bend	W	28–14
Sept. 30	Duke	Ann Arbor	W	52–0
Oct. 7	Arizona	Ann Arbor	W	21–17
Oct. 14	Michigan State	Ann Arbor	L	24–15
Oct. 21	Wisconsin	Madison	W	42–0
Oct. 28	Minnesota	Ann Arbor	W	42–10
Nov. 4	Iowa	Iowa City	W	34–0
Nov. 11	Northwestern	Evanston	W	59–14
Nov. 18	Purdue	Ann Arbor	W	24–6
Nov. 25	Ohio State	Columbus	W	14–3
Jan. 1	Southern California	Rose Bowl	L	17–10

Coach: Glenn E. "Bo" Schembechler   372–105

Captains: Russell Davis, Jerry Meter

Ranking (AP): Preseason No. 6; Postseason No. 5

All-American: Rick Leach

All-Big Ten (first team): Rick Leach, Jon Giesler, John Arbeznik, Russell Davis, Curtis Greer, Ron Simpkins, Mike Jolly, Mike Harden

Leaders: Rushing—Harlan Huckleby (741 yards, 154 carries); Passing—Rick Leach (78 of 158, 1,283 yards); Receiving—Ralph Clayton (25 catches, 546 yards).

The Rose Bowl loss included one of the most controversial calls in college football history when, on second down at the Michigan 3, Southern California running back Charles White appeared to fumble with linebacker Jerry Meter recovering the loose ball. However, a line judge ruled that White had first crossed the goal line for the touchdown. ... Playing in his third straight Rose Bowl, quarterback Rick Leach set career Rose Bowl records for total plays (94), total yards running and passing (523), and most yards passing (452), to be named co-MVP along with White. Leach made 48 consecutive starts, was named All-Big Ten three times, and both All-American and conference MVP his senior season.

1979
8–4

Sept. 8	Northwestern	Ann Arbor	W	49–7
Sept. 15	Notre Dame	Ann Arbor	L	12–10
Sept. 22	Kansas	Ann Arbor	W	28–7
Sept. 29	California	Berkley	W	14–10
Oct. 6	Michigan State	East Lansing	W	21–7
Oct. 13	Minnesota	Ann Arbor	W	31–21
Oct. 20	Illinois	Champaign	W	27–7
Oct. 27	Indiana	Ann Arbor	W	27–21
Nov. 3	Wisconsin	Ann Arbor	W	54–0
Nov. 10	Purdue	West Lafayette	L	24–21
Nov. 17	Ohio State	Ann Arbor	L	18–15
Dec. 28	North Carolina	Gator Bowl	L	17–15

Coach: Glenn E. "Bo" Schembechler   312–151

Captains: John Arbeznik, Ron Simpkins

Ranking (AP): Preseason No. 7; Postseason No. 18

All-American: Curtis Green, Ron Simpkins

All-Big Ten (first team): John Arbeznik, Curtis Greer, Ron Simpkins, Mike Jolly, Mike Trgovac, Butch Woolfolk

Leaders: Rushing—Butch Woolfolk (990 yards, 191 carries); Passing—John Wangler (78 of 130, 1,431 yards); Receiving—Doug Marsh (33 catches, 612 yards).

Radio announcer Bob Ufer made his famous last-second call of "Oh my God! Carter scored!" during the homecoming game against Indiana when from the 45-yard line with six seconds remaining John Wangler hit Anthony Carter with a pass at the 20. Carter then bounced off two defenders and got away from safety Tim Wilbur to score the game-winning touchdown. ... Michigan had passed for 203 yards when quarterback John Wangler sustained a severe knee injury on a sprint out and tackle by North Carolina linebacker Lawrence Taylor in the Gator Bowl. Also hindering the Wolverines were two lost fumbles, two interceptions, and 87 yards in penalties.

Anthony Carter sprints into the end zone against Indiana for his famous touchdown to win the game. He had caught the pass, stumbled, and had to fight through Hoosier tacklers to score.

1980

10–2, Big Ten champions

Sept. 13	Northwestern	Ann Arbor	W	17–10
Sept. 20	Notre Dame	South Bend	L	29–27
Sept. 27	South Carolina	Ann Arbor	L	17–14
Oct. 4	California	Ann Arbor	W	38–13
Oct. 11	Michigan State	Ann Arbor	W	27–23
Oct. 18	Minnesota	Minneapolis	W	37–14
Oct. 25	Illinois	Ann Arbor	W	45–14
Nov. 1	Indiana	Bloomington	W	35–0
Nov. 8	Wisconsin	Madison	W	24–0
Nov. 15	Purdue	Ann Arbor	W	26–0
Nov. 22	Ohio State	Columbus	W	9–3
Jan. 1	Washington	Rose Bowl	W	23–6

Coach: Glenn E. "Bo" Schembechler   322–129

Captains: Andy Cannavino, George Lilja

Ranking (AP): Preseason No. 12; Postseason No. 4

All-American: Anthony Carter, George Lilja

All-Big Ten (first team): Mike Trgovac, Harold "Butch" Woolfolk,
Mel Owens, Andy Cannavino, Anthony Carter, Ed Muransky,
George Lilja, Kurt Becker, Bubba Paris, John Powers

Leaders: Rushing—Harold "Butch" Woolfolk (1,042 yards, 196
carries); Passing—John Wangler (117 of 212, 1,522 yards);
Receiving—Anthony Carter (51 catches, 818 yards).

After a 1–2 start, Michigan got on a roll and
beginning with the Illinois game had a streak of
15 consecutive scoreless quarters en route to its
first Big Ten title outright since 1971. ... Although
Washington's 374 total yards were the most
Michigan yielded all season, a goal-line stand in
the second quarter turned the momentum for
good, and Bo Schembechler recorded his first victory at the Rose Bowl in six visits. During that
stretch the Wolverines were 96–10–3 in regular-season games. ... Teammates selected wide
receiver Anthony Carter as most valuable player,
the first time squad members gave the award to a
sophomore.

1981
9–3

Sept. 12	Wisconsin	Madison	L	21–14
Sept. 19	Notre Dame	Ann Arbor	W	25–7
Sept. 26	Navy	Ann Arbor	W	21–16
Oct. 3	Indiana	Bloomington	W	38–17
Oct. 10	Michigan State	East Lansing	W	38–20
Oct. 17	Iowa	Ann Arbor	L	9–7
Oct. 24	Northwestern	Ann Arbor	W	38–0
Oct. 31	Minnesota	Minneapolis	W	34–13
Nov. 7	Illinois	Ann Arbor	W	70–21
Nov. 14	Purdue	West Lafayette	W	28–10
Nov. 21	Ohio State	Ann Arbor	L	14–9
Dec. 31	UCLA	Bluebonnet Bowl	W	33–14

Coach: Glenn E. "Bo" Schembechler   355–162

Captains: Kurt Becker, Robert Thompson

Ranking (AP): Preseason No. 1; Postseason No. 12

All-American: Kurt Becker, Anthony Carter, Ed Muransky, William "Bubba" Paris, Harold "Butch" Woolfolk

All-Big Ten (first team): Anthony Carter, Ed Muransky, Kurt Becker, William "Bubba" Paris

Leaders: Rushing—Harold "Butch" Woolfolk (1,459 yards, 253 carries); Passing—Steve Smith (97 of 210, 1,661 yards); Receiving—Anthony Carter (50 catches, 952 yards).

Against UCLA in the Bluebonnet Bowl, Michigan accumulated 320 rushing yards while the defense allowed just 33 and 195 total yards. Butch Woolfolk closed his collegiate career with 186 rushing yards, for a four-year total of 3,861, and was named game MVP. Quarterback Steve Smith's 152 passing yards set a Michigan single-season record of 1,661 yards.

1982

8–4, Big Ten champions

Sept. 11	Wisconsin	Ann Arbor	W	20–9
Sept. 18	Notre Dame	South Bend	L	23–17
Sept. 25	UCLA	Ann Arbor	L	31–27
Oct. 2	Indiana	Ann Arbor	W	24–10
Oct. 9	Michigan State	Ann Arbor	W	31–17
Oct. 16	Iowa	Iowa City	W	29–7
Oct. 23	Northwestern	Evanston	W	49–14
Oct. 30	Minnesota	Ann Arbor	W	52–14
Nov. 6	Illinois	Champaign	W	16–10
Nov. 13	Purdue	Ann Arbor	W	52–21
Nov. 20	Ohio State	Columbus	L	24–14
Jan. 1	UCLA	Rose Bowl	L	24–14

Coach: Glenn E. "Bo" Schembechler   345–204

Captains: Anthony Carter, Paul Girgash, Robert Thompson

Ranking (AP): Preseason No. 12; Postseason NR

All-American: Anthony Carter

All-Big Ten (first team): Anthony Carter, Lawrence Ricks, Stefan Humphries, Tom Dixon, Rich Strenger, Robert Thompson, Paul Girgash, Keith Bostic

Leaders: Rushing—Lawrence Ricks (1,388 yards, 266 carries); Passing—Steve Smith (118 of 227, 1,735 yards); Receiving—Anthony Carter (43 catches, 844 yards).

Michigan clinched the Big Ten title before its loss to Ohio State. The Rose Bowl matchup against UCLA was a rematch from earlier in the season and the previous year's Bluebonnet Bowl. ... Anthony Carter was named All-American for the third time and a unanimous selection for the second time. In Heisman Trophy voting he placed 10th, 7th, and 4th. During his career he had 36 touchdowns, with 33 on receptions. He scored 240 points to break Tom Harmon's school record of 237 (1938–40).

1983
9–3

Sept. 10	Washington State	Ann Arbor	W	20–17
Sept. 17	Washington	Seattle	L	25–24
Sept. 24	Wisconsin	Madison	W	38–21
Oct. 1	Indiana	Ann Arbor	W	43–18
Oct. 8	Michigan State	East Lansing	W	42–0
Oct. 15	Northwestern	Ann Arbor	W	35–0
Oct. 22	Iowa	Ann Arbor	W	16–13
Oct. 29	Illinois	Champaign	L	16–6
Nov. 5	Purdue	Ann Arbor	W	42–10
Nov. 12	Minnesota	Minneapolis	W	58–10
Nov. 19	Ohio State	Ann Arbor	W	24–21
Jan. 2	Auburn	Sugar Bowl	L	9–7

Coach: Glenn E. "Bo" Schembechler   355–160

Captains: Stefan Humphries, John Lott

Ranking (AP): Preseason No. 10; Postseason No. 8

All-American: Stefan Humphries, Tom Dixon

All-Big Ten (first team): Stefan Humphries, Tom Dixon, Bob Bergeron, Kevin Brooks, Al Sincich, Evan Cooper

Leaders: Rushing—Rick Rogers (1,002 yards, 209 carries); Passing—Steve Smith (106 of 205, 1,420 yards); Receiving—Sim Nelson (41 catches, 494 yards).

After a narrow early season loss at Washington, Michigan rebounded with back-to-back shutouts of Michigan State and Northwestern followed by a last-second victory against Iowa. The loss to Illinois essentially determined the Big Ten title, but by holding off Ohio State the Wolverines still earned a January bowl bid. ... Running backs Lionel James, Bo Jackson, and Tommy Agee combined for 306 rushing yards, but it was a last-minute field goal by Al Del Greco that gave Auburn the victory in the Sugar Bowl.

1984
6–6

Sept. 8	Miami (Fla.)	Ann Arbor	W	22–14
Sept. 15	Washington	Ann Arbor	L	20–11
Sept. 22	Wisconsin	Ann Arbor	W	20–14
Sept. 29	Indiana	Bloomington	W	14–6
Oct. 6	Michigan State	Ann Arbor	L	19–7
Oct. 13	Northwestern	Ann Arbor	W	31–0
Oct. 20	Iowa	Iowa City	L	26–0
Oct. 27	Illinois	Ann Arbor	W	26–18
Nov. 3	Purdue	West Lafayette	L	31–29
Nov. 10	Minnesota	Ann Arbor	W	31–7
Nov. 17	Ohio State	Columbus	L	21–6
Dec. 21	Brigham Young	Holiday Bowl	L	24–17

Coach: Glenn E. "Bo" Schembechler   214–200

Captains: Doug James, Mike Mallory

Ranking (AP): Preseason No. 14; Postseason NR

All-Big Ten (first team): Kevin Brooks, Mike Mallory

Leaders: Rushing—Jamie Morris (574 yards, 118 carries);
Passing—Jim Harbaugh (60 of 111, 718 yards); Receiving—Sim
Nelson (40 catches, 459 yards).

After upsetting top-ranked Miami in the season
opener, Michigan's season was derailed when
quarterback Jim Harbaugh broke his arm against
Michigan State. Nevertheless, the Wolverines
wound up playing in the game to determine the
national championship, against No. 1 BYU in the
Holiday Bowl. The Cougars accumulated 483
yards in total offense, 32 first downs, and thanks
to two late touchdowns won their 24th consecutive game.

1985
10–1–1

Sept. 14	Notre Dame	Ann Arbor	W	20–12
Sept. 21	South Carolina	Columbia	W	34–3
Sept. 28	Maryland	Ann Arbor	W	20–0
Oct. 5	Wisconsin	Ann Arbor	W	33–6
Oct. 12	Michigan State	East Lansing	W	31–0

Bo Schembechler yells instructions to quarterback Jim Harbaugh. Today, it's Harbaugh that does the yelling: after a great career at Michigan and a decade-long career in the pros, Harbaugh is head coach at Stanford.

Oct. 19	Iowa	Iowa City	L	12–10
Oct. 26	Indiana	Ann Arbor	W	42–15
Nov. 2	Illinois	Champaign	T	3–3
Nov. 9	Purdue	Ann Arbor	W	47–0
Nov. 16	Minnesota	Minneapolis	W	48–7
Nov. 23	Ohio State	Ann Arbor	W	27–17
Jan. 1	Nebraska	Fiesta Bowl	W	27–23

Coach: Glenn E. "Bo" Schembechler — 342–98

Captains: Brad Cochran, Eric Kattus, Mike Mallory

Ranking (AP): Preseason NR; Postseason No. 2

All-American: Mike Hammerstein, Brad Cochran

All-Big Ten (first team): Mike Mallory, Brad Cochran, Mike Hammerstein, Eric Kattus, Mark Messner, Clay Miller

Leaders: Rushing—Jamie Morris (1,030 yards, 197 carries); Passing—Jim Harbaugh (145 of 227, 1,976 yards); Receiving—Eric Kattus (38 catches, 582 yards).

Michigan converted two fumble recoveries into touchdowns, Dave Arnold rushed in untouched to block his third punt of the season to set up a field goal, and quarterback Jim Harbaugh scored twice as the Wolverines scored 24 points in the third quarter to defeat Nebraska in the Fiesta Bowl. Michigan finished No. 2 behind Oklahoma in the final polls.

1986
11–2, Big Ten champions (tie)

Sept. 13	Notre Dame	South Bend	W	24–23
Sept. 20	Oregon State	Ann Arbor	W	31–12
Sept. 27	Florida State	Ann Arbor	W	20–18
Oct. 4	Wisconsin	Madison	W	34–17
Oct. 11	Michigan State	Ann Arbor	W	27–6
Oct. 18	Iowa	Ann Arbor	W	20–17
Oct. 25	Indiana	Bloomington	W	38–14
Nov. 1	Illinois	Ann Arbor	W	69–13
Nov. 8	Purdue	West Lafayette	W	31–7
Nov. 15	Minnesota	Ann Arbor	L	20–17
Nov. 22	Ohio State	Columbus	W	26–24
Dec. 6	Hawaii	Honolulu	W	27–10

Jan. 1	Arizona State	Rose Bowl	L	22–15

Coach: Glenn E. "Bo" Schembechler 379–203

Captains: Jim Harbaugh, Andy Moeller

Ranking (AP): Preseason No. 2; Postseason No. 8

All-American: John Elliott, Jim Harbaugh, Garland Rivers

All-Big Ten (first team): Mark Messner, John Elliott, Mark Hammerstein, Jim Harbaugh, Jamie Morris, Garland Rivers

Leaders: Rushing—Jamie Morris (1,086 yards, 212 carries); Passing—Jim Harbaugh (180 of 277, 2,729 yards); Receiving—Gerald White (38 catches, 408 yards).

Michigan's Rose Bowl troubles continued, but Wolverines fans enjoyed their 32nd Big Ten title and Bo Schembechler's 200th career victory to pass Fielding Yost as the winningest coach in Michigan history. ... The upset loss to Minnesota snapped a 13-game winning streak and 15-game unbeaten streak.

1987
8–4

Sept. 12	Notre Dame	Ann Arbor	L	26–7
Sept. 19	Washington State	Ann Arbor	W	44–18
Sept. 26	Long Beach State	Ann Arbor	W	49–0
Oct. 3	Wisconsin	Ann Arbor	W	49–0
Oct. 10	Michigan State	East Lansing	L	17–11
Oct. 17	Iowa	Ann Arbor	W	37–10
Oct. 24	Indiana	Bloomington	L	14–10
Oct. 31	Northwestern	Ann Arbor	W	29–6
Nov. 7	Minnesota	Minneapolis	W	30–20
Nov. 14	Illinois	Champaign	W	17–14
Nov. 21	Ohio State	Ann Arbor	L	23–20
Jan. 2	Alabama	Hall of Fame Bowl	W	28–24

Coach: Glenn E. "Bo" Schembechler 331–172

Captains: Doug Mallory, Jamie Morris

Ranking (AP): Preseason No. 7; Postseason No. 19

All-American: John Elliott, Mark Messner

All-Big Ten (first team): Mark Messner, John Elliott, Jamie Morris, John Vitale, Mike Husar

Jamie Morris breaks through an Arizona State tackle in the Rose Bowl to score a touchdown. Morris saved his best for big games, racking up 234 yards in the Hall of Fame Bowl the next year and finishing his Michigan career with 4,393 rushing yards.

Leaders: Rushing—Jamie Morris (1,703 yards, 282 carries); Passing—Demetrius Brown (80 of 168, 1,251 yards); Receiving—Greg McMurtry (21 catches, 474 yards).

Bo Schembechler underwent quadruple bypass heart surgery in early December so offensive coordinator Gary Moeller coached the Wolverines against Alabama in the Hall of Fame Bowl. Jamie Morris' 234 rushing yards set both a Hall of Fame Bowl and Michigan bowl record. He also broke the Wolverines' single-season rushing record with 1,703 yards and ended his career with 4,393 rushing yards, the third best in Big Ten history.

1988
9–2–1, Big Ten champions

Sept. 10	Notre Dame	South Bend	L	19–17
Sept. 17	Miami (Fla.)	Ann Arbor	L	31–30
Sept. 24	Wake Forest	Ann Arbor	W	19–9
Oct. 1	Wisconsin	Madison	W	62–14
Oct. 8	Michigan State	Ann Arbor	W	17–3
Oct. 15	Iowa	Iowa City	T	17–17
Oct. 22	Indiana	Ann Arbor	W	31–6
Oct. 29	Northwestern	Evanston	W	52–7
Nov. 5	Minnesota	Ann Arbor	W	22–7
Nov. 12	Illinois	Ann Arbor	W	38–9
Nov. 19	Ohio State	Columbus	W	34–31
Jan. 2	Southern California	Rose Bowl	W	22–14

Coach: Glenn E. "Bo" Schembechler   361–167

Captains: Mark Messner, John Vitale

Ranking (AP): Preseason No. 11; Postseason No. 4

All-American: John Vitale

All-Big Ten (first team): Mark Messner, John Vitale, Mike Husar, John Kolesar, Tony Boles, Mike Gillette, David Arnold

Leaders: Rushing—Tony Boles (1,408 yards, 262 carries); Passing—Michael Taylor (76 of 122, 957 yards); Receiving—Greg McMurtry (27 catches, 470 yards).

After Michigan opened the regular season with close losses to Notre Dame and Miami, Michigan didn't lose another game and captured the Big Ten title. The tough victory against Ohio State made

many wonder if the Wolverines would find more heartache against Southern California, which featured a strong defense and Heisman Trophy runner-up Rodney Peete, at the Rose Bowl. Leroy Hoard had 142 rushing yards on 19 carries and scored two touchdowns as Bo Schembechler enjoyed his second victory in Pasadena.

1989

10–2, Big Ten champions

Sept. 16	Notre Dame	Ann Arbor	L	24–19
Sept. 24	UCLA	Los Angeles	W	24–23
Sept. 30	Maryland	Ann Arbor	W	41–21
Oct. 7	Wisconsin	Ann Arbor	W	24–0
Oct. 14	Michigan State	East Lansing	W	10–7
Oct. 21	Iowa	Iowa City	W	26–12
Oct. 28	Indiana	Bloomington	W	38–10
Nov. 4	Purdue	Ann Arbor	W	42–27
Nov. 11	Illinois	Champaign	W	24–10
Nov. 18	Minnesota	Minneapolis	W	49–15
Nov. 25	Ohio State	Ann Arbor	W	28–18
Jan. 2	Southern California	Rose Bowl	L	17–10

Coach: Glenn E. "Bo" Schembechler 335–184

Captains: J.J. Grant, Derrick Walker

Ranking (AP): Preseason No. 1; Postseason No. 7

All-American: Tripp Welborne

All-Big Ten (first team): Tony Boles, J.D. Carlson, Dean Dingman, Derrick Walker, Tripp Welborne

Leaders: Rushing—Tony Boles (839 yards, 131 carries); Passing—Michael Taylor (74 of 121, 1,081 yards); Receiving—Greg McMurtry (41 catches, 711 yards).

Bo Schembechler's final game was against Southern California in the Rose Bowl. The key play came with 12 minutes remaining, on fourth-and-2 at the Michigan 46, when Chris Stapleton's fake punt for a first down was nullified by holding and unsportsmanlike-conduct penalties. The Trojans took advantage and drove 75 yards in 13 plays for the game-winning touchdown. ... Schembechler, who never had a losing season, retired as the win-ningest active coach in the nation (234–65–8) and fifth on the all-time list, behind Paul "Bear" Bryant, Amos Alonzo Stagg, Glen "Pop" Warner, and Woody Hayes. ... Michigan was the preseason No. 1 but fell to No. 2 after Notre Dame opened with a 36–13 victory against Virginia. However, it still set up a season-opening No. 1 vs. No. 2 matchup for the Wolverines.

1990

9–3, Big Ten champions (tie)

Sept. 15	Notre Dame	South Bend	L	28–24
Sept. 22	UCLA	Ann Arbor	W	38–15
Sept. 29	Maryland	Ann Arbor	W	45–17
Oct. 6	Wisconsin	Madison	W	41–3
Oct. 13	Michigan State	Ann Arbor	L	28–27
Oct. 20	Iowa	Ann Arbor	L	24–23
Oct. 27	Indiana	Bloomington	W	45–19
Nov. 3	Purdue	West Lafayette	W	38–13
Nov. 10	Illinois	Ann Arbor	W	22–17
Nov. 17	Minnesota	Ann Arbor	W	35–18
Nov. 24	Ohio State	Columbus	W	16–13
Jan. 1	Ole Miss	Gator Bowl	W	35–3

Coach: Gary Moeller | 389–198

Captains: Jarrod Bunch, John Milligan

Ranking (AP): Preseason 6; Postseason 7

All-American: Dean Dingman, Greg Skrepanek, Tripp Welborne

All-Big Ten (first team): J.D. Carlson, Dean Dingman, Tripp Welborne, Jon Vaughn, Greg Skrepenak, Desmond Howard, Tom Dohring, Erick Anderson

Leaders: Rushing—Jon Vaughn (1,416 yards, 216 carries); Passing—Elvis Grbac (155 of 266, 1,911 yards); Receiving—Desmond Howard (63 catches, 1,025 yards).

Taking over for Bo Schembechler was Gary Moeller, who had made the move with Schembechler from Miami (Ohio) in 1969 and served as defensive ends coach until promoted to defensive coordinator in 1973. Moeller led Michigan to five bowl games during his five-year tenure. Ironically, he graduated from Ohio State in 1963. ... Although quarterback Elvis Grbac threw four touchdown passes, a Michigan bowl

record, against Ole Miss, offensive linemen Dean
Dingman, Tom Dohring, Greg Skrepenak, Matt
Elliott, and Steve Everitt shared MVP honors after
the Wolverines tallied 715 total yards in the Gator
Bowl.

1991

10–2, Big Ten champions

Sept. 7	Boston College	Chestnut Hill	W	35–13
Sept. 14	Notre Dame	Ann Arbor	W	24–14
Sept. 28	Florida State	Ann Arbor	L	51–31
Oct. 5	Iowa	Iowa City	W	43–24
Oct. 12	Michigan State	East Lansing	W	45–28
Oct. 19	Indiana	Ann Arbor	W	24–16
Oct. 25	Minnesota	Minneapolis	W	52–6
Nov. 2	Purdue	Ann Arbor	W	42–0
Nov. 9	Northwestern	Ann Arbor	W	59–14
Nov. 16	Illinois	Champaign	W	20–0
Nov. 23	Ohio State	Ann Arbor	W	31–3
Jan. 1	Washington	Rose Bowl	L	34–14
Coach: Gary Moeller				420–203

Captains: Erick Anderson, Greg Skrepenak

Ranking (AP): Preseason 2; Postseason 6

Major Awards: Desmond Howard, Heisman Trophy, Walter
Camp Award, Maxwell Award; Erick Anderson, Dick Butkus
Award

All-American: Erick Anderson, Matt Elliott, Desmond Howard,
Greg Skrepenak

All-Big Ten (first team): J.D. Carlson, Greg Skrepenak, Desmond
Howard, Erick Anderson, Matt Elliott, Mike Evans, Ricky Powers,
Elvis Grbac, Chris Hutchinson

Leaders: Rushing—Ricky Powers (1,364 yards, 240 carries);
Passing—Elvis Grbac (165 of 254, 2,085 yards); Receiving—
Desmond Howard (62 catches, 985 yards).

Desmond Howard became the first receiver to
lead the Big Ten in scoring (90 points) and won
the Heisman Trophy. His 640 first-place votes
(85 percent) were the most ever for a Heisman
winner. ... Erick Anderson won the first Butkus
Award in Michigan history. ... Michigan's bid

A pair of Michigan head coaches watch from the sideline during the 1990 Rose Bowl. Bo Schembechler is animated in his last game at the helm, which Gary Moeller was content to watch before taking over the next year.

for the national championship was derailed by Washington, which had the nation's top-rated defense, in the Rose Bowl. The Huskies (12–0) held the Wolverines to just 72 yards and sacked quarterback Elvis Grbac five times while limiting Heisman winner Desmond Howard to one pass reception.

1992
9–0–3, Big Ten champions

Sept. 12	Notre Dame	South Bend	T	17–17
Sept. 19	Oklahoma State	Ann Arbor	W	35–3
Sept. 26	Houston	Ann Arbor	W	61–7
Oct. 3	Iowa	Ann Arbor	W	52–28
Oct. 10	Michigan State	Ann Arbor	W	35–10
Oct. 17	Indiana	Bloomington	W	31–3
Oct. 24	Minnesota	Ann Arbor	W	63–13
Oct. 31	Purdue	West Lafayette	W	24–17
Nov. 7	Northwestern	Evanston	W	40–7
Nov. 14	Illinois	Ann Arbor	T	22–22
Nov. 21	Ohio State	Columbus	T	13–13
Jan. 1	Washington	Rose Bowl	W	38–31
Coach: Gary Moeller				431–171

Captains: Corwin Brown, Elvis Grbac, Chris Hutchinson

Ranking (AP): Preseason No. 6; Postseason No. 5

All-American: Derrick Alexander, Joe Cocozzo, Chris Hutchinson

All-Big Ten (first team): Elvis Grbac, Chris Hutchinson, Derrick Alexander, Corwin Brown, Joe Cocozzo, Rob Doherty, Matt Dyson, Steve Everitt, Tony McGee, Shonte Peoples, Doug Skene, Tyrone Wheatley

Leaders: Rushing—Tyrone Wheatley (1,357 yards, 185 carries); Passing—Elvis Grbac (129 of 199, 1,640 yards); Receiving—Derrick Alexander (50 catches, 740 yards).

Even though Michigan had three ties, it set a Big Ten record by winning 19 consecutive confer-ence games from 1990–92. ... The Wolverines were able to avenge the previous year's loss to Washington in the Rose Bowl with a wild 38–31 victory. The game-winning points came on an 80-yard drive, with Elvis Grbac, on third-and-short

from the Huskies' 15, hitting Tony McGee at the 2 as he fell into the end zone for the only score of the fourth quarter. Tyrone Wheatley had 235 rushing yards, including touchdown runs of 56, 88, and 24 yards.

1993
8–4

Sept. 4	Washington State	Ann Arbor	W	41–14
Sept. 11	Notre Dame	Ann Arbor	L	27–23
Sept. 25	Houston	Ann Arbor	W	42–21
Oct. 2	Iowa	Ann Arbor	W	24–7
Oct. 9	Michigan State	East Lansing	L	17–7
Oct. 16	Penn State	University Park	W	21–13
Oct. 23	Illinois	Ann Arbor	L	24–21
Oct. 30	Wisconsin	Madison	L	13–10
Nov. 6	Purdue	Ann Arbor	W	25–10
Nov. 13	Minnesota	Minneapolis	W	58–7
Nov. 20	Ohio State	Ann Arbor	W	28–0
Jan. 1	North Carolina State	Hall of Fame Bowl	W	42–7
Coach: Gary Moeller				342–160

Captains: Ricky Powers, Buster Stanley

Ranking (AP): Preseason No. 3; Postseason No. 21

All-Big Ten (first team): Ty Law, Buster Stanley, Tyrone Wheatley

Leaders: Rushing—Tyrone Wheatley (1,129 yards, 207 carries); Passing—Todd Collins (189 of 296, 2,509 yards); Receiving—Derrick Alexander (35 catches, 621 yards).

Running back Tyrone Wheatley was named game MVP of the Hall of Fame Bowl after rushing for 124 yards on 18 carries, including touchdown runs of 26 and 18 yards. The final score marked his 35th career rushing touchdown, which broke Rick Leach's school record, and was his 40th overall, tying Anthony Carter's mark.

Through the Years

1994
8–4

Sept. 3	Boston College	Ann Arbor	W	34–26
Sept. 10	Notre Dame	South Bend	W	26–24
Sept. 24	Colorado	Ann Arbor	L	27–26
Oct. 1	Iowa	Iowa City	W	29–14
Oct. 8	Michigan State	Ann Arbor	W	40–20
Oct. 15	Penn State	Ann Arbor	L	31–24
Oct. 22	Illinois	Champaign	W	19–14
Oct. 29	Wisconsin	Ann Arbor	L	31–19
Nov. 5	Purdue	West Lafayette	W	45–23
Nov. 12	Minnesota	Ann Arbor	W	38–22
Nov. 19	Ohio State	Columbus	L	22–6
Dec. 30	Colorado State	Holiday Bowl	W	24–14
Coach: Gary Moeller				330–268

Captains: Steve Morrison, Walter Smith

Ranking (AP): Preseason No. 5; Postseason No. 12

All-American: Remy Hamilton, Ty Law

All-Big Ten (first team): Tyrone Wheatley, Ty Law, Remy Hamilton, Steve Morrison, Amani Toomer, Jason Horn

Leaders: Rushing—Tyrone Wheatley (1,144 yards, 210 carries); Passing—Todd Collins (186 of 288, 2,518 yards); Receiving—Amani Toomer (54 catches, 1,096 yards).

With six seconds remaining, Colorado pulled off the miracle "Rocket Left" touchdown when quarterback Kordell Stewart threw a pass 73 yards into the wind, and Blake Anderson tipped the ball over Michigan defenders to Michael Westbrook for the touchdown. The Buffaloes were coached by former Michigan assistant Bill McCartney. ... Against Colorado State in the Holiday Bowl, quarterback Todd Collins threw for 162 yards (14 of 24) and two touchdowns to earn offensive MVP honors. Meanwhile, the defense had 11 tackles for a loss as Michigan never trailed.

1995
9–4

Aug. 26	Virginia	Pigskin Classic	W	18–17
Sept. 2	Illinois	Champaign	W	38–14
Sept. 9	Memphis	Ann Arbor	W	24–7
Sept. 16	Boston College	Chestnut Hill	W	23–13
Sept. 30	Miami (Ohio)	Ann Arbor	W	38–19
Oct. 7	Northwestern	Ann Arbor	L	19–13
Oct. 21	Indiana	Bloomington	W	34–17
Oct. 28	Minnesota	Ann Arbor	W	52–17
Nov. 4	Michigan State	East Lansing	L	28–25
Nov. 11	Purdue	Ann Arbor	W	5–0
Nov. 18	Penn State	University Park	L	27–17
Nov. 25	Ohio State	Ann Arbor	W	31–23
Dec. 28	Texas A&M	Alamo Bowl	L	22–20
Coach: Lloyd Carr				338–223

Captains: Jarrett Irons, Joe Marinaro

Ranking (AP): Preseason No. 14; Postseason No. 17

All-American: Jason Horn, Jon Runyan

All-Big Ten (first team): Jason Horn, Jarrett Irons, Jon Runyan, Clarence Thompson, Charles Woodson, Rod Payne

Leaders: Rushing—Tim Biakabutuka (1,818 yards, 303 carries); Passing—Brian Griese (127 of 238, 1,577 yards); Receiving—Mercury Hayes (48 catches, 923 yards).

Lloyd Carr entered the season as interim head coach, which didn't become permanent until November 13. He had been on the Wolverines' coaching staff for 28 years before his final promotion. … Michigan was done in by five field goals by Texas A&M's Kyle Bryant (27, 49, 47, 31, and 37 yards), the last of which occurred with 23 seconds remaining at the Alamo Bowl.

1996
8–4

Aug. 31	Illinois	Ann Arbor	W	20–8
Sept. 14	Colorado	Boulder	W	20–13
Sept. 21	Boston College	Ann Arbor	W	20–14
Sept. 28	UCLA	Ann Arbor	W	38–9
Oct. 5	Northwestern	Evanston	L	17–16
Oct. 19	Indiana	Ann Arbor	W	27–20
Oct. 22	Minnesota	Minneapolis	W	44–10
Oct. 26	Michigan State	Ann Arbor	W	45–29
Nov. 2	Purdue	West Lafayette	L	9–3
Nov. 9	Penn State	Ann Arbor	L	29–17
Nov. 23	Ohio State	Columbus	W	13–9
Jan. 1	Alabama	Outback Bowl	L	17–14
Coach: Lloyd Carr			287–184	

Captains: Jarrett Irons, Rod Payne

Ranking (AP): Preseason No. 14; Postseason No. 20

All-American: William Carr, Jarrett Irons, Rod Payne, Charles Woodson

All-Big Ten (first team): Jarret Irons, Rod Payne, David Bowens, William Carr, Damon Denson, Marcus Ray, Jerame Tuman, Charles Woodson

Leaders: Rushing—Clarence Williams (837 yards, 202 carries); Passing—Scott Dreisbach (149 of 269, 2,025 yards); Receiving—Tai Streets (44 catches, 730 yards).

Michigan dominated statistically—415 yards of total offense compared to 247—but struggled to find the end zone against Alabama in the Outback Bowl. Three times the Wolverines had the ball inside Alabama's 35-yard line, but failed to score. Quarterback Brian Griese completed 21 of 37 passes for 287 yards, with one touchdown. His one interception was returned 88 yards for a touchdown by linebacker Dwayne Rudd. In Gene Stallings' last game coaching the Crimson Tide, Alabama put the game away when Shaun Alexander scored on a 46-yard touchdown with 2:15 remaining in the game.

1997

12–0, National champions, Big Ten champions

Sept. 13	Colorado	Ann Arbor	W	27–3
Sept. 20	Baylor	Ann Arbor	W	38–3
Sept. 27	Notre Dame	Ann Arbor	W	21–14
Oct. 4	Indiana	Bloomington	W	37–0
Oct. 11	Northwestern	Ann Arbor	W	23–6
Oct. 18	Iowa	Ann Arbor	W	28–24
Oct. 25	Michigan State	East Lansing	W	23–7
Nov. 1	Minnesota	Ann Arbor	W	24–3
Nov. 8	Penn State	University Park	W	34–8
Nov. 15	Wisconsin	Madison	W	26–16
Nov. 22	Ohio State	Ann Arbor	W	20–14
Jan. 1	Washington State	Rose Bowl	W	21–16
Coach: Lloyd Carr				322–144

Captains: Jon Jansen, Eric Mayes

Ranking (AP): Preseason No. 14; Postseason No. 1

Major Awards: Charles Woodson, Heisman Trophy, Walter Camp Award, Jim Thorpe Award, Bronko Nagurski Award, Chuck Bednarik Award

All-American: Glen Steele, Jerame Tuman, Charles Woodson

All-Big Ten (first team): Charles Woodson, Marcus Ray, Jerame Tuman, Brian Griese, Zach Adami, Steve Hutchinson, Jon Jansen, Glen Steele, Sam Sword, Andre Weathers

Leaders: Rushing—Chris Howard (938 yards, 199 carries); Passing—Brian Griese (193 of 307, 2,293 yards); Receiving—Chris Howard (37 catches, 276 yards).

Michigan's No. 1-ranked defense limited Washington State to its lowest scoring output of the season at the Rose Bowl. Game MVP Brian Griese completed 18 of 30 passes for 251 yards and three touchdowns, and split end Tai Streets had touchdown receptions of 53 and 58 yards. ... Although Michigan was No. 1 in both polls prior to the Rose Bowl, Wolverines fans were outraged when the coaches' poll preferred Nebraska by a very narrow margin, resulting in a spilt title. ... Defensive back Charles Woodson, who had eight

interceptions and also saw time at wide receiver and punt returner, won Michigan's third Heisman Trophy, edging Tennessee quarterback Peyton Manning for the award.

1998

10–3, Big Ten champions (tie)

Sept. 5	Notre Dame	South Bend	L	36–20
Sept. 12	Syracuse	Ann Arbor	L	38–28
Sept. 19	Eastern Michigan	Ann Arbor	W	59–20
Sept. 26	Michigan State	Ann Arbor	W	29–17
Oct. 3	Iowa	Iowa City	W	12–9
Oct. 17	Northwestern	Evanston	W	12–6
Oct. 24	Indiana	Ann Arbor	W	21–10
Oct. 31	Minnesota	Minneapolis	W	15–10
Nov. 7	Penn State	Ann Arbor	W	27–0
Nov. 14	Wisconsin	Ann Arbor	W	27–10
Nov. 21	Ohio State	Columbus	L	31–16
Nov. 28	Hawaii	Honolulu	W	48–17
Jan. 1	Arkansas	Florida Citrus Bowl	W	45–31
Coach: Lloyd Carr				359–235

Captains: Juaquin Feazell, Jon Jansen

Ranking (AP): Preseason No. 5; Postseason No. 12

All-American: Jon Jansen

All-Big Ten (first team): Steve Hutchinson, Jon Jansen, Jerame Tuman

Leaders: Rushing—Anthony Thomas (893 yards, 167 carries); Passing—Tom Brady (214 of 350, 2,636 yards); Receiving—Tai Streets (67 catches, 1,035 yards).

After trailing 31–24 with just 5:49 remaining in the game, Michigan rallied to score 21 points in a span of 4:02 to defeat Arkansas and become the first Big Ten team to win at the Florida Citrus Bowl in five years. Running back Anthony Thomas led the Wolverines with 139 rushing yards and three touchdowns, and linebacker Sam Sword made 11 tackles.

Heisman winner Charles Woodson gestures into the sky during the Rose Bowl. Just the third Michigan player to win college football's highest honor, Woodson is also the last defensive player to win the award.

1999
10–2

Sept. 4	Notre Dame	Ann Arbor	W	26–22
Sept. 11	Rice	Ann Arbor	W	37–3
Sept. 18	Syracuse	Syracuse	W	18–13
Sept. 25	Wisconsin	Madison	W	21–16
Oct. 2	Purdue	Ann Arbor	W	38–12
Oct. 9	Michigan State	East Lansing	L	34–31
Oct. 23	Illinois	Ann Arbor	L	35–29
Oct. 30	Indiana	Bloomington	W	34–31
Nov. 6	Northwestern	Ann Arbor	W	37–3
Nov. 13	Penn State	University Park	W	31–27
Nov. 20	Ohio State	Ann Arbor	W	24–17
Jan. 1	Alabama	Orange Bowl	W OT	35–34
Coach: Lloyd Carr				361–247

Captains: Tom Brady, Steve Hutchinson, Rob Renes

Ranking (AP): Preseason No. 8; Postseason No. 5

All-American: Rob Renes

All-Big Ten (first team): Steve Hutchinson, David Terrell, Rob Renes, Ian Gold, Tommy Hendricks, Jeff Backus

Leaders: Rushing—Anthony Thomas (1,297 yards, 301 carries); Passing—Tom Brady (214 of 341, 2,586 yards); Receiving—David Terrell (71 catches, 1,038 yards).

Michigan erased a pair of 14-point deficits to send the Orange Bowl into overtime, the first in school history. Quarterback Tom Brady set up a score on the first play with a 25-yard pass to tight end Shawn Thompson, and Hayden Epstein made the extra point. After Alabama's Andrew Zow connected with Antonio Carter for a 21-yard touchdown, kicker Ryan Pflugner sent the extra-point attempt wide right. Wide receiver David Terrell set career highs in receiving yards (150) and receiving touchdowns (three) and tied his career high in receptions (10). Brady went 34-for-46 with four touchdown passes and a Michigan bowl-record 369 passing yards.

2000

9–3, Big Ten champions (tie)

Sept. 2	Bowling Green	Ann Arbor	W	42–7
Sept. 9	Rice	Ann Arbor	W	38–7
Sept. 16	UCLA	Los Angeles	L	23–20
Sept. 23	Illinois	Champaign	W	35–31
Sept. 30	Wisconsin	Ann Arbor	W	13–10
Oct. 7	Purdue	West Lafayette	L	32–31
Oct. 14	Indiana	Ann Arbor	W	58–0
Oct. 21	Michigan State	Ann Arbor	W	14–0
Nov. 4	Northwestern	Evanston	L	54–51
Nov. 11	Penn State	Ann Arbor	W	33–11
Nov. 18	Ohio State	Columbus	W	38–26
Jan. 1	Auburn	Florida Citrus Bowl	W	31–28

Coach: Lloyd Carr — 404–229

Captains: Steve Hutchinson, Anthony Thomas, Eric Wilson

Ranking (AP): Preseason No. 6; Postseason No. 11

All-American: Steve Hutchinson, David Terrell

All-Big Ten (first team): Steve Hutchinson, David Terrell, Jeff Backus, Anthony Thomas, Larry Foote

Leaders: Rushing—Anthony Thomas (1,733 yards, 319 carries); Passing—Drew Henson (146 of 237, 2,146 yards); Receiving—David Terrell (67 catches, 1,130 yards).

After defeating Ohio State, Michigan received its second invitation in three years to play in the Florida Citrus Bowl. Quarterback Drew Henson completed 15 of 20 passes for 294 yards and two touchdowns, while running back Anthony Thomas had 32 carries for 182 yards and two touchdowns against Auburn. Sophomore safety Julius Curry and senior safety DeWayne Patmon both made interceptions, and junior linebacker Eric Brackins had 13 tackles.

Through the Years

Marquise Walker pulls free from a Purdue tackler in
2001. Walker accounted for 249 total yards in the game
and was named an All-American after the season.

2001
8–4

Sept. 1	Miami (Ohio)	Ann Arbor	W	31–13
Sept. 8	Washington	Seattle	L	23–18
Sept. 22	Western Michigan	Ann Arbor	W	38–21
Sept. 29	Illinois	Ann Arbor	W	45–20
Oct. 6	Penn State	University Park	W	20–0
Oct. 13	Purdue	Ann Arbor	W	24–10
Oct. 27	Iowa	Iowa City	W	32–26
Nov. 3	Michigan State	East Lansing	L	26–24
Nov. 10	Minnesota	Ann Arbor	W	31–10
Nov. 17	Wisconsin	Madison	W	20–17
Nov. 24	Ohio State	Ann Arbor	L	26–20
Jan. 1	Tennessee	Florida Citrus Bowl	L	45–17
Coach: Lloyd Carr				320–237

Captains: Eric Brackins, Shawn Thompson

Ranking (AP): Preseason 12; Postseason 20

All-American: Larry Foote, Marquise Walker

All-Big Ten (first team): Larry Foote, Jonathan Goodwin, Dan Rumishek, Marquise Walker

Leaders: Rushing—B.J. Askew (902 yards, 199 carries); Passing—John Navarre (207 of 385, 2,435 yards); Receiving—Marquise Walker (86 catches, 1,143 yards).

The Michigan State game was known as "Clockgate" due to a controversy involving the timekeeper. On fourth-and-goal, with one second remaining, Michigan State quarterback Jeff Smoker threw a touchdown pass to T. J. Duckett as time expired. However, Michigan fans claimed the clock should have run out prior to the winning play (while Spartans fans counter that the penalty for Michigan having too many men on the field should have stopped the clock with 36 seconds remaining). Following a petition from Coach Lloyd Carr, NCAA officials began keeping time on the field. Duckett set a Michigan State record for most rushing yards against Michigan (211), while the Wolverines sacked Smoker 11 times. ...

The game against Tennessee was the first meeting between the two schools. The loss snapped Michigan's four-game winning streak in January bowl games.

2002
10–3

Aug. 31	Washington	Ann Arbor	W	31–29
Sept. 7	Western Michigan	Ann Arbor	W	35–12
Sept. 14	Notre Dame	South Bend	L	25–23
Sept. 21	Utah	Salt Lake City	W	10–7
Sept. 28	Illinois	Champaign	W	45–28
Oct. 12	Penn State	Ann Arbor	W OT	27–24
Oct. 19	Purdue	West Lafayette	W	23–21
Oct. 26	Iowa	Ann Arbor	L	34–9
Nov. 2	Michigan State	Ann Arbor	W	49–3
Nov. 9	Minnesota	Minneapolis	W	41–24
Nov. 16	Wisconsin	Ann Arbor	W	21–14
Nov. 23	Ohio State	Columbus	L	14–9
Dec. 22	Florida	Outback Bowl	W	38–30
Coach: Lloyd Carr				361–265

Captains: Victor Hobson, Bennie Joppru

Ranking (AP): Preseason No. 12; Postseason No. 9

All-American: Marlin Jackson, Bennie Joppru

All-Big Ten (first team): David Baas, Victor Hobson, Marlin Jackson, Tony Pape

Leaders: Rushing—Chris Perry (1,110 yards, 267 carries); Passing—John Navarre (248 of 448, 2,905 yards); Receiving—Braylon Edwards (67 catches, 1,035 yards).

Tailback Chris Perry had 28 carries for 85 yards and four touchdowns and also had a career-best six receptions for 108 yards, in the Outback Bowl. Quarterback John Navarre completed 21 of 36 passes for a career-high 319 yards and one touchdown as Michigan won the roller-coaster game. Victor Hobson sealed the victory with an interception on Florida's final drive and also had 12 tackles, including two for a loss.

2003

10–3, Big Ten champions

Aug. 30	Central Michigan	Ann Arbor	W	45–7
Sept. 6	Houston	Ann Arbor	W	50–3
Sept. 13	Notre Dame	Ann Arbor	W	38–0
Sept. 20	Oregon	Eugene	L	31–27
Sept. 27	Indiana	Ann Arbor	W	31–17
Oct. 4	Iowa	Iowa City	L	30–27
Oct. 10	Minnesota	Minneapolis	W	38–35
Oct. 18	Illinois	Ann Arbor	W	56–14
Oct. 25	Purdue	Ann Arbor	W	31–3
Nov. 1	Michigan State	East Lansing	W	27–20
Nov. 15	Northwestern	Evanston	W	41–10
Nov. 22	Ohio State	Ann Arbor	W	35–21
Jan. 1	Southern California	Rose Bowl	L	28–14
Coach: Lloyd Carr				460–219

Captains: Grant Bowman, Carl Diggs, John Navarre

Ranking (AP): Preseason No. 4; Postseason No. 6

Major Awards: Chris Perry, Doak Walker Award

All-American: Marlin Jackson, Chris Perry

All-Big Ten (first team): David Baas, Marlin Edwards, Braylon Edwards, John Navarre, Tony Pape, Chris Perry

Leaders: Rushing—Chris Perry (1,674 yards, 338 carries); Passing—John Navarre (270 of 456, 3,331 yards); Receiving—Braylon Edwards (85 catches, 1,138 yards).

Through the Years

Southern California was ranked No. 1 but had been excluded from the Bowl Championship Series title game, sending the Trojans back to the Rose Bowl to meet No. 4 Michigan. Although the Wolverines defense was sixth in the nation against the pass, Matt Leinart completed 23 of 34 passes for 327 yards and three touchdowns (two to Keary Colvert). Southern California registered nine sacks for 69 yards against a Michigan offensive line that had surrendered just 15 sacks all season. "You have to give the guys up front the credit for the havoc they created," Lloyd Carr said. Despite the constant pressure, quarterback John Navarre completed 27 of 46 passes for 271 yards and one touchdown, and Braylon Edwards

had 10 receptions for 107 yards. ... Michigan scored 31 points in the fourth quarter to edge No. 17 Minnesota, 38–35. "We still don't know what happened," Wolverines defensive end Larry Stevens said.

2004

9–3, Big Ten champions (tie)

Sept. 4	Miami (Ohio)	Ann Arbor	W	43–10
Sept. 11	Notre Dame	South Bend	L	28–20
Sept. 18	San Diego State	Ann Arbor	W	24–21
Sept. 25	Iowa	Ann Arbor	W	30–17
Oct. 2	Indiana	Bloomington	W	35–14
Oct. 9	Minnesota	Ann Arbor	W	27–24
Oct. 16	Illinois	Champaign	W	30–19
Oct. 23	Purdue	West Lafayette	W	16–14
Oct. 30	Michigan State	Ann Arbor	W 3OT	45–37
Nov. 13	Northwestern	Ann Arbor	W	42–20
Nov. 20	Ohio State	Columbus	L	37–21
Jan. 1	Texas	Rose Bowl	L	38–37
Coach: Lloyd Carr			370–279	

Captains: David Baas, Marlin Jackson

Ranking (AP): Preseason No. 8; Postseason No. 14

Major Awards: Braylon Edwards, Fred Biletnikoff Award; David Baas, Dave Rimington Trophy

All-American: David Baas, Braylon Edwards, Marlin Jackson, Ernest Shazor

All-Big Ten (first team): David Baas, Braylon Edwards, Mike Hart, Matt Lentz, Adam Stenavich, Tim Massaquoi, Gabe Watson, Marlin Jackson, Ernest Shazor

Leaders: Rushing—Mike Hart (1,455 yards, 282 carries); Passing—Chad Henne (240 of 399, 2,743 yards); Receiving—Braylon Edwards (97 catches, 1,330 yards).

With No. 1 Southern California playing the Bowl Championship Series title game, Texas was invited to Pasadena for its first meeting with Michigan. The game went down to the final play, a 37-yard field goal by Dusty Magnum as time expired to give the Longhorns a 38–37 victory. Texas quarterback Vince Young accumulated 372 yards of total offense (192 rushing) and accounted for all five UT touchdowns. Michigan quarterback Chad Henne passed for 227 yards and a Rose Bowl-record four touchdown passes. All-American wide receiver Braylon Edwards had 10 catches for 109 yards and three touchdown receptions, also a Rose Bowl record. Wide receiver/kick returner Steve Breaston had a Rose Bowl-record 315 all-purpose yards, including 221 on six kickoff returns, plus a 50-yard touchdown reception.

2005
7–5, Big Ten champions

Sept. 3	Northern Illinois	Ann Arbor	W	33–17
Sept. 10	Notre Dame	Ann Arbor	L	17–10
Sept. 17	Eastern Michigan	Ann Arbor	W	55–0
Sept. 24	Wisconsin	Madison	L	23–20
Oct. 1	Michigan State	East Lansing	W OT	34–31
Oct. 8	Minnesota	Ann Arbor	L	23–20
Oct. 15	Penn State	Ann Arbor	W	27–25
Oct. 22	Iowa	Iowa City	W OT	23–20
Oct. 29	Northwestern	Evanston	W	33–17
Nov. 12	Indiana	Ann Arbor	W	41–14
Nov. 19	Ohio State	Ann Arbor	L	25–21
Dec. 28	Nebraska	Alamo Bowl	L	32–28
Coach: Lloyd Carr				345–244

Captains: Jason Avant, Pat Massey

Ranking (AP): Preseason No. 4; Postseason NR

All-Big Ten (first team): Jason Avant, Matt Lentz, Adam Stenavich, Gabe Watson, Mike Hart

Leaders: Rushing—Mike Hart (662 yards, 150 carries); Passing—Chad Henne (223 of 382, 2,526 yards); Receiving—Jason Avant (82 catches, 1,007 yards).

The season ended on a bizarre play, with Michigan's Chad Henne throwing a short pass and his teammates lateraling eight times up and down the field before Titus Brothers shoved Tyler Ecker out of bounds at the Nebraska 13 to conclude the Alamo Bowl. Extra players and some coaches from both teams were on the field as the play

Jake Long blocks an Eastern Michigan defensive lineman in 2007. A two-year captain, Long was widely considered the finest offensive lineman in the country as early as his junior season. He was the top overall pick at the 2008 NFL Draft, making him just the fifth offensive lineman to be selected in that spot.

concluded. "We just didn't finish," Michigan running back Mike Hart said. "That's been a problem all year."

2006
11–2

Sept. 2	Vanderbilt	Ann Arbor	W	27–7
Sept. 9	Central Michigan	Ann Arbor	W	41–17
Sept. 16	Notre Dame	South Bend	W	47–21
Sept. 23	Wisconsin	Ann Arbor	W	27–13
Sept. 30	Minnesota	Minneapolis	W	28–14
Oct. 7	Michigan State	Ann Arbor	W	31–13
Oct. 14	Penn State	University Park	W	17–10
Oct. 21	Iowa	Ann Arbor	W	20–6
Oct. 28	Northwestern	Ann Arbor	W	17–3
Nov. 4	Ball State	Ann Arbor	W	34–26
Nov. 11	Indiana	Bloomington	W	34–3
Nov. 18	Ohio State	Columbus	L	42–39
Jan. 1	Southern California	Rose Bowl	L	32–18
Coach: Lloyd Carr				380–210

Captains: Jake Long, LaMarr Woodley

Ranking (AP): Preseason No. 14; Postseason No. 6

Major Awards: LaMarr Woodley, Rotary Lombardi Award, Ted Hendricks Award

All-American: Leon Hall, Jake Long, LaMarr Woodley

All-Big Ten (first team): Alan Branch, David Harris, Leon Hall, Adam Kraus, Mike Hart, Jake Long, Mario Manningham, Garret Rivas, LaMarr Woodley

Leaders: Rushing—Mike Hart (1,562 yards, 318 carries); Passing—Chad Henne (203 of 328, 2,508 yards); Receiving—Mario Manningham (38 catches, 703 yards).

The game against Ohio State was the first No. 1 vs. No. 2 meeting in the rivalry and was played a day after the death of former Michigan Coach Bo Schembechler (who graduated from Ohio State). It was the second-highest scoring game in the 103-game series (the most was in 1902, won by Michigan 86–0). Although running back Mike Hart accumulated 142 rushing yards and had three touchdowns, Ohio State quarterback Troy Smith finished 29-of-41 for 316 yards with four touchdowns and one interception to essentially lock up the Heisman Trophy. Michigan wasn't given the opportunity for a rematch and looked flat at the Rose Bowl, a 32–18 loss to Southern California. Meanwhile, Ohio State was crushed by Florida in the BCS title game, 41–14. ... It was the fourth straight bowl loss for Lloyd Carr, and Michigan ended the season with a two-game losing streak for the third consecutive year. ... Steve Breaston led the team in catches with 58 receptions but only accumulated 670 yards.

2007
9–4

Sept. 1	Appalachian State	Ann Arbor	L	34–32
Sept. 8	Oregon	Ann Arbor	L	39–7
Sept. 15	Notre Dame	Ann Arbor	W	38–0
Sept. 22	Penn State	Ann Arbor	W	14–9
Sept, 29	Northwestern	East Lansing	W	28–16
Oct. 6	Eastern Michigan	Ann Arbor	W	33–22
Oct. 13	Purdue	Ann Arbor	W	48–21
Oct. 20	Illinois	Champaign	W	27–17
Oct. 27	Minnesota	Ann Arbor	W	34–10
Nov. 3	Michigan State	East Lansing	W	28–24
Nov. 10	Wisconsin	Madison	L	37–21
Nov. 17	Ohio State	Ann Arbor	L	14–3
Jan. 1	Florida	Capital One Bowl	W	41–35
Coach: Lloyd Carr				354–278

Captains: Jake Long, Mike Hart, Shawn Crable

Ranking (AP): Preseason No. 1; Postseason No. 18

All-American: Jake Long

All-Big Ten (first team): Adam Kraus, Jake Long, Mario Manningham, Chad Henne

Leaders: Rushing—Mike Hart (1,361 yards, 265 carries); Passing—Chad Henne (162 of 278, 1,938 yards); Receiving—Mario Manningham (72 catches, 1,174 yards).

Lloyd Carr announced his retirement before the Capital One Bowl, where Michigan snapped its

Morgan Trent drops Appalachian State's Dexter Jackson in 2007. Trent had a breakout season that year, setting him up for a fine campaign in 2008. The loss was the first of two to open the season, but the Wolverines bounced back to win nine straight.

four-game bowl losing streak with a 41–35 victory over Florida. Quarterback Chad Henne threw for 373 yards and three touchdowns, and running back Mike Hart ran for 129 yards and two scores. "What they did in this game and this environment, well, I love them to death," Carr said. Carr's overall record was 122–40 and 81–23 in Big Ten play. His 122 victories trailed only Fielding H. Yost (165–29–10) and Bo Schembechler (194–48–5) at Michigan. He's the first Wolverines coach to win four straight bowl games and the third, joining Yost and Schembechler, to claim five or more Big Ten titles (1997, 1998, 2000, 2003, 2004). ... Michigan's loss to Appalachian State in the opener was the first loss by a ranked I-A (Bowl Subdivision) team to a I-AA (Football Championship Subdivision) opponent.

2008
3-9

Aug. 30	Utah	Ann Arbor	L	25–23
Sept. 6	Miami (Ohio)	Ann Arbor	W	16–6
Sept. 13	Notre Dame	South Bend	L	35–17
Sept. 27	Wisconsin	Ann Arbor	W	27–25
Oct. 4	Illinois	Ann Arbor	L	45–20
Oct. 11	Toledo	Ann Arbor	L	13–10
Oct. 18	Penn State	University Park	L	46–17
Oct. 25	Michigan State	Ann Arbor	L	35–21
Nov. 1	Purdue	West Lafayette	L	48–42
Nov. 8	Minnesota	Minneapolis	W	29–6
Nov. 15	Northwestern	Ann Arbor	L	21–14
Nov. 22	Ohio State	Columbus	L	42–7
Coach: Rich Rodriguez				243–347

Captains: Mike Massey, Tim Jamison, Will Johnson, Terrance Taylor

All-Big Ten (first team): Zoltan Mesko

Leaders: Rushing—Brandon Minor (533 yards, 103 carries); Passing—Steven Threet (102 of 200, 1,105 yards); Receiving—Martavious Odoms (49 catches, 443 yards).

The Wolverines lost the most games in school history, missed a bowl trip for the first time in 34 years, and had their first losing season in 41 years. The offense ranked 109th in the nation (290.8 yards per game), and the defense gave up more points (28.9 per game) than any Michigan team since statistics have been kept. ... Ohio State won its fifth straight over Michigan to claim the Buckeyes' longest streak in the history of the rivalry. The 35-point win was Ohio State's third largest over Michigan and the largest since 1968. Michigan mustered just 198 yards and punted 12 times.

Wins for Michigan against Minne-sota in the Metrodome. The Wol-verines never lost the Little Brown Jug in the building and will look to maintain that tradition when Min-nesota moves to its new stadium in 2009.

Michigan Bowl Games

(Won 19, Lost 20)

Date	Bowl	Opponent	Result	
Jan. 1, 1902	Rose	Stanford	W	49–0
Jan. 1, 1948	Rose	Southern California	W	49–0
Jan. 1, 1951	Rose	California	W	14–6
Jan. 1, 1965	Rose	Oregon State	W	34–7
Jan. 1, 1970	Rose	Southern California	L	10–3
Jan. 1, 1972	Rose	Stanford	L	13–12
Jan. 1, 1976	Orange	Oklahoma	L	14–6
Jan. 1, 1977	Rose	Southern California	L	14–6
Jan. 2, 1978	Rose	Washington	L	27–20
Jan. 1, 1979	Rose	Southern California	L	17–10
Dec. 28, 1979	Gator	North Carolina	L	17–15
Jan. 1, 1981	Rose	Washington	W	23–6
Dec. 31, 1981	Bluebonnet	UCLA	W	33–14
Jan. 1, 1983	Rose	UCLA	L	24–14
Jan. 2, 1984	Sugar	Auburn	L	9–7
Dec. 21, 1984	Holiday	Brigham Young	L	24–17
Jan. 1, 1986	Fiesta	Nebraska	W	27–23
Jan. 1, 1987	Rose	Arizona State	L	22–15
Jan. 2, 1988	Hall of Fame	Alabama	W	28–24
Jan. 2, 1989	Rose	Southern California	W	22–14
Jan. 1, 1990	Rose	Southern California	L	17–10
Jan. 1, 1991	Gator	Ole Miss	W	35–3
Jan. 1, 1992	Rose	Washington	L	34–14
Jan. 1, 1993	Rose	Washington	W	38–31
Jan. 1, 1994	Hall of Fame	NC State	W	42–7
Dec. 30, 1994	Holiday	Colorado State	W	24–14
Dec. 28, 1995	Alamo	Texas A&M	L	22–20
Jan. 1, 1997	Outback	Alabama	L	17–14
Jan. 1, 1998	Rose	Washington State	W	21–16
Jan. 1, 1999	Citrus	Arkansas	W	45–31
Jan. 1, 2000	Orange	Alabama	W OT	35–34
Jan. 1, 2001	Citrus	Auburn	W	31–28
Jan. 1, 2002	Citrus	Tennessee	L	45–17
Jan. 1, 2003	Outback	Florida	W	38–30
Jan. 1, 2004	Rose	Southern California	L	28–14
Jan. 1, 2005	Rose	Texas	L	38–37

Dec. 28, 2005	Alamo	Nebraska	L 32–28
Jan. 1, 2007	Rose	Southern California	L 32–18
Jan. 1, 2008	Capital One	Florida	W 41–35

All-Time Record vs. Opponents

Team	First	Last	Record
Adelbert	1895	1895	1-0-0
Adrian	1894	1894	1-0-0
Air Force	1964	1964	1-0-0
Alabama	1987	1999	2-1-0
Albion	1884	1929	16-1-0
American Medical	1904	1904	1-0-0
Ann Arbor H.S.	1891	1891	1-0-0
Appalachian State	2007	2007	0-1-0
Arizona	1970	1978	2-0-0
Arizona State	1986	1986	0-1-0
Arkansas	1998	1998	1-0-0
Army	1945	1962	4-5-0
Auburn	1983	2000	1-1-0
Ball State	2006	2006	1-0-0
Baylor	1975	1997	1-0-1
Beloit	1898	1903	3-0-0
Boston College	1991	1996	4-0-0
Bowling Green	2000	2000	1-0-0
Brigham Young	1984	1984	0-1-0
Buffalo	1901	1901	1-0-0
Butler	1891	1891	1-0-0
California	1940	1980	6-2-0
Camp Grant	1943	1943	1-0-0
Carlisle	1901	1901	1-0-0
Carroll	1916	1916	1-0-0
Case	1894	1923	26-0-1
Central Michigan	1931	2006	2-1-0
Chicago	1892	1939	19-7-0
Chicago A.A.	1889	1889	0-1-0
Chicago Athletic Club	1891	1891	0-1-0
U. Club (Chicago)	1884	1888	1-1-0

Cleveland A.A.	1891	1891	0-1-0
Colorado	1974	1997	3-1-0
Colorado State	1994	1994	1-0-0
Columbia	1935	1941	3-0-0
Cornell	1889	1915	6-12-0
Dartmouth	1950	1950	1-0-0
Denison	1930	1930	1-0-0
DePauw	1892	1914	3-0-0
Detroit	1917	1917	1-0-0
Detroit Athletic Club	1888	1895	5-0-0
Detroit Industrial	1883	1883	1-0-0
Drake	1903	1905	3-0-0
Duke	1960	1978	6-0-0
Eastern Michigan	1896	2007	8-0-0
Ferris State	1903	1903	1-0-0
Florida	2002	2007	2-0-0
Florida State	1986	1991	1-1-0
Georgia	1957	1965	1-1-0
Georgia Tech	1934	1934	1-0-0
Grand Rapids	1896	1896	1-0-0
Great Lakes	1942	1945	2-0-0
Harvard	1881	1942	4-4-0
Harvard Club (Chi.)	1887	1887	1-0-0
Hawaii	1986	1998	2-0-0
Hillsdale	1899	1900	2-0-0
Houston	1992	2003	3-0-0
Illinois	1898	2008	66-22-4
Indiana	1900	2006	50-9-0
Iowa	1900	2006	40-10-4
Iowa Pre-Flight	1942	1944	1-1-0
Kalamazoo	1899	1917	5-0-0
Kansas	1893	1979	3-0-0
Kentucky	1908	1908	1-0-0
Kenyon	1898	1898	1-0-0
Lawrence	1915	1915	1-0-0
Lehigh	1896	1896	1-0-0
Long Beach State	1987	1987	1-0-0
Marietta	1915	1916	2-0-0
Marquette	1909	1944	2-0-0

Maryland	1985	1990	3-0-0
Memphis	1995	1995	1-0-0
Miami (Fla.)	1984	1988	1-1-0
Miami (Ohio)	1924	2008	5-0-0
Michigan A.A.	1892	1892	2-0-0
Michigan M.A.	1894	1895	2-0-1
Michigan State	1898	2008	67-29-5
Minnesota	1892	2008	70-24-3
Ole Miss	1990	1990	1-0-0
Missouri	1955	1975	2-2-0
Mount Union	1913	1929	7-0-0
Navy	1925	1981	12-5-1
Nebraska	1905	2005	3-2-1
North Carolina	1965	1979	1-2-0
North Carolina St.	1993	1993	1-0-0
Northern Illinois	2005	2005	1-0-0
Northwestern	1892	2008	52-15-2
Notre Dame	1887	2008	20-15-1
Oberlin	1891	1905	9-0-0
Ohio Northern	1903	1905	3-0-0
Ohio State	1897	2008	57-42-6
Ohio Wesleyan	1897	1928	2-1-1
Oklahoma	1975	1975	0-1-0
Oklahoma State	1926	1992	2-0-0
Olivet	1891	1894	2-0-0
Oregon	1948	2007	3-2-
Oregon State	1959	1986	4-0-0
P&S Chicago	1896	1904	2-0-0
Peninsulars	1885	1885	1-0-0
Pennsylvania	1899	1953	11-8-2
Penn State	1993	2008	10-4-0
Pittsburgh	1941	1947	2-0-0
Princeton	1881	1932	2-1-0
Purdue	1890	2008	42-13-0
Quantico Marines	1923	1923	1-0-0
Racine	1923	1923	1-0-0
Rice	1999	2000	2-0-0
Rush Lake Forest	1895	1896	2-0-0
San Diego State	2004	2004	1-0-0

South Carolina	1980	1985	1-1-0
South Dakota	1912	1912	1-0-0
Southern California	1947	2006	4-6-0
Southern Methodist	1963	1963	1-0-0
Stanford	1901	1976	6-3-1
Stevens Institute	1883	1883	1-0-0
Syracuse	1908	1999	6-5-1
Tennessee	2001	2001	0-1-0
Texas	2004	2004	0-1-0
Texas A&M	1970	1995	2-1-0
Toledo	2008	2008	0-1-0
Toronto	1879	1880	1-0-1
Tulane	1920	1972	3-0-0
UCLA	1956	2000	8-3-0
Utah	2002	2008	1-1-0
Vanderbilt	1905	2006	10-0-1
Virginia	1899	1995	3-0-0
Wabash	1907	1907	1-0-0
Wake Forest	1976	1988	2-0-0
Washington	1953	2002	7-5-0
Washington State	1983	1997	4-0-0
Washington U. (Mo.)	1916	1916	1-0-0
Wesleyan	1883	1883	0-1-0
West Virginia	1904	1904	1-0-0
Western Michigan	1917	2002	4-0-0
Western Reserve	1898	1899	2-0-0
Windsor Club	1885	1885	2-0-0
Wisconsin	1892	2008	49-12-1
Wittenberg	1896	1897	2-0-0
Yale	1881	1939	2-2-0

Mike Hart powers through a Vanderbilt tackler in 2006. The Commodores have had 11 shots at the Wolverines but failed each time—Michigan's win that season made it 10-0-1 all time against the squad from Nashville.

THE GREATEST PLAYERS

Neil Snow
(End-Fullback, 1898–1901)

Neil Snow played both fullback and end at Michigan. He was an All-American and captain of Fielding H. Yost's 1901 team as a senior. He capped off his playing career by scoring five touchdowns in the Wolverines' 49–0 rout of Stanford in the inaugural Tournament of Roses Game, known today as the Rose Bowl.

Willie Heston
(Halfback, 1901–04)

Willie Heston followed Fielding H. Yost from the West Coast and spearheaded his point-a-minute juggernauts. During Heston's playing career, the Wolverines won four national titles and never lost a game, going 43–0–1. Yost referred to the best playmakers as his "Heston Backfield." Heston was the fastest of the group and scored 93 touchdowns. The left halfback played for Michigan teams that scored 2,326 points, compared to just 40 for the opposition.

Adolph "Germany" Schulz
(Center, 1904–08)

When legendary sportswriter Grantland Rice named his all-time team, Germany Schulz was the center. "Schulz stands as the fastest giant who ever played football, a human bulwark fast enough to tackle at either end, as he brought down his man after the manner of a hawk snaring a quail," Rice wrote in 1928. Schulz dominated games on both sides on the line of scrimmage, backing up the line on defense. He was a 1907 All-American and a member of the AP All-Time Team picked in 1951.

Albert Benbrook
(Guard, 1908–10)

Albert Benbrook was the first of the great pulling guards. At 240 pounds, which was extremely large at the time, Benbrook could outrun most backs. He was a two-time All-American of whom Walter Camp remarked, "He leads his mates across the line with his quick, ripping charge that simply smothers the opposition."

Harry Kipke
(Halfback, 1921–23)

Harry Kipke was an All-American halfback in 1922 who also earned letters in basketball and baseball. Kipke excelled as a ball carrier, passer, blocker, kicker, and defensive player and was known as one of the best punters in the nation. He was captain of the 8-0 national champion Wolverines as a senior in 1923, and he later returned to Ann Arbor as head coach (1929–37).

Benny Friedman
(Quarterback, 1923–26)

Benny Friedman, a charter member of the College Football Hall of Fame, was considered the greatest passer of his day. Said George Little, a Fielding Yost assistant who left to become head coach at Wisconsin before Friedman's senior year, "I should have waited until Benny graduated. In my first year as head coach at Madison, we lost only one game—to Michigan, 21-0—and Benny figured in all of the touchdowns. He was unstoppable." Friedman was a two-year All-American (1925–26). "In Benny Friedman, I have one of the greatest passers and smartest quarterbacks in history," Yost once said. "He never makes a mistake."

The Greatest Players

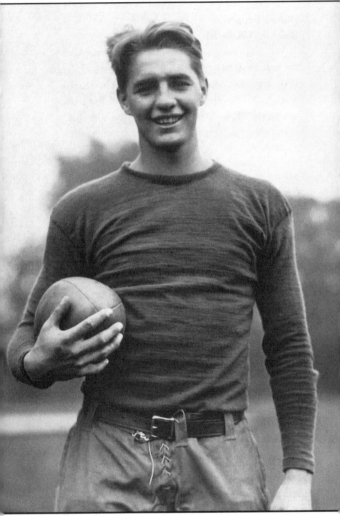

Smiling for a photo, Bennie Oosterbaan did it all in his Michigan days. He earned nine varsity letters: he was a three-time All-American in football, an All-American in basketball, and he also played baseball. He went on to coach all three sports at UM.

Bennie Oosterbaan
(End, 1924–27)

In 1948 Oosterbaan became the only man to win a national championship in his first year as a head coach and held that distinction for 53 years, until 2001. As a player, Oosterbaan was an outstanding receiver, a three-time All-American (1925–27), and was selected to the All-Time All-America team in 1951. The Benny Friedman-to-Oosterbaan connection was one of the first great passing combinations, and as an end on defense Oosterbaan consistently frustrated opposing ball carriers, including Red Grange.

The Wisterts: Francis, Albert, and Alvin
(Tackles, 1931–33, 1940–42, 1946–49)

Francis, Albert, and Alvin Wistert are the only trio of brothers to all be named first-team All-Americans. All three were tackles and wore No. 11, which has since been retired in their honor. Francis "Whitey" Wistert was an All-American as a senior in 1933, when Coach Harry Kipke's Wolverines won the national championship. During his four years, Michigan went 31–1–3. Albert, also known as "Ox," was an All-American and team MVP in 1942, before enjoying an All-Pro career with the Philadelphia Eagles. Alvin "Moose" Wistert was the oldest Michigan football player ever, thanks in large part to a four-year stint in the marines during World War II before enrolling in 1946 at age 30. Alvin was a two-time All-American, in 1948 and '49.

Tom Harmon
(Halfback, 1938–40)

Known as "Old 98," Tom Harmon finished second in Heisman Trophy balloting in 1939, won it in 1940, and led the nation in scoring both seasons. "He was better than Red Grange, the "Galloping Ghost," Coach Fritz Crisler said. "Tom could do more things. He ran, passed, punted, blocked, kicked off, and kicked extra points and field goals. He was a superb defensive player." During his three seasons in Ann Arbor, Harmon ran for 2,134 yards, scored 33 touchdowns, and threw 16 touchdown passes. In his last game for the Maize and Blue—the 1940 Ohio State showdown—he had 139 rushing yards and two touchdowns, completed 11 of 12 passes for 151 yards and two more touchdowns, intercepted three passes, running one back for a score, and averaged 50 yards per punt in the 40–0 victory. After serving as a pilot in World War II, Harmon married film star Elyse Knox and became one of the nation's top sports broadcasters and directors.

Bob Chappuis
(Halfback, 1942, 1946–47)

Bob Chappuis had his collegiate football career interrupted by World War II, where he was an aerial gunner and shot down on a mission over Italy (he later escaped captivity). After returning to Ann Arbor in 1946, the triple-threat halfback was named an All-American and runner-up for the 1947 Heisman Trophy. He capped his career by setting Rose Bowl records for total offense and pass completions. "You have to smell where to go on pass defense, and my sniffer's not too good," Chappuis said about his biggest weakness, pass defense.

Chalmers "Bump" Elliott
(Halfback, 1946–47)

Although halfback Bob Chappuis was in the same backfield, Bump Elliott was also named All-American. Coach Fritz Crisler called Elliott the greatest right halfback he ever saw. His 54 points as a senior led the conference, earning him MVP honors. He later returned to Michigan as head coach and led the Maize and Blue to the Big Ten and Rose Bowl titles in 1964.

Ron Kramer
(End, 1954–56)

Ron Kramer earned nine letters at Michigan, three each in football, basketball, and track, and led both the football and basketball teams in scoring for two seasons. "To top off his marvelous physical gifts of size and speed and strength, plus an uncanny coordination, Kramer was one of the fiercest competitors I've ever seen," Coach Bennie Oosterbaan said. "Nothing was impossible for him; the impossible was only a challenge." Although a standout on both sides of the ball, the two-time All-American end was particularly dangerous as a receiver. His football jersey No. 87 was retired following his senior year, and Kramer went on to an impressive pro career with Vince Lombardi's Green Bay Packers.

Bob Timberlake
(Quarterback, 1962–64)

Bob Timberlake quarterbacked Michigan to the Big Ten and Rose Bowl titles in 1964. He was MVP of the Big Ten, a consensus All-American, and finished fourth in that year's Heisman Trophy voting.

The Greatest Players

The Greatest Players

Bill Yearby
(Tackle, 1963–65)

Bill Yearby was one of the best defensive tackles in the nation in the mid-1960s. Blessed with both strength and speed, he was best known for his prowess in pursuit. Yearby was twice named an All-American (1964–65).

Ron Johnson
(Halfback, 1966–68)

During his three-year collegiate career, Ron Johnson broke nearly every Michigan rushing record, including single season and career rushing yards. He also established eight Big Ten records. Johnson was a two-time team MVP and was named both an All-American and Big Ten MVP in 1968. The 347 yards he gained against Wisconsin in 1968 set an NCAA record at the time.

Thomas Curtis
(Defensive Back, 1967–69)

During his three-year career with the Wolverines, Thomas Curtis intercepted 25 passes. He started off quickly his sophomore year, tying a then-Big Ten record with seven interceptions. He broke that record the following season with 10 pickoffs and had eight more as a senior during Bo Schembechler's first season as head coach in 1969. Curtis also made 45 unassisted tackles and was named an All-American as a senior. The 6-foot-1 defensive back was a two-time All-Big Ten selection and set a then-NCAA record with 431 return yards on his interceptions.

Dan Dierdorf
(Offensive Tackle, 1968–70)

Dan Dierdorf was a two-time All–Big Ten selection and a 1970 All-American offensive tackle. After his collegiate career, he went on to an All-Pro career with the

Bob Timberlake looks forward with steely resolve in 1964. A consensus All-American that season, Timberlake finished fourth in Heisman Trophy voting and led the Wolverines to a Big Ten title.

St. Louis Cardinals and was twice named the NFL's top offensive lineman.

Reggie McKenzie
(Offensive Guard, 1969–71)

A consensus All-American as a senior in 1971, Reggie McKenzie is recognized as one of the game's greatest pulling guards. McKenzie helped lead the Wolverines to two Big Ten titles and Rose Bowl appearances.

Billy Taylor
(Halfback, 1969–71)

Billy Taylor was MVP of the 1971 Big Ten champion Wolverine team that finished with a perfect 11–0 regular season before dropping the Rose Bowl game by one point. He exited Michigan after his senior year with the school's career rushing record of 3,072 yards and was second only to Tom Harmon with 32 touchdowns. Taylor was a three-time All-Big Ten selection and a 1971 All-American.

Thom Darden
(Defensive Back, 1969–71)

One of the best punt returners in program history, Thom Darden was a three-year regular in the defensive backfield, starting and excelling at all four positions. Of his 11 career interceptions, Darden notched touchdown returns of 92 and 60 yards.

Dave Brown
(Defensive Halfback, 1972–74)

Dave Brown intercepted nine passes during his collegiate career and also had an 88-yard punt return to his credit. He was cocaptain of Bo Schembechler's 1974 Big Ten champions, was a three-time all-conference pick and a two-year All-American (1973–74).

Rob Lytle
(Running Back, 1974–76)

Rob Lytle set Michigan records for both single season and careering rushing yards, to be named a consensus All-American, the Big Ten's MVP, and third-highest Heisman vote-getter in 1976. In the Michigan State game as a senior, Lytle averaged 18 yards on 10 carries.

Mark Donahue
(Offensive Guard, 1975–77)

Mark Donahue was a two-time consensus All-American—the 13th Michigan player to be so honored twice—and was considered one of the greatest pulling guards in program history.

Rick Leach
(Quarterback, 1975–78)

Rick Leach broke all of Michigan's career passing, total offense, and touchdown records in the 1970s. He was a three-time All-Big Ten selection and during his senior year was named an All-American, finished third in Heisman Trophy voting, and was the Big Ten MVP.

Anthony Carter
(Wide Receiver, 1979–82)

The Big Ten hadn't had a three-time All-American in 36 years until Michigan wide receiver Anthony Carter (1980–82). He was the first 3,000-yard receiver in conference history, finishing with 161 catches for 3,076 yards and 37 touchdowns (40 TDs overall). Carter set an NCAA all-purpose running mark with a 17.4-yard average, and during his senior season he finished fourth in Heisman Trophy voting. "The best player I ever coached," Bo Schembechler said.

The Greatest Players

John Elliott
(Offensive Tackle, 1984–87)

John "Jumbo" Elliott was a four-year starting offensive tackle and a two-year consensus All-American. He was a first-round pick in the 1988 NFL Draft and enjoyed a 14-year pro career with the New York Giants and Jets.

Jim Harbaugh
(Quarterback, 1983–86)

Quarterback Jim Harbaugh led the nation in pass efficiency in 1985, and his 2,729 passing yards in 1986 set a school record that stood until 2002. He quarterbacked the Wolverines to a Fiesta Bowl victory following the 1985 season and the Big Ten title in 1986. As a senior in 1986, Harbaugh was chosen Big Ten Player of the Year and finished third in the Heisman Trophy voting.

Mark Messner
(Defensive Tackle, 1985–88)

Messner was a two-year All-American defensive tackle who graduated from Michigan with more tackles for loss (70) for more lost yardage (376) than anyone who had gone before him. Messner started all 49 games of his college career and led the Wolverines in sacks three straight years.

Tripp Welborne
(Safety, 1987–1990)

A converted wide receiver after his freshman season, Sullivan A. "Tripp" Welborne tallied nine career interceptions and 238 tackles as a defensive back. He was a record-breaking punt returner and a two-year All-American (1989–90).

Desmond Howard
(Wide Receiver, 1989–1991)

After watching Desmond Howard's 93-yard punt return vs. Ohio State, ending with his famous pose in the end zone, announcer Keith Jackson could only proclaim, "Hello, Heisman!" Sure enough, he became just the second Michigan Heisman winner in 1991, joining Tom Harmon. Howard was the first receiver to lead the Big Ten in scoring, and he also set a handful of NCAA records. Howard received more first-place Heisman votes than anyone else before him and also won the Walter Camp and Maxwell Awards as a junior.

Greg Skrepenak
(Offensive Tackle, 1988–1991)

Greg Skrepenak was a four-year offensive tackle for Michigan, and his 48 consecutive starts set a school record. He was a two-year All-American and a finalist for both the Outland Trophy and Lombardi Award.

Charles Woodson
(Cornerback, Receiver, 1995–1997)

In 1997 Charles Woodson became the first primarily defensive player to win the Heisman Trophy and was twice named the Big Ten's player of the year. He took over as a starter in the second game of his freshman year and later became an offensive force as well. He was on the field for a staggering 83 plays in the 20–14 win over the No. 4 Buckeyes, and he punctuated his Heisman bid against Ohio State with a 78-yard punt return for a touchdown and an interception in the end zone. "You know what feeling you get when you win. You know what feeling you get when you lose. You learn that early on. You either get used to the feeling of losing, or you do something to win," Woodson once said.

The Greatest Players

Steve Hutchinson
(Guard, 1997–2000)

Steve Hutchinson was a four-year starter at guard and a two-time team captain. He was first-team All–Big Ten four straight years, did not allow a sack in either of his final two seasons, and was a two-year All-American.

Braylon Edwards
(Wide Receiver, 2001–04)

Braylon Edwards believed it was his destiny to wear the prestigious No. 1 uniform. The son of former Michigan running back Stanley Edwards, he finally convinced Coach Lloyd Carr to give it to him after his sophomore season. He proved worthy by setting school records for career receptions (252), receiving yards (3,542), receiving touchdowns (39), and consecutive games with a reception (38). He won the Biletnikoff Award as the nation's outstanding wide receiver as a senior, catching 97 passes for 1,330 yards and 15 touchdowns.

1 Receivers in Big Ten history to have three consecutive 1,000-yard seasons. Braylon Edwards is the only player from the conference to accomplish the feat, and was just the third player in NCAA history to do so.

Elevating after scoring his second touchdown of the game against Michigan State in 2003, Braylon Edwards is among the finest receivers to ever don the maize and blue. He holds nearly every school receiving record.

Major Awards

Heisman Trophies (3): Tom Harmon, 1940; Desmond Howard, 1991; Charles Woodson, 1997

Walter Camp Award (outstanding player): Desmond Howard, 1991; Charles Woodson, 1997

Maxwell Award (outstanding player): Tom Harmon, 1940; Desmond Howard, 1991

Rotary Lombardi Award (outstanding lineman): LaMarr Woodley, 2006

Dick Butkus Award (best linebacker): Erick Anderson, 1991

Jim Thorpe Award (best defensive back): Charles Woodson, 1997

Bronko Nagurski Award (top defensive player): Charles Woodson, 1997

Chuck Bednarik Award (defensive): Charles Woodson, 1997

Doak Walker Award (best running back): Chris Perry, 2003

Fred Biletnikoff Award (top wide receiver): Braylon Edwards, 2004

Dave Rimington Trophy (top center): David Baas (cowinner), 2004

Ted Hendricks Award (defensive end): LaMarr Woodley, 2006

Retired Jerseys

No. 11: Francis Wistert, 1931–33, tackle; Albert Wistert, 1940–42, tackle; Alvin Wistert, 1947–49, tackle

No. 47: Bennie Oosterbaan, 1925–27, end

No. 48: Gerald Ford, 1932–34, center

No. 87: Ron Kramer, 1954–56, end

No. 98: Tom Harmon, 1938–40, halfback

College Football Hall of Fame

(player, years, position, inducted)

Albert Brenbrook, 1908–10, guard, 1971

David Brown, 1972–74, defensive back, 2007

Anthony Carter, 1979–82, wide receiver, 2001

Bob Chappuis, 1942–47, halfback, 1988

Fritz Crisler, 1937–47, coach, 1954

Tom Curtis, 1967–69, defensive back, 2005

Dan Dierdorf, 1967–72, tackle, 2000

Chalmers "Bump" Elliott, 1946–47, halfback, 1989

Pete Elliott, 1945–48, quarterback, 1994

Benny Friedman, 1923–26, quarterback, 1951

Tom Harmon, 1937–40, halfback, 1954

Willie Heston, 1901–04, halfback, 1954

Elroy Hirsch, 1943, halfback, 1974

Ron Johnson, 1965–68, halfback, 1992

Harry Kipke, 1920–23, halfback, 1958

Ron Kramer, 1953–56, end, 1978

George Little, 1922–24, coach, 1955

Jim Mandich, 1966–69, end, 2005

John Maulbetsch, 1914–16, halfback, 1973

Reggie McKenzie, 1968–71, guard, 2002

Harry Newman, 1931–33, quarterback, 1975

Bennie Oosterbaan, 1924–27, end, 1954

Merv Pregulman, 1940–43, guard/tackle, 1982

Glen E. "Bo" Schembechler, 1969–89, coach, 1993

Adolph "Germany" Schulz, 1904–08, center, 1951

Neil Snow, 1898–1901, end/fullback, 1960

Ernie Vick, 1917–21, center, 1983

Elton "Tad" Weiman, 1921–28, coach, 1956

Bob Westfall, 1938–41, fullback, 1987

Albert Wistert, 1938–42, tackle, 1968

Alvin Wistert, 1946–49, tackle, 1981

Francis Wistert, 1930–33, tackle, 1967

Fielding Yost, 1901–24, 1926, coach, 1951

The Greatest Players

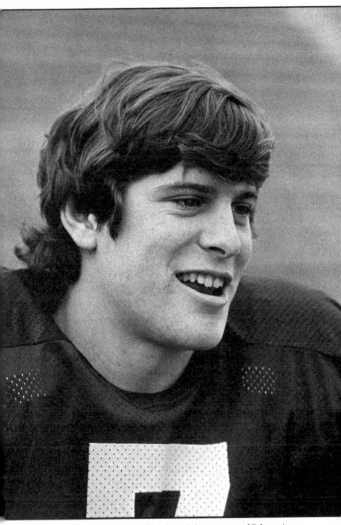

The All-American boy Rick Leach became an All-American player in 1978 after posting stellar numbers as a dual-threat quarterback. He finished third in Heisman Trophy voting but elected for a career in pro baseball, where he spent a decade playing with four different teams.

First-Team All-Americans

(Source: NCAA. * consensus, # unanimous selection)

William Cunningham, C, *1898; Neil Snow, E, *1901; Willie Heston, HB, *1903, *1904; Adolph Schulz, C, *1907; Albert Benbrook, G, *1909, *1910; Stanfield Wells, E, *1910; Miller Pontius, T, *1913; Jim Craig, HB, *1913; John Maulbetsch, HB, *1914; Frank Culver, G, 1917; Frank Steketee, FB, 1918; Henry Vick, C, 1921; Harry Kipke, HB, *1922; Jack Blott, C, *1923; Edliff Slaughter, G, 1924; Robert Brown, C, 1925; Benny Friedman, QB, *1925, *1926; Bennie Oosterbaan, E, *1925, *1926, #*1927; Otto Pommerening, T, *1928; Maynard Morrison, C, 1931; Chuck Bernard, C, 1932, #*1933; Harry Newman, QB, #*1932; Ted Petoskey, E, 1932, 1933; Francis Wistert, T, *1933; Ralph Heikkinen, G, #*1938; Tom Harmon, HB, *1939, #*1940; Ed Frutig, E, 1940; Bob Westfall, FB, *1941; Albert Wistert, T, *1942; Julie Franks, G, *1942; Bill Daley, FB, #*1943; Merv Pregulman, T, 1943; Elmer Madar, E, 1946; Bob Chappuis, HB, #*1947; Bump Elliott, HB, 1947; Pete Elliott, QB, 1948; Dick Rifenburg, E, *1948; Alvin Wistert, T, *1948, *1949; Allen Wahl, T, 1949, 1950; Lowell Perry, E, 1951; Art Walker, T, 1954; Ron Kramer, E, *1955, #*1956; Jim Pace, HB, 1957; Bob Timberlake, QB, 1964; Bill Yearby, DT, 1964, *1965; Jack Clancy, E, #*1966; Ron Johnson, HB, 1968; Tom Curtis, DB, *1969; Jim Mandich, TE, #*1969; Dan Dierdorf, OT, *1970; Henry Hill, MG, 1970; Marty Huff, LB, 1970; Tom Darden, DB, 1971; Reggie McKenzie, OG, *1971; Mike Taylor, LB, #*1971; Randy Logan, DB, *1972; Paul Seymour, OT, *1972; Dave Brown, DB, *1973, #*1974; Dave Gallagher, DT, *1973; Don Dufek Jr., DB, 1975; Mark Donahue, OG, *1976, #*1977; Rob Lytle, RB, *1976; Calvin O'Neal, LB, 1976; Jim Smith, WR, 1976; John Anderson, LB, 1977; Walt Downing, C, 1977; Rick Leach, QB, 1978; Curtis Greer, DT, 1979; Ron Simpkins, LB, *1979; Anthony Carter, WR, 1980, #*1981, #*1982; Kurt Becker, OG, *1981; Ed Muransky, OT, *1981; Tom Dixon, C, 1983; Stefan Humphries, OG, 1983; Brad Cochran, DB, *1985; Mike Hammerstein, DT, *1985; John Elliott, OT, 1986, *1987; Garland Rivers, DB, *1986; Mark Messner, DT, #*1988; John Vitale, C, *1988; Tripp Welborne, DB, #*1989,

The Greatest Players

#*1990; Dean Dingman, OL, 1990; Greg Skrepanek, OL, 1990, #*1991; Erick Anderson, LB, 1991; Desmond Howard, WR, #*1991; Chris Hutchinson, DL, 1992; Remy Hamilton, PK, 1994; Ty Law, DB, 1994; Jason Horn, DL, 1995; Jarrett Irons, LB, *1996; Rod Payne, C, 1996; Charles Woodson, DB, 1996, #*1997; Glen Steele, DL, 1997; Jerame Tuman, TE, 1997; Jon Jenson, OL, 1998; Rob Renes, DT, 1999; Steve Hutchinson, OL, #*2000; Larry Foote, LB, 2001; Marquise Walker, WR, 2001; Chris Perry, RB, *2003; David Baas, OL, *2004; Braylon Edwards, WR, #*2004; Marlin Jackson, DB, *2004; Ernest Shazor, DB, *2004; Leon Hall, DB, *2006; Jake Long, OL, 2006, *2007; LaMarr Woodley, DL, #*2006

Academic All-Americans

Dick Balzhiser, fullback, 1952; Jim Orwig, offensive line, 1955, 1957; Bob Timberlake, quarterback, 1964; Dave Fisher, fullback, 1966; Dick Vidmer, quarterback, 1966; Jim Mandich, tight end, 1969; Phil Seymour, defensive end, 1970; Bruce Elliott, defensive back, 1971; Bill Hart, center, 1972; Kirk Lewis, offensive line, 1974; Dan Jilek, defensive end, 1975; Norm Betts, tight end, 1981; Stefan Humphries, offensive line, 1982; Robert Thompson, linebacker, 1982; Stefan Humphries, offensive line, 1983, Clay Miller, offensive line, 1985; Kenneth Higgins, wide receiver, 1986; Rob Renes, nose tackle, 1999

Bob Timberlake always took his education seriously, and he remains active in education today. He teaches courses at Marquette University in Milwaukee and contributes time and effort to Habitat for Humanity.

All-Time
NFL Draft Selections

Year, Round, Name, Position, Team, (Overall Pick)

1937: 9, Matt Patanelli, E, Pittsburgh Steelers (85)

1938: None

1939: 12, Ralph Heikkenen, G, Brooklyn Dodgers (105); 19, John Brennan, G, Green Bay Packers (179)

1940: 15, Archie Kodros, C, Green Bay Packers

1941: 1, Tom Harmon, B, Chicago Bears (1); 1, Forest Evashevski, B, Washington Redskins (10); 3, Ed Frutig, E, Green Bay Packers (37); 10, Ralph Fritz, G, Pittsburgh Steelers (82)

1942: 1, Bob Westfall, B, Detroit Lions (5); 6, Joe Rogers, E, Green Bay Packers (69); 18, Bob Ingalls, C, Green Bay Packers (169)

1943: 3, George Ceithaml, B, Brooklyn Dodgers (19); 5, Al "Whitey" Wistert, T, Philadelphia Eagles (32); 12, Bob Kolesar, G, Detroit Lions (101)

1944: 1, Merv Pregulman, G, Green Bay Packers (7); 3, Tom Kuzma, B, Green Bay Packers (22); 3, Rudy Smeja, E, Chicago Bears (24); 5, John Greene, T, Detroit Lions (35); 11, Paul White, B, Detroit Lions (101); 14, Bill Pritula, T, Detroit Lions (134); 29, Bob Derleth, T, Detroit Lions (299)

1945: 1, Elroy Hirsch, B, Cleveland Rams (5); 1, Don Lund, B, Chicago Bears (7); 2, Milan Lazetich, T, Cleveland Rams (16); 5, Bob Wiese, B, Detroit Lions (39); 30, Don Robinson, B, Chicago Bears (314)

1946: 3, Bob Nussbaumer, B, Green Bay Packers (21); 7, Art Renner, E, Green Bay Packers (56); 8, Joe Ponsetto, B, Pittsburgh Steelers (63); 17, Milton Prashaw, T, Washington Redskins (159)

1947: 5, Bob Chappuis, B, Detroit Lions (26); 10, Chalmers "Bump" Elliott, B, Detroit Lions (76); 16, Ralph Chubb, B, Los Angeles Rams (143); 20, Elmer Madar, E, Detroit Lions (176); 21, J.T. White, E, Detroit Lions (186); 21, Joe Ponsetto, B, New York Giants (194); 31, Bob Callahan, C, Chicago Cardinals (389). AAFC: 1, Elmer Madar, E, Miami Seahawks (1); 1, Bob Chappuis, B, Cleveland Browns (8); 2, Bob Wiese, B, San Francisco 49ers (14); 3, Bob Derleth, T, Chicago Rockets (20); 3, Jack Carpenter, T, Cleveland Browns (24); 11, Jim Brieske, C, Miami Seahawks (81)

The Greatest Players

The Greatest Players

1948: 6, Jack Weisenburger, B, Washington Redskins (38); 12B, Jim Brieske, C, New York Giants (97); 14, Dick Kempthorn, B, Philadelphia Eagles (123); 15, Pete Elliott, B, Detroit Lions (Future Pick) (127); 15, Dick Rifenburg, E, Philadelphia Eagles (132); 17, Quentin Sickels, G, Detroit Lions (147); 17, Ralph Kohl, T, Philadelphia Eagles (153); 30, Bruce Hilkene, T, Pittsburgh Steelers (283). AAFC: 3, Len Ford, E, Los Angeles Dons (14); 11, Jack Weisenberger, B, New York Yankees (64); 14, J.T. White, C, Brooklyn Dodgers (84); 15, Dan Dworsky, B, Cleveland Browns (97, pick declared ineligible); 18, Bill Pritula, T, San Francisco 49ers (118)

1949: 2, Dan Dworsky, C, Green Bay Packers (15); 9, Joe Soboleski, G, New York Giants (86); 9, Ed McNeill, E, Washington Redskins (88); 15, Ed Sobczak, E, Pittsburgh Steelers (145); 16, Al Wahl, T, Chicago Bears (159, pick declared ineligible); 17, Wally Teninga, B, New York Giants (166); 24, Oswald Clark, E, Detroit Lions (232). AAFC Secret Draft: 1, Dan Dworsky, C, Los Angeles Dons; 1B, Pete Elliott, B, Chicago Rockets; 1, Gene Derricotte, B, Cleveland Browns; 2, Dick Kempthorn, B, Cleveland Browns. AAFC: 4, Dick Rifenburg, E, New York Yankees (24); 4, Ralph Kohl, T, Baltimore Colts (25); 5, Ed McNeill, E, Cleveland Browns (37); 29, Joe Soboleski, T, Cleveland Browns (192)

1950: 10, Al Wahl, T, Chicago Bears (128)

1951: 2, Chuck Ortmann, B, Pittsburgh Steelers (20); 5, Anton Momsen, C, Los Angeles Rams (59); 9, Dick McWilliams, T, Green Bay Packers (99); 12, Carl Kreager, C, Green Bay Packers (136); 17, Don Dufek, B, Chicago Bears (205); 27, Harry Allis, E, Detroit Lions (322)

1952: 6, Tom Johnson, T, Green Bay Packers (63); 17, Don Peterson, B, Green Bay Packers (196)

1953: 5, Roger Zatkoff, T, Green Bay Packers (55); 8, Lowell Perry, E, Pittsburgh Steelers (90); 15, Ted Topor, B, Detroit Lions (181); 22, Larry LeClaire, B, Philadelphia Eagles (261)

1954: 10, Gene Knutson, E, Green Bay Packers (111); 13, Bob Topp, E, New York Giants (148)

1955: 12, Art Walker, T, Green Bay Packers (137); 14, Fred Baer, B, Green Bay Packers (161); 20, Ron Geyer, T, Washington Redskins (231); 26, Duncan McDonald, B, Detroit Lions (312)

1956: 10A, Lou Baldacci, B, Pittsburgh Steelers (111); 23, Tony Branoff, B, Chicago Cardinals (269); 28, John Morrow, T, Los Angeles Rams (336)

1957: 1, Ron Kramer, E, Green Bay Packers (4); 2, Tom Maentz, E, Chicago Cardinals (22); 3, Terry Barr, B, Detroit Lions (36); 7B, Mike Rotunno, C, Cleveland Browns (82); 21, Charley Brooks, E, Philadelphia Eagles (242); 25, Jerry Goebel, C, New York Giants (301); 28, Clem Corona, G, Philadelphia Eagles (326)

1958: 1A, Jim Pace, B, San Francisco 49ers (8); 5, Jim VanPelt, QB, Washington Redskins (54); 28, Gordy Morrow, C, Los Angeles Rams (331)

1959: 4A, Gary Prahst, E, Cleveland Browns (37); 8A, Bob Ptacek, QB, Cleveland Browns (87); 8B, Willie Smith, T, Chicago Bears (94); 11, Jerry Marciniak, G, Washington Redskins (124); 21, John Herrnstein, B, Baltimore Colts (252)

1960: 15, Darrell Harper, HB, Detroit Lions (171). AFL: 1st Tier, Don Deskins, T, Minneapolis; 1st Tier, George Genyk, G, New York Titans; 2nd Tier, Darrell Harper, HB, Buffalo Bills.

1961: 15, Bob Johnson, E, Washington Redskins (199). AFL: 22, Bob Johnson, E, Boston Patriots; 28, Bill Stine, G, Dallas Texans

1962: 2B, Bennie McRae, B, Chicago Bears (21); 5B, Bill Tunnicliff, FB, Chicago Bears (63); 5B, Jon Schopf, G, Green Bay Packers (70); 8, Ken Tureaud, B, Dallas Cowboys (102); 9, Todd Grant, C, Detroit Lions (122); 14, George Mans, E, St. Louis Cardinals (187); 20, Bob Brown, E, Detroit Lions (future pick) (276). AFL: 7, George Mans, E, New York Titans (53); 7, John Schopf, T, Boston Patriots (54); 8, Benny McRae, HB, Boston Patriots (62); 17, Scott Maentz, E, Boston Patriots (134); 21, Bill Tunnicliff, FB, Oakland Raiders (161); 23, Ken Tureaud, HB, Denver Broncos (178)

1963: 9, Dave Raimey, B, Cleveland Browns (121). AFL: 17, Tom Neumann, HB, Boston Patriots (135)

1964: 3C, Joe O'Donnell, G, Green Bay Packers (40); 4B, Tom Keating, T, Minnesota Vikings (53); 15, John Houtman, T, Cleveland Browns (207). AFL: 5A, Tom Keating, T, Kansas City Chiefs (34); 13, Joe O'Donnell, G, Buffalo Bills (101)

1965: 3B, Bob Timberlake, QB, New York Giants (33); 5, John Henderson, E, Philadelphia Eagles (63); 6A, Arnie Simkus, T, Cleveland Browns (72); 16, Mel Anthony, FB, Cleveland Browns (223). AFL: 13, Bob Timberlake, QB, Buffalo Bills; 17, John Henderson, E, Buffalo Bills

1966: 1, Tom Mack, T, Los Angeles Rams (2); 5B, Steve Smith, E, San Francisco 49ers (71); 5, Jack Clancy, FL, St. Louis Cardinals (73); 18, Chuck Kines, T, Chicago Bears (272). AFL: 1, Bill Yearby, T, New York Jets; 16, Steve Smith, DE, Houston Oilers. AFL

Bob Timberlake throws out a stiff arm on an Oregon
State tackler in the Rose Bowl. He was drafted by both
major pro football leagues in 1965 and played one year in
the NFL before retiring to become a minister.

Redshirt: 3, Jack Clancy, E, Miami Dolphins

1967: 1B, Jim Detwiler, HB, Baltimore Colts (20); 2, Rick Volk, DB, Baltimore Colts (45); 3A, Frank Nunley, LB, San Francisco 49ers (62); 3, John Rowser, DB, Green Bay Packers (78); 4A, Carl Ward, HB, Cleveland Browns (83); 12, Mike Bass, DB, Green Bay Packers (314)

1968: 5, Rocky Rosema, LB, St. Louis Cardinals (123); 7A, Ray Phillips, G, New Orleans Saints (169); 9, David Porter, DT, Cleveland Browns (238)

1969: 1, Ron Johnson, RB, Cleveland Browns (20); 3A, Tom Stinic, LB, Dallas Cowboys (68); 14, George Hoey, FL, Detroit Lions (346)

1970: 2, Jim Mandich, TE, Miami Dolphins (29); 5, Cecil Pryor, DE, Green Bay Packers (120); 5B, Barry Pierson, DB, St. Louis Cardinals (127); 14, Garvie Craw, RB/TE, Boston Patriots (343); 14, Tom Curtis, DB, Baltimore Colts (356); 17, Brian Healy, DB, Minnesota Vikings (441)

1971: 2, Dan Dierdorf, T, St. Louis Cardinals (43); 3A, Paul Staroba, WR, Cleveland Browns (66); 5, Pete Newell, G, Detroit Lions (125); 5C, Marty Huff, LB, San Francisco 49ers (127); 6, Don Moorhead, RB, New Orleans Saints (132); 10, Jim Bettis, DB, New York Jets (240); 14, John Harpring, G, New York Jets (344)

1972: 1, Thom Darden, DB, Cleveland Browns (18); 1B, Mike Taylor, LB, New York Jets (20); 2, Reggie McKenzie, G, Buffalo Bills (27); 2B, Glenn Doughty, WR, Baltimore Colts (47); 3, Tom Beckman, DE, St. Louis Cardinals (57); 3A, Mike Keller, LB, Dallas Cowboys (64); 5A, Billy Taylor, RB, Atlanta Falcons (109); 10, Mike Oldham, WR, Wash. Redskins (255); 16, Guy Murdock, C, Houston Oilers (396); 17, Fritz Seyferth, RB, New York Giants (419)

1973: 1A, Paul Seymour, T, Buffalo Bills (7); 3, Randy Logan, DB, Philadelphia Eagles (55); 4, Bo Rather, WR, Miami Dolphins (104); 5, Fred Grambau, DE, Kansas City Chiefs (120); 13B, Clint Spearman, LB, Los Angeles Rams (323); 16, Bill Hart, C, Chicago Bears (395)

1974: 1B, Dave Gallagher, DE/DT, Chicago Bears (20); 2, Paul Seal, TE, New Orleans Saints (36); 2B, Ed Shuttlesworth, RB, Baltimore Colts (37); 4A, Clint Haslerig, WR, San Francisco 49ers (83); 7, James Coode, T/G, Atlanta Falcons (173); 10, Doug Troszak, DT, Green Bay Packers (246); 11, Bob Thornbladh, RB, Kansas City Chiefs (275); 14, Walt Williamson, DE, San Fran. 49ers (347); 15, Larry Cipa, QB, New Orleans Saints (373); 16, Don Coleman, LB, New Orleans Saints (398)

1975: 1, Dave Brown, DB, Pittsburgh Steelers (26); 6C, Dennis Franklin, QB/WR, Detroit Lions (144); 7A, Gil Chapman, RB, Buffalo Bills (166); 7C, Harry Banks, DB, Buffalo Bills (175); 8B, Greg Denboer, TE, Baltimore Colts (187); 9, Steve Strinko, LB, Detroit Lions (219); 10, Chuck Heater, RB, New Orleans Saints (241); 11, Tom Drake, DB, Buffalo Bills (279); 13, Carl Russ, LB, Atlanta Falcons (315)

1976: 4A, Gordon Bell, RB, New York Giants (104); 4, Dan Jilek, LB, Buffalo Bills (110); 5A, Don Dufek Jr., DB, Seattle Seahawks (126); 5, Steve King, T, New York Jets (129); 9A, Jim Czirr, C, Denver Broncos (252); 10, Jeff Perlinger, DE, San Diego Chargers (268); 13, Waymon Britt, DB/WR, Wash. Redskins (364)

1977: 2, Rob Lytle, RB, Denver Broncos (45); 3B, Jim Smith, WR, Pittsburgh Steelers (75); 6, Calvin O'Neal, LB, Baltimore Colts (163); 8, Greg Morton, DT, Buffalo Bills (197); 9, Jerry Vogele, LB, New England Patriots (249); 10, John Hennessy, DE, New York Jets (256)

1978: 1, Mike Kenn, T, Atlanta Falcons (13); 1B, John Anderson, LB, Green Bay Packers (26); 2B, Walt Downing, G, San Francisco 49ers (47); 6A, Dwight Hicks, DB, Detroit Lions (150); 11B, Mark Donahue, G, Cincinnati Bengals (294)

1979: 1, Jon Giesler, T, Miami Dolphins (24); 4A, Russell Davis, RB, Pittsburgh Steelers (86); 5A, Tom Seabron, LB, San Francisco 49ers (111); 5, Harlan Huckleby, RB, New Orleans Saints (120); 5, Jerry Meter, LB, Minnesota Vikings (129); 5, Rick Leach, QB, Denver Broncos (132); 6, Bill Dufek, G, New York Jets (149)

1980: 1, Curtis Greer, DE, St. Louis Cardinals (6); 2, Doug Marsh, TE, St. Louis Cardinals (33); 2B, Ralph Clayton, WR/RB, New York Jets (47); 4, Mike Jolly, DB, New Orleans Saints (96); 5A, Mike Harden, DB, Denver Broncos (131); 7A, Ron Simpkins, LB, Cincinnati Bengals (167)

1981: 1A, Mel Owens, LB, Los Angeles Rams (9); 4A, George Lilja, C, Los Angeles Rams (104); 8A, John Powers, G, New York Giants (197); 10, Andy Cannavino, LB, Detroit Lions

1982: 1, Butch Woolfolk, RB, New York Giants (18); 2A, Bubba Paris, T, San Francisco 49ers (29); 3B, Stan Edwards, RB, Houston Oilers (72); 4, Ed Muransky, T, Oakland Raiders (91); 4, Brian Carpenter, DB, Dallas Cowboys (101); 6, Kurt Becker, G, Chicago Bears (146); 7, Ben Needham, LB, Cincinnati Bengals (194)

1983: 2, Rick Strenger, T, Detroit Lions (40); 2B, Keith Bostic, DB, Houston Oilers (42); 8, Robert Thompson, LB, Houston Oilers (198); 8B, Craig Dunaway, TE, Pittsburgh Steelers (218); 8, Lawrence Ricks,

RB, Dallas Cowboys (220); 9, Ali Haji-Sheikh, PK, New York Giants (237); 12, Anthony Carter, WR, Miami Dolphins (334)

1984: 3, Stefan Humphries, G, Chicago Bears (71); 4, Evan Cooper, DB, Philadelphia Eagles (88); Supplemental: 2, Steve Smith, QB, San Diego Chargers (33); 2, Tom Dixon, C, Pittsburgh Steelers (52)

1985: 1, Kevin Brooks, DE, Dallas Cowboys (17)

1986: 3B, Mike Hammerstein, DT, Cincinnati Bengals (65); 3, Brad Cochran, DB, Los Angeles Raiders (80); 4A, Eric Kattus, TE, Cincinnati Bengals (91); 12A, Clay Miller, G, Tampa Bay Bucanneers (306)

1987: 1, Jim Harbaugh, QB, Chicago Bears (26); 3, Bob Perryman, FB, New England Patriots (79); 4, Garland Rivers, DB, Detroit Lions (92); 5, Paul Jokisch, WR, San Francisco 49ers (134); 9, Thomas Wilcher, RB, San Diego Chargers (226)

1988: 2, John Elliott, OT, New York Giants (36); 4, Monte Robbins, P, Tampa Bay Buccaneers (107); 4, Jamie Morris, RB, Washington Redskins (109)

1989: 4, John Kolesar, FLK, Buffalo Bills (109); 5, David Arnold, DB, Pittsburgh Steelers (118); 6, Mark Messner, DT, Los Angeles Rams (161)

1990: 2, Leroy Hoard, RB, Cleveland Browns (45); 3, Greg McMurtry, SE, New England Patriots (80); 4, Chris Calloway, FLK, Pittsburgh Steelers (97); 6, Derrick Walker, TE, San Diego Chargers (163); 11, Brent White, DT, Chicago Bears (284)

1991: 1, Jarrod Bunch, FB, New York Giants (27); 5, Jon Vaughn, RB, New England Patriots (112); 6, David Key, DB, New England Patriots (140); 7, Tripp Welborne, DB, Minnesota Vikings (180); 8, Dean Dingman, OL, Pittsburgh Steelers (212); 8, Tom Dohring, OT, Kansas City Chiefs (218); 11, Tony Boles, RB, Dallas Cowboys (291)

1992: 1, Desmond Howard, FLK, Washington Redskins (4); 2, Greg Skrepenak, OT, Los Angeles Raiders (32); 4, Mike Evans, DL, Kansas City Chiefs (101); 7, Erick Anderson, ILB, Kansas City Chiefs (186); 9, Brian Townsend, OLB, Los Angeles Rams (281); 12, Matt Elliott, OL, Washington Redskins (336)

1993: 1, Steve Everitt, C, Cleveland Browns (14); 2, Tony McGee, TE, Cincinnati Bengals (37); 3, Joe Cocozzo, OG, San Diego Chargers (64); 4, Corwin Brown, S, New England Patriots (110); 8, Doug Skene, OT, Philadelphia Eagles (217); 8, Elvis Grbac, QB, San Francisco 49ers (219)

1994: 1, Derrick Alexander, WR, Cleveland Browns (29)

David Terrell celebrates his fourth-quarter touchdown that gave the Wolverines a come-from-behind win over Wisconsin in 2000.

1995: 1, Tyrone Wheatley, RB, New York Giants (17); 1, Ty Law, DB, New England Patriots (23); 1, Trezelle Jenkins, OT, Kansas City Chiefs (31); 2, Todd Collins, QB, Buffalo Bills (45); 4, Matt Dyson, LB, Los Angeles Raiders (138)

1996: 1, Tshimanga Biakabutuka, RB, Carolina Panthers (8); 2, Amani Toomer, WR, New York Giants (34); 4, Jon Runyan, OT, Houston Oilers (109); 5, Mercury Hayes, WR, New Orleans Saints (136); 7, Jay Riemersma, TE, Buffalo Bills (244)

1997: 3, Rod Payne, C, Cincinnati Bengals (76); 4, Damon Denson, OG, New England Patriots (97); 7, William Carr, NT, Cincinnati Bengals (217)

1998: 1, Charles Woodson, CB, Oakland Raiders (4); 3, Chris Floyd, FB, New England Patriots (81); 3, Brian Griese, QB, Denver Broncos (91); 4, Glen Steele, DT, Cincinnati Bengals (105); 5, Chris Howard, RB, Denver Broncos (153)

1999: 2, Jon Jansen, OT, Washington Redskins (37); 5, Jerame Tuman, TE, Pittsburgh Steelers (136); 6, Tai Streets, WR, San Francisco 49ers (171); 6, Andre Weathers, CB, New York Giants (205)

2000: 2, Ian Gold, LB, Denver Broncos (40); 4, Aaron Shea, FB, Cleveland Browns (110); 4, Josh Williams, DL, Indianapolis Colts (122); 6, Dhani Jones, LB, New York Giants (177); 6, Tom Brady, QB, New England Patriots (199); 7, Rob Renes, NT, Indianapolis Colts (235)

2001: 1, David Terrell, WR, Chicago Bears (8); 1, Steve Hutchinson, OG, Seattle Seahawks (17); 1, Jeff Backus, OT, Detroit Lions (18); 2, Anthony Thomas, TB, Chicago Bears (38); 2, Maurice Williams, OT, Jacksonville Jaguars (43)

2002: 3, Marquise Walker, WR, Tampa Bay Buccaneers (86); 4, Larry Foote, LB, Pittsburgh Steelers (128); 5, Jonathan Goodwin, OG, New York Jets (154); 7, Hayden Epstein, PK/P, Jacksonville Jaguars (247)

2003: 2, Bennie Joppru, TE, Houston Texans (41); 2, Victor Hobson, LB, New York Jets (53); 3, B.J. Askew, RB, New York Jets (85); 6, Drew Henson, QB, Houston Texans (192); 6, Cato June, S, Indianapolis Colts (198); 7, Charles Drake, S, New York Giants (240)

2004: 1, Chris Perry, RB, Cincinnati Bengals (26); 3, Jeremy LeSueur, CB, Denver Broncos (85); 7, John Navarre, QB, Arizona Cardinals (202); 7, Tony Pape, OT, Miami Dolphins (221)

2005: 1, Braylon Edwards, WR, Cleveland Browns (3); 1, Marlin Jackson, CB, Indianapolis Colts (29); 2, David Baas, OG/C, San

Francisco 49ers (33)

2006: 4, Gabe Watson, DT, Arizona Cardinals (107); 4, Jason Avant, WR, Philadelphia Eagles (109); 7, Tim Massaquoi, TE, Tampa Bay Buccaneers (244)

2007: 1, Leon Hall, CB, Cincinnati Bengals (18); 2, Alan Branch, DT, Arizona Cardinals (33); 2, LaMarr Woodley, DE/OLB, Pittsburgh Steelers (46); 2, David Harris, ILB, New York Jets (47); 5, Steve Breaston, WR/RS, Arizona Cardinals (142); 6, Prescott Burgess, LB, Baltimore Ravens (207); 7, Tyler Ecker, TE, Washington Redskins (216).

2008: 1, Jake Long, T, Miami Dolphins (1); 2, Chad Henne, QB, Miami Dolphins (57); 3, Shawn Crable, OLB, New England Patriots (78); 3, Mario Manningham, WR, New York Giants (95); 6, Mike Hart, RB, Indianapolis Colts (202); 7, Adrian Arrington, WR, New Orleans Saints (237)

2009: 4, Terrance Taylor, DT, Indianapolis Colts (136); 6, Morgan Trent, CB, Cincinnati Bengals (179)

All-Centennial Team

(Determined by fan vote on the school's athletic website)

Offense: Dan Dierdrof, OL; Reggie McKenzie, OL; John "Jumbo" Elliott, OL; Greg Skrepenak, OL; Jon Jansen, OL; Bennie Oosterbaan, WR; Anthony Carter, WR; Desmond Howard, WR; Rick Leach, QB; Tom Harmon, RB; Tyrone Wheatley, RB; Remy Hamilton, K

Defense: Mark Messner, DL; Glen Steele, DL; Chris Hutchinson, DL; Erick Anderson, LB; Jarrett Irons, LB; Ron Simpkins, LF; Sam Sword, LB; Charles Woodson, DB; Ty Law, DB; Tripp Welborne, DB; Tom Curtis, DB; Monte Robbins, P

Coach: Bo Schembechler

The Bo Schembechler Award

(Team Most Valuable Player)

1926: Benny Friedman, QB

1927: Bennie Oosterbaan, L

1928: Otto Pommerening, L

1929: James Simrall, QB

1930: Jack Wheeler, QB

1931: Bill Hewitt, L

1932: Harry Newman, QB

1933: Herman Everhardus, RB

1934: Gerald Ford, L

1935: Bill Renner, QB

1936: Matt Patanelli, L

1937: Ralph Heikkinen, L

1938: Ralph Heikkinen, L

1939: Tom Harmon, RB

1940: Tom Harmon, RB

1941: Reuben Kelto, L

1942: Al Wistert, L

1943: Bob Wiese, RB

1944: Don Lund, RB

1945: Harold Watts, L

1946: Bob Chappuis, RB

1947: Chalmers "Bump" Elliott, RB

1948: Dominic Tomasi, L

1949: Dick Kempthorn, RB

1950: Don Dufek, RB

1951: Don Peterson, RB

1952: Ted Topor, QB

1953: Tony Branoff, RB

1954: Fred Baer, RB

1955: Terry Barr, RB

1956: Dick Hill, L

1957: Jim Pace, RB

1958: Bob Ptacek, RB

1959: Tony Rio, FB

1960: Dennis Fitzgerald, RB

1961: John Walker, L

1962: Dave Raimey, RB

1963: Tom Keating, L

1964: Bob Timberlake, QB

1965: Bill Yearby, L

1966: Jack Clancy, TE

1967: Ron Johnson, RB

1968: Ron Johnson, RB

1969: Jim Mandich, TE

1970: Don Moorhead, QB; Henry Hill, RB

1971: Billy Taylor, RB

1972: Randy Logan, DB

1973: Paul Seal, TE

1974: Steve Strinko, LB

1975: Gordon Bell, RB

1976: Rob Lytle, RB

1977: Russell Davis, FB

1978: Rick Leach, QB

1979: Ron Simpkins, LB

1980: Anthony Carter, WR

1981: Butch Woolfolk, RB

1982: Anthony Carter, WR

1983: Steve Smith, QB

1984: Mike Mallory, LB

1985: Mike Hammerstein, DL

1986: Jim Harbaugh, QB

1987: Jamie Morris, RB

1988: Mark Messner, DL

1989: Tony Boles, RB

1990: Tripp Welbourne, DB

1991: Desmond Howard, WR

1992: Chris Hutchinson, OL

1993: Buster Stanley, DL

1994: Todd Collins, QB

1995: Tshimanga Biakabutuka, RB

1996: Rod Payne, C

1997: Charles Woodson, CB

1998: Tai Streets, WR

1999: Tom Brady, QB

2000: Anthony Thomas, RB

2001: Marquise Walker, WR

2002: B.J. Askew, RB

2003: Chris Perry, RB

2004: Braylon Edwards, WR

2005: Jason Avant, WR

2006: Mike Hart, RB; David Harris, ILB

2007: Mike Hart, RB

2008: Brandon Graham, DE

The Greatest Players

RECORDS & LEADERS
Rushing
Game

Name	Yards	Opponent
1. Ron Johnson	347	Wisconsin, Nov. 16, 1968
2. Tshimanga Biakabutuka	313	Ohio State, Nov. 25, 1995
3. Jon Vaughn	288	UCLA, Sept. 22, 1990
4. Ron Johnson	270	Navy, Oct. 7, 1967
5. Butch Woolfolk	253	at Michigan State, Oct. 10, 1981
6. Tyrone Wheatley	235	Washington, Jan. 1, 1993
7. Jamie Morris	234	Alabama, Jan. 2, 1988
(tie) Mike Hart	234	at Illinois, Oct. 16, 2004
9. Chris Perry	232	Central Michigan, Aug. 30, 2003
10. Anthony Thomas	228	at Illinois, Sept. 23, 2000

Season

Name	Yards	Year
1. Tshimanga Biakabutuka	1,818	1995
2. Anthony Thomas	1,733	2000
3. Jamie Morris	1,703	1987
4. Chris Perry	1,674	2003
5. Mike Hart	1,562	2006
6. Rob Lytle	1,469	1976
7. Butch Woolfolk	1,459	1981
8. Mike Hart	1,455	2004
9. Tony Boles	1,408	1988
10. Ron Johnson	1,391	1968

Career

Name	Yards	Years
1. Mike Hart	5,040	2004–07
2. Anthony Thomas	4,472	1997–00
3. Jamie Morris	4,393	1984–87

On his finest day in maize and blue, Tim Biakabutuka high steps past a diving Ohio State player in 1995 to add to his rushing total for the day. He finished with 313 yards, which was second best in school history.

4. Tyrone Wheatley	4,178	1991–94
5. Butch Woolfolk	3,861	1978–81
6. Chris Perry	3,696	2000–03
7. Rob Lytle	3,317	1973–76
8. Billy Taylor	3,072	1969–71
9. Gordon Bell	2,900	1973–75
10. Tshimanga Biakabutuka	2,810	1993–95

Passing

Game

Name	Yards	Opponent
1. John Navarre	389	at Iowa, Oct. 4, 2003
2. Tom Brady	375	at Ohio State, Nov. 21, 1998
3. Scott Dreisbach	372	Virginia, Aug. 26, 1995
4. Tom Brady	369	vs. Alabama, Jan. 1, 2000
5. John Navarre	360	at Oregon, Sept. 20, 2003
6. John Navarre	353	at Minnesota, Oct. 10, 2003
7. Todd Collins	352	Minnesota, Nov. 12, 1994
8. Chad Henne	328	Minnesota Oct. 9, 2004
(tie) Chad Henne	328	at Ohio State Nov. 20, 2004
10. Brian Griese	323	Penn State Nov. 18, 1995

Season

Name	Yards	Year
1. John Navarre	3,331	2003
2. John Navarre	2,905	2002
3. Chad Henne	2,743	2004
4. Jim Harbaugh	2,729	1986
5. Tom Brady	2,636	1998
6. Tom Brady	2,586	1999
7. Chad Henne	2,526	2005
8. Todd Collins	2,518	1994
9. Todd Collins	2,509	1993
10. Chad Henne	2,508	2006

Career

Name	Yards	Years
1. Chad Henne	9,715	2004–07
2. John Navarre	9,254	2000–03
3. Elvis Grbac	6,460	1989–92
4. Todd Collins	5,858	1991–94
5. Jim Harbaugh	5,449	1983–86
6. Tom Brady	5,351	1996–99
7. Steve Smith	4,860	1980–83
8. Brian Griese	4,383	1994–97
9. Rick Leach	4,284	1975–78
10. John Wangler	2,994	1976–80

Receiving

Game

Name	Yards	Opponent
1. Jack Clancy	197	Oregon State, Sept. 17, 1966
2. Tai Streets	192	at Minnesota, Oct. 31, 1998
3. Braylon Edwards	189	Michigan State, Oct. 30, 2004
4. Derrick Alexander	188	Illinois, Oct. 23, 1993
5. Jim Smith	184	Purdue, Nov. 8, 1975
6. Mercury Hayes	179	Virginia Aug. 26, 1995
(tie) Amani Toomer	179	Boston College Sept. 3, 1994
(tie) Jack Clancy	179	Illinois Nov. 5, 1966
9. Paul Staroba	178	at Wisconsin Oct. 31, 1970
10. Amani Toomer	177	Minnesota Oct. 28, 1995

Season

Name	Yards	Year
1. Braylon Edwards	1,330	2004
2. Mario Manningham	1,174	2007
3. Marquise Walker	1,143	2001
4. Braylon Edwards	1,138	2003

The Greatest Players

5. David Terrell	1,130	2000
6. Amani Toomer	1,096	1994
7. Jack Clancy	1,077	1966
8. David Terrell	1,038	1999
9. Tai Streets	1,035	1998
(tie) Braylon Edwards	1,035	2002

Career

Name	Yards	Years
1. Braylon Edwards	3,541	2001–04
2. Anthony Carter	3,076	1979–82
3. Amani Toomer	2,657	1992–95
4. David Terrell	2,317	1998–00
5. Mario Manningham	2,310	2005–07
6. Tai Streets	2,284	1995–98
7. Marquise Walker	2,269	1998–01
8. Jason Avant	2,247	2002–05
9. Greg McMurtry	2,163	1986–89
10. Desmond Howard	2,146	1989–91
11. Mercury Hayes	2,144	1992–95

Other Records

Points, game: Ron Johnson, 30, Wisconsin, Nov. 16, 1968

Points, season: Desmond Howard, 138, 1991

Points, career: Garrett Rivas, 354, 2003–06

All-purpose yards, game: Ron Johnson, 387, Wisconsin, Nov. 16, 1968

All-purpose, season: Chris Perry, 2,041, 2003

All-purpose, career: Jamie Morris, 6,201, 1984–87

Interceptions, game: 3, 10 different players

Braylon Edwards hauls in a 38-yard touchdown pass in 2004 against the Indiana Hoosiers. Among Edwards' career records at Michigan is the one for total receiving yards: 3,541.

Interceptions, season: Tom Curtis, 10, 1968

Interceptions, career: Tom Curtis, 25, 1967–69

Tackles, game: Calvin O'Neal, 24, at Purdue, Nov. 6, 1976

Tackles, season: Ron Simpkins, 174, 1977

Tackles, career: Ron Simpkins, 516, 1976–79

Sacks, game: Mark Messner, 5 (25), Northwestern, Oct. 31, 1987

Sacks, season: David Bowens, 12, 1996; LaMarr Woodley, 12, 2006

Sacks, career: Mark Messner, 36, 1985–88

The Greatest Players

11.5

Sacks by LaMarr Woodley in his breakout 2008 season with the Pittsburgh Steelers, just a half sack shy of the mark he set at Michigan. Woodley also scored his first pro touchdown in 2008 on a fumble recovery.

THE COACHES

Head Coaches

Name	Year	Record
Murphy/Crawford	1891	4–5
Frank Barbour	1892–93	14–8–0
William McCauley	1894–95	17–2–1
William Ward	1896	9–1–0
Gustave Ferbert	1897–99	24–3–1
Langdon Lea	1900	7–2–1
Fielding Yost	1901–23, 25–26	165–29–10
George Little	1924	6–2–0
Elton Wieman	1927–28	9–6–1
Harry Kipke	1929–37	46–24–4
Fritz Crisler	1938–47	71–16–3
Bennie Oosterbaan	1948–58	63–33–4
Bump Elliott	1959–68	51–42–2
Bo Schembechler	1969–89	194–48–5
Gary Moeller	1990–94	44–13–3
Lloyd Carr	1995–07	122–40
Rich Rodriguez	2008–	

Fielding H. Yost
1901–1926

Fielding H. "Hurry Up" Yost came to Michigan from Stanford in 1901 as a result of the Pacific Coast Conference's adoption of a rule forbidding schools to employ nonalumni as coaches. Yost took his first Michigan team out to California to play Stanford in the first-ever Rose Bowl game, on January 1, 1902, and crushed his previous employer 49–0. Yost coached 25 seasons at Michigan, 1901–26 with a one-year hiatus in 1924, and compiled a record of 165–29–10. He earned his nickname from his constant exhortations to his players during practice to "Hurry up! Hurry up!" He won his reputation as a legend by coaching his immortal "point-a-minute" teams of 1901 to 1905 to four national championships in five years. Eight of his

Michigan teams finished unbeaten. Yost also served as Michigan's athletics director (1921–41).

Yost at Michigan

Year	Overall	Big Ten/Place	Bowl
1901	11–0*	4–0/1st	Rose
1902	11–0*	5–0/1st	
1903	11–0–1*	3–0–1/1st	
1904	10–0*	2–0/1st	
1905	12–1	2–1/2nd	
1906	4–1	1–0/1st	
1907	5–1	N/A	
1908	5–2–1	N/A	
1909	6–1	N/A	
1910	3–0–3	N/A	
1911	5–1–2	N/A	
1912	5–2	N/A	
1913	6–1	N/A	
1914	6–3	N/A	
1915	4–3–1	N/A	
1916	7–2	N/A	
1917	8–2	0–1/8th	
1918	5–0*	2–0/1st	
1919	3–4	1–4/7th	
1920	5–2	2–2/6th	
1921	5–1–1	2–1–1/5th	
1922	6–0–1	4–0/1st	
1923	8–0*	4–0/1st	
1925	7–1	5–1/1st	
1926	7–1	5–0/1st	
Total	165–29–10 (.833)	42–10–2 (.778)	

*Claimed National Championship

(Note: Michigan was not in the Big Ten 1907–16)

Fritz Crisler accepts his National Coach of the Year Award in 1947 from New York governor Thomas Dewey, who was running for president at the time. Crisler coached at both Minnesota and Princeton before arriving in Ann Arbor and is also credited for bringing the famous winged helmet to Michigan.

Herbert O. "Fritz" Crisler
1938–47

Fritz Crisler's winning percentage of .805 (71–16–3) during his 10 seasons ranks second in school history (minimum of 50 games coached), behind only Fielding Yost's .833. His 1947 team finished 10–0, won the national title, and beat Southern California 49–0 in the Rose Bowl. Crisler played football at the University of Chicago under Amos Alonzo Stagg and stayed on as an assistant for eight years. He held head coaching positions at Minnesota and Princeton before bringing his innovative approach, and the winged helmet, to Ann Arbor. At a time when most teams were switching to the T formation, Crisler stuck faithfully to the single wing. His buck lateral and spinner-cycle offense, requiring precise timing, ball-handling, and execution, still excited fans.

Crisler at Michigan

Year	Overall	Big Ten/Place	Bowl
1938	6–1–1	3–1–1/2nd	
1939	6–2	3–2/4th	
1940	7–1	3–1/2nd	
1941	6–1–1	3–1–1/2nd	
1942	7–3	3–2/3rd	
1943	8–1	6–0/1st	
1944	8–2	5–2/2nd	
1945	7–3	5–1/2nd	
1946	6–2–1	5–1–1/2nd	
1947	10–0	6–0/1st	Rose
Total	71–16–3 (.805)	42–11–3 (.777)	

Glenn E. "Bo" Schembechler
1969–89

Although he last roamed the sideline at Michigan Stadium as a coach in 1989, Glenn "Bo" Schembechler remains the most recognizable coach in the state. Tough, blunt, opinionated, and wildly successful during his 21 seasons as Michigan's head coach, Schembechler led the Wolverines to 13 Big Ten championships, 10 Rose Bowls, and 194 wins. The victory total is a program record.

When Schembechler was named head coach prior to the 1969 season, no one knew what to expect from the former Woody Hayes assistant, who was coming off six years at his alma mater, Miami of Ohio.

Nevertheless, in his first meeting against Hayes, Michigan stunned the No. 1 Buckeyes, 24–12, costing Ohio State a shot at the national championship.

Schembechler's hard-driving style didn't suit every player, but that never bothered him. He hung a sign in the Michigan locker room that stated: "Those who stay will be champions."

During the 1970s, the Wolverines had a nation-best 96–10–3 record. Michigan never had a losing record in the 1980s, either, before Schembechler retired for health reasons. He served as the school's director of athletics between 1988 and 1990, and the school's football offices are named after him.

When he retired in 1989, Schembechler was the fifth-winningest coach in Division I-A history, with 234 career victories.

The day before the 2006 meeting with Ohio State, Schembechler collapsed and died during the taping of a television show. He was 77.

Schembechler at Michigan

Year	Overall	Big Ten/Place	Bowl
1969	8–3	6–1/1st*	Rose
1970	9–1	6–1/2nd	
1971	11–1	8–0/1st	Rose
1972	10–1	7–1/1st*	
1973	10–0–1	7–0–1/1st*	
1974	10–1	7–1/1st*	
1975	8–2–2	7–1/2nd	Orange
1976	10–2	7–1/1st*	Rose
1977	10–2	7–1/1st*	Rose
1978	10–2	7–1/1st*	Rose
1979	8–4	6–2/3rd	Gator
1980	10–2	8–0/1st	Rose
1981	9–3	6–3/3rd	Bluebonnet
1982	8–4	8–1/1st	Rose
1983	9–3	8–1/2nd	Sugar
1984	6–6	5–4/6th	Holiday
1985	10–1–1	6–1–1/2nd	Fiesta
1986	11–2	7–1/1st	Rose
1987	8–4	5–3/4th	Hall of Fame
1988	9–2–1	7–0–1/1st	Rose
1989	10–2	8–0/1st	Rose
Total	194–48–5 (.796)	143–24–3 (.850)	

*Shared conference championship

The Coaches

Lloyd Carr
1995–2007

Lloyd Carr saw his first Michigan football game in 1969, when he was an assistant high school coach at Detroit Nativity. Little did he know that he'd eventually become the face of Michigan football for more than a decade.

"I cried more tears than I knew I had," said Carr, who after 28 seasons on the Michigan coaching staff announced his retirement in 2007. "And I've never laughed so hard in my life because there were so many memories."

Carr gradually climbed through the coaching ranks and landed at Michigan in 1980, when Bo Schembechler hired him as a defensive backs coach. He was the school's defensive coordinator for eight years before he was named head coach prior to the 1995 season. In his third season in 1997, Carr led the team to a 12–0 record and the Associated Press national championship, earning him numerous national coach of the year awards.

Overall, Carr compiled a record of 122–40 and led the Wolverines to a bowl game every season, including four Rose Bowls, five Big Ten titles, and six 10-win seasons. His teams never placed lower than third in the Big Ten. In 2003 Carr joined Fielding Yost, Bennie Oosterbaan, and Schembechler as the only Michigan head coaches to coach more than 100 games.

"His legacy in football is unbelievable, and he did it with integrity," Michigan offensive coordinator Mike DeBord said. "There has never been an NCAA person come here to question anything about football."

The Coaches

Carr at Michigan

Year	Overall	Big Ten/Place	Bowl
1995	9–4	5–3/3rd	Alamo
1996	8–4	5–3/5th	Outback
1997	12–0**	8–0/1st	Rose
1998	10–3	7–1/1st*	Citrus
1999	10–2	6–2/2nd	Orange
2000	9–3	6–2/1st*	Citrus
2001	8–4	6–2/2nd	Citrus
2002	10–3	6–2/3rd	Outback
2003	10–3	7–1/1st	Rose
2004	9–3	7–1/1st*	Rose
2005	7–5	5–3/3rd	Alamo

2006	11–2	7–1/2nd	Rose
2007	9–4	6–2/2nd	Capital One
Total	122–40 (.753)	81–23 (.779)	

*Shared conference championship

**National champions

Coaching Awards:

GTE Coach of the Year (American Football Coaches' Association): Fritz Crisler, 1947; Bennie Oosterbaan, 1948; Bo Schembechler, 1969; Lloyd Carr, 1997

Paul "Bear" Bryant Coach of the Year: Lloyd Carr, 1997, 2003

Walter Camp Coach of the Year: Bo Schembechler, 1969; Lloyd Carr, 1997

Bobby Dodd Coach of the Year: Bo Schembechler, 1977; Lloyd Carr, 2007

AFCA (American Football Coaches Association) Coach of the Year: Fritz Crisler, 1947; Bennie Oosterbaan, 1948; Bo Schembechler, 1969; Lloyd Carr, 1998

Eddie Robinson Coach of the Year: Bo Schembechler, 1969

Broyles Award (Assistant Coach of the Year): Jim Herrmann, 1997

2009 Coaching Staff

Rich Rodriguez	Head Coach
Tony Dews	Wide Receivers
Tony Gibson	Assistant Head Coach/Secondary
Fred Jackson	Running Backs
Bruce Tall	Defensive Line
Calvin Magee	Associate Head Coach/Offensive Coordinator
Greg Frey	Offensive Line
Jay Hopson	Linebackers
Greg Robinson	Defensive Coordinator
Rod Smith	Quarterbacks

Freshman Morgan Trent upends Iowa running back Albert Young in 2005. The two teams shared the Big Ten title the year before even though the Wolverines beat the Hawkeyes in Ann Arbor.

THE BIG TEN CONFERENCE

Illinois

Location: Urbana-Champaign
Founded: 1867
Enrollment: 27,770
Nickname: Fighting Illini
Colors: Orange and blue
Mascot: Chief Illinwek
Stadium: Memorial Stadium (69,249 capacity)
Coach: Ron Zook
Consensus National Championships: None
Other National Championships (4): 1914, 1919, 1923, 1927
Big Ten Championships (15): 1910, 1914, 1915, 1918, 1919, 1923, 1927, 1928, 1946, 1951, 1953, 1963, 1983, 1990, 2001
First season: 1890
Heisman Winners: None
Retired Jerseys: 50 Dick Butkus, 77 Red Grange

Indiana

Location: Bloomington
Founded: 1820
Enrollment: 38,903
Nickname: Hoosiers
Colors: Cream and crimson
Mascot: None
Stadium: Memorial Stadium (52,354 capacity)
Coach: Bill Lynch
Consensus National Championships: None
Other National Championships: None
Big Ten Championships (2): 1945, 1967
First season: 1887
Heisman Winners: None
Retired Jerseys: 32 Anthony Thompson

Iowa

Location: Iowa City
Founded: 1847
Enrollment: 29,979
Nickname: Hawkeyes

Big Ten

Colors: Old gold and black
Mascot: Herky the Hawk
Stadium: Kinnick Stadium (70,397 capacity)
Coach: Kirk Ferentz
Consensus National Championships: None
Other National Championships (1): 1958
Big Ten Championships (11): 1900, 1921, 1922, 1956, 1958, 1960, 1981, 1985, 1990, 2002, 2004
First season: 1889
Heisman Winners (1): Nile Kinnick, 1939
Retired Jerseys: 24 Nile Kinnick, 62 Cal Jones

Michigan

Location: Ann Arbor
Founded: 1817
Enrollment: 38,006
Nickname: Wolverines
Colors: Maize and blue

Mascot: None. The original live wolverine was named "Biff."
Stadium: Michigan Stadium (107,501 capacity, with ongoing renovations scheduled to be completed in 2010), nicknamed the "Big House"
Coach: Rich Rodriguez
Consensus National Championships (3): 1947, 1948, 1997
Other National Championships (8): 1901, 1902, 1903, 1904, 1918, 1923, 1932, 1933
Big Ten Championships (42): 1898, 1901, 1902, 1903, 1904, 1906, 1918, 1922, 1923, 1925, 1926, 1930, 1931, 1932, 1933, 1943, 1947, 1948, 1949, 1950, 1964, 1969, 1971, 1972, 1973, 1974, 1976, 1977, 1978, 1980, 1982, 1986, 1988, 1989, 1990, 1991, 1992, 1997, 1998, 2000, 2003, 2004
First season: 1879
Heisman Winners (3): Tom Harmon, 1940; Desmond Howard, 1991; Charles Woodson, 1997
Retired Jerseys: 11 Francis Wistert, Albert Wistert, and Alvin Wistert; 47 Bennie Oosterbaan; 48 Gerald Ford; 87 Ron Kramer; 98 Tom Harmon

Michigan State

Location: East Lansing
Founded: 1855
Enrollment: 45,520
Nickname: Spartans

Big Ten

Colors: Green and white
Mascot: Sparty (although during 1909 it was a live brown bear named Brewer's Bruin)
Stadium: Spartan Stadium (75,005 capacity)
Coach: Mark Dantonio
Consensus National Championships (2): 1952, 1965
Other National Championships (4): 1951, 1955, 1957, 1966
Big Ten Championships (6): 1953, 1965, 1966, 1978, 1987, 1990
First season: 1896
Heisman Winners: None
Retired Jerseys: 46 John Hannah, 78 Don Coleman, 90 George Webster, 95 Charles "Bubba" Smith

Minnesota

Location: Minneapolis
Founded: 1851
Enrollment: 46,618
Nickname: Golden Gophers
Colors: Maroon and gold
Mascot: Goldy the Gopher
Stadium: TCF Bank Stadium (50,300 capacity)
Coach: Tim Brewster
Consensus National Championships (4): 1936, 1940, 1941, 1960
Other National Championships (2): 1934, 1935
Big Ten Championships (18): 1900, 1903, 1904, 1906, 1909, 1910, 1911, 1915, 1927, 1933, 1934, 1935, 1937, 1938, 1940, 1941, 1960, 1967
First season: 1882
Heisman Winners (1): Bruce Smith, 1941
Retired Jerseys: 10 Paul Giel, 15 Sandy Stephens, 54 Bruce Smith, 79 Bronko Nagurski

Northwestern

Location: Evanston, Illinois
Founded: 1851
Enrollment: 7,840
Nickname: Wildcats
Colors: Purple and white
Mascot: Willie the Wildcat
Stadium: Ryan Field (47,130 capacity)
Coach: Pat Fitzgerald
Consensus National Championships: None

Big Ten

Fullback B.J. Askew plows through a Purdue tackler in 2001. He had one of his best days in a Michigan uniform, rushing for 63 yards and a pair of touchdowns in the Michigan victory.

Other National Championships: None
Big Ten Championships (8): 1903, 1926, 1930, 1931, 1936, 1995, 1996, 2000
First season: 1876
Heisman Winners: None
Retired Jerseys: None

Penn State

Location: University Park, Pennsylvania
Founded: 1855
Enrollment: 42,000
Nickname: Nittany Lions
Colors: Blue and white
Mascot: The Nittany Lion
Stadium: Beaver Stadium (107,782 capacity)
Coach: Joe Paterno
Consensus National Championships (2): 1982, 1986
Other National Championships: None
Big Ten Championships (3): 1994, 2005, 2007
First season: 1887
Heisman Winners (1): John Cappelletti, 1973
Retired Jerseys: None

Purdue

Location: West Lafayette, Indiana
Founded: 1869
Enrollment: 39,228
Nickname: Boilermakers
Colors: Old gold and black
Mascot: Purdue Pete, special mascot train
Stadium: Ross-Ade Stadium (62,500 capacity)
Coach: Joe Tiller
Consensus National Championships: None
Other National Championships: None
Big Ten Championships (8): 1918, 1929, 1931, 1932, 1943, 1952, 1967, 2000
First season: 1887
Heisman Winners: None
Retired Jerseys: None

Big Ten

Wisconsin

Location: Madison
Founded: 1848
Enrollment: 41,169

Nickname: Badgers
Colors: Cardinal and white
Mascot: Bucky Badger
Stadium: Camp Randall Stadium (80,321 capacity)
Coach: Bret Bielema
Consensus National Championships: None
Other National Championships: None
Big Ten Championships (11): 1896, 1897, 1901, 1906, 1912, 1952, 1959, 1962, 1993, 1998, 1999
First season: 1889
Heisman Winners (2): Alan Ameche, 1954; Ron Dayne, 1999
Retired Jerseys: 33 Ron Dayne, 35 Alan Ameche, 40 Elroy "Crazylegs" Hirsch, 80 Dave Schreiner, 83 Allan Shafer, 88 Pat Richter

BIG TEN TROPHY GAMES

Trophy	Teams	First Year
Little Brown Jug	Michigan-Minnesota	1909
Old Oaken Bucket	Purdue-Indiana	1925
Illibuck	Ohio State-Illinois	1925
Floyd of Rosedale	Minnesota-Iowa	1935
Purdue Cannon	Purdue-Illinois	1943
Sweet Sioux Tomahawk	Illinois-Northwestern	1945
Paul Bunyan's Axe	Wisconsin-Minnesota	1948
Megaphone	Michigan State-Notre Dame	1949
Old Brass Spittoon	Michigan State-Indiana	1950
Paul Bunyan-Governor of Michigan	Michigan-Michigan State	1953
Shillelagh	Purdue-Notre Dame	1958
Cy-Hawk	Iowa-Iowa State	1977
Governor's Victory Bell	Penn State-Minnesota	1993
Land Grant Trophy	Penn State-Michigan State	1993
The Heartland Trophy	Iowa-Wisconsin	2004

Big Ten Champions

Year	Team(s)	Record
1896	Wisconsin	2–0–1
1897	Wisconsin	3–0–0
1898	Michigan	3–0–0
1899	Chicago	4–0–0
1900	Iowa	2–0–1
	Minnesota	3–0–1
1901	Michigan	4–0–0
	Wisconsin	2–0–0
1902	Michigan	5–0–0
1903	Michigan	3–0–1
	Minnesota	3–0–1
	Northwestern	1–0–2
1904	Michigan	2–0–0
	Minnesota	3–0–0
1905	Chicago	7–0–0
1906	Michigan	1–0–0
	Minnesota	2–0–0
	Wisconsin	3–0–0
1907	Chicago	4–0–0
1908	Chicago	5–0–0
1909	Minnesota	3–0–0
1910	Illinois	4–0–0
	Minnesota	2–0–0
1911	Minnesota	3–0–1
1912	Wisconsin	5–0–0
1913	Chicago	7–0–0
1914	Illinois	6–0–0
1915	Illinois	3–0–2
	Minnesota	3–0–1
1916	Ohio State	4–0–0
1917	Ohio State	4–0–0
1918	Illinois	4–0–0
	Michigan	2–0–0
	Purdue	1–0–0
1919	Illinois	6–1–0
1920	Ohio State	5–0–0
1921	Iowa	5–0–0
1922	Iowa	5–0–0
	Michigan	4–0–0
1923	Illinois	5–0–0
	Michigan	4–0–0
1924	Chicago	3–0–3
1925	Michigan	5–1–0
1926	Michigan	5–0–0
	Northwestern	5–0–0
1927	Illinois	5–0–0
1928	Illinois	4–1–0
1929	Purdue	5–0–0
1930	Michigan	5–0–0
	Northwestern	5–0–0
1931	Michigan	5–1–0
	Northwestern	5–1–0
	Purdue	5–1–0
1932	Michigan	6–0–0
1933	Michigan	5–0–1
1934	Minnesota	5–0–0
1935	Minnesota	5–0–0
	Ohio State	5–0–0
1936	Northwestern	6–0–0
1937	Minnesota	5–0–0
1938	Minnesota	4–1–0
1939	Ohio State	5–1–0
1940	Minnesota	6–0–0
1941	Minnesota	5–0–0
1942	Ohio State	5–1–0
1943	Michigan	6–0–0
	Purdue	6–0–0
1944	Ohio State	6–0–0
1945	Indiana	5–0–1
1946	Illinois	6–1–0

Year	Team	Record
1947	Michigan	6–0–0
1948	Michigan	6–0–0
1949	Michigan	4–1–1
	Ohio State	4–1–1
1950	Michigan	4–1–1
1951	Illinois	5–0–1
1952	Purdue	4–1–1
	Wisconsin	4–1–1
1953	Illinois	5–1–0
	Michigan State	5–1–0
1954	Ohio State	7–0–0
1955	Ohio State	6–0–0
1956	Iowa	5–1–0
1957	Ohio State	7–0–0
1958	Iowa	5–1–0
1959	Wisconsin	5–2–0
1960	Iowa	5–1–0
	Minnesota	5–1–0
1961	Ohio State	6–0–0
1962	Wisconsin	6–1–0
1963	Illinois	5–1–1
1964	Michigan	6–1–0
1965	Michigan State	7–0–0
1966	Michigan State	7–0–0
1967	Indiana	6–1–0
	Minnesota	6–1–0
	Purdue	6–1–0
1968	Ohio State	7–0–0
1969	Michigan	6–1–0
	Ohio State	6–1–0
1970	Ohio State	7–0–0
1971	Michigan	8–0–0
1972	Michigan	7–1–0
	Ohio State	7–1–0
1973	Michigan	7–0–1
	Ohio State	7–0–1
1974	Michigan	7–1–0
	Ohio State	7–1–0
1975	Ohio State	8–0–0
1976	Michigan	7–1–0
	Ohio State	7–1–0
1977	Michigan	7–1–0
	Ohio State	7–1–0
1978	Michigan	7–1–0
	Michigan State	7–1–0
1979	Ohio State	8–0–0
1980	Michigan	8–0–0
1981	Iowa	6–2–0
	Ohio State	6–2–0
1982	Michigan	8–1–0
1983	Illinois	9–0–0
1984	Ohio State	7–2–0
1985	Iowa	7–1–0
1986	Michigan	7–1–0
	Ohio State	7–1–0
1987	Michigan State	7–0–1
1988	Michigan	7–0–1
1989	Michigan	8–0–0
1990	Illinois	6–2–0
	Iowa	6–2–0
	Michigan	6–2–0
	Michigan State	6–2–0
1991	Michigan	8–0–0
1992	Michigan	6–0–2
1993	Ohio State	6–1–1
	Wisconsin	6–1–1
1994	Penn State	8–0–0
1995	Northwestern	8–0–0
1996	Northwestern	7–1
	Ohio State	7–1
1997	Michigan	8–0
1998	Michigan	7–1
	Ohio State	7–1
	Wisconsin	7–1
1999	Wisconsin	7–1

Big Ten Season Summaries
2000

| | Conference | | Season | |
	W–L	Pct.	W–L	Pct.
Purdue	6–2	.750	8–4	.667
Michigan	6–2	.750	9–3	.750
Northwestern	6–2	.750	8–4	.667
Ohio State	5–3	.625	8–4	.667
Minnesota	4–4	.500	6–6	.500
Penn State	4–4	.500	5–7	.417
Wisconsin	4–4	.500	9–4	.692
Iowa	3–5	.375	3–9	.250
Illinois	2–6	.250	5–6	.455
Indiana	2–6	.250	3–8	.273
Michigan State	2–6	.250	5–6	.455

Bowls: Rose—Washington 34, Purdue 24; Florida Citrus—Michigan 31, Auburn 28; Outback—South Carolina 24, Ohio State 7; Alamo—Nebraska 66, Northwestern 17; Sun—Wisconsin 21, UCLA 20; Micronpc.com—N.C. State 38, Minnesota 30

All-Big Ten

Offense: QB Drew Brees, Purdue; RB Damien Anderson, Northwestern; RB Anthony Thomas, Michigan; WR David Terrell, Michigan; WR Vinny Sutherland, Purdue; C Ben Hamilton, Minnesota; G Steve Hutchinson, Michigan; G Casey Rabach, Wisconsin; T Jeff Backus, Michigan; T Matt Light, Purdue; TE Tim Stratton, Purdue; K Dan Stultz, Ohio State

Defense: DL Wendell Bryant, Wisconsin; DL Dwayne Missouri, Northwestern; DL Karon Riley, Minnesota; DL Fred Wakefield, Illinois; LB Joe Cooper, Ohio State; LB Larry Foote, Michigan; LB Josh Thornhill, Michigan State; DB Nate Clements, Ohio State; DB Jamar Fletcher, Wisconsin; DB Renaldo Hill, Michigan State; DB Willie Middlebrooks, Minnesota; P Kevin Stemke, Wisconsin

Big Ten

Marquise Walker leaps above fellow All-Big Ten selection Bob Sanders to make an incredible touchdown reception at Iowa in 2001. Walker briefly held most Michigan receiving records, but they later fell to 2001 teammate Braylon Edwards.

2001

	Conference		Season	
	W–L	Pct.	W–L	Pct.
Illinois	7–1	.875	10–1	.833
Michigan	6–2	.750	8–3	.667
Ohio State	5–3	.625	7–4	.583
Iowa	4–4	.500	7–5	.583
Purdue	4–4	.500	6–6	.500
Penn State	4–4	.500	5–6	.455
Indiana	4–4	.500	5–6	.455
Michigan State	3–5	.375	7–5	.583
Wisconsin	3–5	.375	5–7	.417
Northwestern	2–6	.250	4–7	.364
Minnesota	2–6	.250	4–7	.364

Bowls: Sugar—LSU 47, Illinois 34; Florida Citrus—Tennessee 45, Michigan 17; Outback—South Carolina 31, Ohio State 28; Alamo—Iowa 19, Texas Tech 16; Sun—Washington State 33, Purdue 27; Silicon Valley—Michigan State 44, Fresno State 35

All-Big Ten

Offense: QB Antwaan Randle El, Indiana; RB Anthony Davis, Wisconsin; RB Levron Williams, Indiana; WR Lee Evans, Wisconsin; WR Marquise Walker, Michigan; C LeCharles Bentley, Ohio State; G Jay Kulaga, Illinois; G Eric Steinbach, Iowa; T Tony Pashos, Illinois; T Tyson Walter, Ohio State; TE Mark Anelli, Wisconsin; K Travis Dorsch, Purdue

Defense: DL Akin Ayodele, Purdue; DL Wendell Bryant, Wisconsin; DL Jimmy Kennedy, Penn State; DL Matt Mitrione, Purdue; LB Larry Foote, Michigan; LB Nick Greisen, Wisconsin; LB Josh Thornhill, Michigan State; DB Mike Doss, Ohio State; DB Mike Echols, Wisconsin; DB Bob Sanders, Iowa; DB Eugene Wilson, Illinois; P Travis Dorsch, Purdue

Big Ten

Despite the interference from Illinois' Mark Kornfeld, Marlin Jackson was in perfect position to pick off this Illini pass in 2002. Jackson went on to be named All-American the next two seasons.

2002

	Conference		Season	
	W–L	**Pct.**	**W–L**	**Pct.**
Ohio State	8–0	1.00	14–0	1.00
Iowa	8–0	1.00	11–2	.846
Michigan	6–2	.750	10–3	.769
Penn State	5–3	.625	9–4	.692
Purdue	4–4	.500	7–6	.538
Illinois	4–4	.500	5–7	.417
Minnesota	3–5	.375	8–5	.615
Wisconsin	2–6	.250	8–6	.571
Michigan State	2–6	.250	4–8	.333
Indiana	1–7	.125	3–9	.250
Northwestern	1–7	.125	3–9	.250

Bowls: Fiesta—Ohio State 31, Miami (Fla.) 24, 2OT; Orange—Southern California 38, Iowa 17; Capital One—Auburn 13, Penn State 9; Outback—Michigan 38, Florida 30; Alamo—Wisconsin 31, Colorado 28, OT; Sun—Purdue 34, Washington 24; Music City—Minnesota 29, Arkansas 14

All-Big Ten

Offense: QB Brad Banks, Iowa; RB Fred Russell, Iowa; RB Larry Johnson, Penn State; WR Charles Rogers, Michigan State; WR Bryant Johnson, Penn State; C Bruce Nelson, Iowa; G Eric Steinbach, Iowa; G David Baas, Michigan; T Robert Gallery, Iowa; T Tony Pape, Michigan; TE Dallas Clark, Iowa; K Nate Keiding, Iowa

Defense: DL Colin Cole, Iowa; DL Darrion Scott, Ohio State; DL Michael Haynes, Penn State; DL Jimmy Kennedy, Penn State; LB Fred Barr, Iowa; LB Victor Hobson, Michigan; LB Matt Wilhelm, Ohio State; DB Bob Sanders, Iowa; DB Marlin Jackson, Michigan; DB Michael Doss, Ohio State; DB Chris Gamble, Ohio State; P Andy Groom, Ohio State

2003

	Conference		Season	
	W–L	**Pct.**	**W–L**	**Pct.**
Michigan	7–1	.875	10–3	.769
Ohio State	6–2	.750	11–2	.846
Purdue	6–2	.750	9–4	.692

	W–L	Pct.	W–L	Pct.
Iowa	5–3	.625	10–3	.769
Minnesota	5–3	.625	10–3	.769
Michigan State	5–3	.625	8–5	.615
Wisconsin	4–4	.500	7–6	.538
Northwestern	4–4	.500	6–7	.462
Penn State	1–7	.125	3–9	.250
Indiana	1–7	.125	2–10	.167
Illinois	0–8	.000	1–11	.083

Bowls: Rose—Southern California 28, Michigan 14; Fiesta—Ohio State 35, Kansas State 28; Capital One—Georgia 34, Purdue 27, OT; Outback—Iowa 37, Florida 17; Alamo—Nebraska 17, Michigan State 3; Sun—Minnesota 31, Oregon 30; Music City—Auburn 28, Wisconsin 14; Motor City—Bowling Green 28, Northwestern 24

All-Big Ten

Offense: QB John Navarre, Michigan; RB Chris Perry, Michigan; RB Marion Barber III, Minnesota; WR Braylon Edwards, Michigan; WR Lee Evans, Wisconsin; C Greg Eslinger, Minnesota; G David Baas, Michigan; G Alex Stepanovich, Ohio State; T Robert Gallery, Iowa; T Tony Pape, Michigan; TE Ben Utecht, Minnesota; K Nate Kaeding, Iowa

Defense: DL Matt Roth, Iowa; DL Tim Anderson, Ohio State; DL Will Smith, Ohio State; DL Shaun Phillips, Purdue; LB A.J. Hawk, Ohio State; LB Niko Koutouvides, Purdue; LB Alex Lewis, Wisconsin; DB Bob Sanders, Iowa; DB Will Allen, Ohio State; DB Stuart Schweigert, Purdue; DB Jim Leonhard, Wisconsin; P B.J. Sander, Ohio State

2004

	Conference		Season	
	W–L	Pct.	W–L	Pct.
Michigan	7–1	.875	9–3	.750
Iowa	7–1	.875	10–2	.833
Wisconsin	6–2	.750	9–3	.750
Northwestern	5–3	.625	6–6	.500
Ohio State	4–4	.500	8–4	.667

Big Ten

John Navarre launches a pass downfield against Western Michigan in 2001. Navarre started all four seasons of his college career and set many of the school's all-time passing records.

Purdue	4–4	.500	7–5	.583
Michigan State	4–4	.500	5–7	.417
Minnesota	3–5	.375	7–5	.583
Penn State	2–6	.250	4–7	.364
Illinois	1–7	.125	3–8	.273
Indiana	1–7	.125	3–8	.273

Bowls: Rose—Texas 38, Michigan 37; Capital One—Iowa 30, LSU 25; Outback—Georgia 24, Wisconsin 21; Alamo—Ohio State 33, Oklahoma State 7; Sun—Arizona State 27, Purdue 23; Music City—Minnesota 20, Alabama 16

All-Big Ten

Offense: QB Drew Tate, Iowa; RB Michael Hart, Michigan; RB Laurence Maroney, Minnesota; WR Braylon Edwards, Michigan; WR Taylor Stubblefield, Purdue; C Greg Eslinger, Minnesota (tie); G David Baas, Michigan (tie); G Matt Lentz, Michigan; G Dan Buenning, Wisconsin; T Adam Stenavich, Michigan; T Rian Melander, Minnesota; TE Tim Massaquoi, Michigan; K Mike Nugent, Ohio State

Defense: DL Matt Roth, Iowa; DL Gabe Watson, Michigan; DL Anttaj Hawthorne, Wisconsin; DL Erasmus James, Wisconsin; LB Chad Greenway, Iowa; LB Abdul Hodge, Iowa; LB A.J. Hawk, Ohio State; DB Marlin Jackson, Michigan; DB Ernest Shazor, Michigan; DB Jim Leonhard, Wisconsin; DB Scott Starks, Wisconsin; P Steve Weatherford, Illinois

2005

	Conference		Season	
	W–L	Pct.	W–L	Pct.
Penn State	7–1	.875	11–1	.917
Ohio State	7–1	.875	10–2	.833
Wisconsin	5–3	.625	10–3	.769
Michigan	5–3	.625	7–5	.583
Northwestern	5–3	.625	7–5	.583
Iowa	5–3	.625	7–5	.583
Minnesota	4–4	.500	7–5	.583
Purdue	3–5	.375	5–6	.455
Michigan State	2–6	.250	5–6	.455
Indiana	1–7	.125	4–7	.364
Illinois	0–8	.000	2–9	.182

Bowls: Orange—Penn State 26, Florida State 23, 3OT; Fiesta— Ohio State 34, Notre Dame 20; Capital One—Wisconsin 24, Auburn 10; Outback—Florida 31, Iowa 24; Alamo—Nebraska 32, Michigan 28; Sun—UCLA 50, Northwestern 38; Music City— Virginia 34, Minnesota 31

All-Big Ten

Offense: QB Brett Basanez, Northwestern; RB Laurence Maroney, Minnesota; RB Brian Calhoun, Wisconsin; WR Jason Avant, Michigan; WR Santonio Holmes, Ohio State; C Greg Eslinger, Minnesota; G Mark Setterstrom, Minnesota; G Rob Sims, Ohio State; T Levi Brown, Penn State; T Joe Thomas, Wisconsin; TE Matt Spaeth, Minnesota; K Josh Huston, Ohio State

Defense: DL Gabe Watson, Michigan; DL Mike Kudla, Ohio State; DL Tamba Hali, Penn State; DL Scott Paxson, Penn State; LB Chad Greenway, Iowa; LB A.J. Hawk, Ohio State; LB Paul Posluszny, Penn State; DB Nate Salley, Ohio State; DB Donte Whitner, Ohio State; DB Ashton Youboty, Ohio State (tie); DB Calvin Lowry, Penn State (tie); DB Alan Zemaitis, Penn State; P Ken Debauche, Wisconsin

2006

	Conference		Season	
	W–L	**Pct.**	**W–L**	**Pct.**
Ohio State	8–0	1.000	12–1	.923
Michigan	7–1	.875	11–2	.846
Wisconsin	7–1	.875	12–1	.923
Penn State	5–3	.625	9–4	.692
Purdue	5–3	.625	8–6	.571
Minnesota	3–5	.375	6–7	.462
Indiana	3–5	.375	5–7	.417
Northwestern	2–6	.250	4–8	.333
Iowa	2–6	.250	6–7	.462
Illinois	1–7	.125	2–10	.167
Michigan State	1–7	.125	4–8	.333

Bowls: BCS Championship—Florida 41, Ohio State 14; Rose— Southern California 32, Michigan 18; Capital One—Wisconsin 17, Arkansas 14; Outback—Penn State 20, Tennessee 10; Alamo—Texas 26, Iowa 24; Champs Sport—Maryland 24, Purdue 7; Insight—Texas Tech 44, Minnesota 41, OT

All-Big Ten

Offense: QB Troy Smith, Ohio State; RB Mike Hart, Michigan; RB Antonio Pittman, Ohio State; WR Mario Manningham, Michigan; WR Anthony Gonzalez, Ohio State; C Doug Datish, Ohio State; G Mike Jones, Iowa; G T.J. Downing, Ohio State; T Jake Long, Michigan; T Joe Thomas, Wisconsin; TE Matt Spaeth, Minnesota; K Garrett Rivas, Michigan

Defense: DL Alan Branch, Michigan; DL LaMarr Woodley, Michigan; DL Quinn Pitcock, Ohio State; DL Anthony Spencer, Purdue; LB David Harris, Michigan; LB James Laurinaitis, Ohio State; LB Paul Posluszny, Penn State; DB Leon Hall, Michigan; DB Malcolm Jenkins, Ohio State; DB Antonio Smith, Ohio State; DB Jack Ikegwuonu, Wisconsin; P Brandon Fields, Michigan State

2007

	Conference		Season	
	W–L	Pct.	W–L	Pct.
Ohio State	7–1	.875	11–2	.846
Illinois	6–2	.750	9–4	.692
Michigan	6–2	.750	9–4	.692
Wisconsin	5–3	.625	9–4	.692
Penn State	4–4	.500	9–4	.692
Iowa	4–4	.500	6–6	.500
Purdue	3–5	.375	8–5	.615
Indiana	3–5	.375	7–6	.538
Michigan State	3–5	.375	7–6	.538
Northwestern	3–5	.375	6–6	.500
Minnesota	0–8	.000	1–11	.083

Bowls: BCS Championship—LSU 38, Ohio State 24; Rose—Southern California 49, Illinois 17; Capital One—Michigan 41, Florida 35; Outback—Tennessee 21, Wisconsin 17; Insight—Oklahoma State 49, Indiana 33; Alamo Bowl—Penn State 24, Texas A&M 17; Champs Sports—Boston College 24, Michigan State 21; Motor City—Purdue 51, Central Michigan 48

MICHIGAN FOOTBALL

All-Big Ten

Offense: QB Chad Henne, Michigan; RB Rashard Mendenhall, Illinois; RB Chris "Beanie" Wells, Ohio State; WR James Hardy, Indiana; WR Mario Manningham, Michigan; C A.Q. Shipley, Penn State; G Martin O'Donnell, Illinois; G Adam Kraus, Michigan; T Jake Long, Michigan; T Kirk Barton, Ohio State; TE Travis Beckum, Wisconsin; K Taylor Mehlhaff, Wisconsin

Defense: DL Greg Middleton, Indiana; DL Mitch King, Iowa; DL Vernon Gholston, Ohio State; DL Maurice Evans, Penn State; LB J. Leman, Illinois; LB James Laurinaitis, Ohio State; LB Dan Connor, Penn State; DB Vontae Davis, Illinois; DB Malcolm Jenkins, Ohio State; DB Justin King, Penn State; DB Jack Ikegwuonu, Wisconsin; P Jeremy Boone, Penn State

2008

| | Conference | | Season | |
	W–L	Pct.	W–L	Pct.
Penn State	7–1	.875	11–2	.846
Ohio State	7–1	.875	10–4	.769
Michigan State	6–2	.750	9–4	.692
Iowa	5–3	.625	9–4	.692
Northwestern	5–3	.625	9–4	.692
Minnesota	3–5	.375	7–6	.538
Wisconsin	3–5	.375	7–6	.538
Illinois	3–5	.375	5–7	.417
Purdue	2–6	.250	4–8	.333
Michigan	2–6	.250	3–9	.250
Indiana	1–7	.125	3–9	.250

Bowls: Fiesta—Texas 24, Ohio State 21; Rose—Southern California 38, Penn State 24; Capital One—Georgia 24, Michigan State 12; Outback—Iowa 31, South Carolina 10; Insight—Kansas 42, Minnesota 21; Alamo—Missouri 30, Northwestern 23 OT; Champs Sports—Florida State 42, Wisconsin 13

All-Big Ten

Offense: QB Daryll Clark, Penn State; RB Shonn Greene, Iowa; RB Javon Ringer, Michigan State; WR Eric Decker, Minnesota; WR Derrick Williams, Penn State; C A.Q. Shipley, Penn State; G Seth Olsen, Iowa; G Rich Ohrnberger, Penn State; T Alex Boone, Ohio State; T Gerald Cadogan, Penn State; TE Brandon Myers, Iowa; K Kevin Kelly, Penn State

Defense: DL Mitch King, Iowa; DL Corey Wootton, Northwestern; DL Aaron Maybin, Penn State; DL Jared Odrick, Penn State; LB Greg Jones, Michigan State; LB James Laurinaitis, Ohio State; LB Navorro Bowman, Penn State; DB Vontae Davis, Illinois; DB Otis Wiley, Michigan State; DB Malcolm Jenkins, Ohio State; DB Anthony Scirrotto, Penn State; P Zoltan Mesko, Michigan

Big Ten Awards

Player of the Year (Selected by media)

1982:	Anthony Carter
1986:	Jim Harbaugh

Offensive Player of the Year (Selected by coaches and media)

1990:	Jon Vaughn (coaches)
1991:	Desmond Howard (coaches and media)
1992:	Tyrone Wheatley (coaches and media)
2003:	Chris Perry (coaches and media)
2004:	Braylon Edwards (coaches and media)

Offensive Lineman of the Year (Selected by Big Ten radio broadcasters until 1991; coaches since)

1991:	Greg Skrepenak
1998:	Jon Jansen
2000:	Steve Hutchinson
2004:	David Baas
2006:	Jake Long
2007:	Jake Long

Big Ten

Defensive Player of the Year (Selected by coaches and media)

1997: Charles Woodson (coaches and media)

2001: Larry Foote (coaches and media)

2006: LaMarr Woodley (coaches and media)

Defensive Lineman of the Year (Selected by radio broadcasters until 1991; coaches since)

1985: Mike Hammerstein

1988: Mark Messner

1992: Chris Hutchinson

2006: LaMarr Woodley

Freshman of the Year (Selected by coaches and media)

1995: Charles Woodson (coaches)

1997: Anthony Thomas (coaches and media)

2003: Steve Breaston (coaches)

2004: Mike Hart (coaches and media)

Dave McClain Coach of the Year (Selected by media)

1972: Bo Schembechler

1976: Bo Schembechler

1980: Bo Schembechler

1985: Bo Schembechler

1991: Gary Moeller

1992: Gary Moeller

Big Ten

THE RIVALRIES

Michigan vs. Ohio State

They may not be in the same state, or representing different facets of the military, but when it comes to college football rivalries, perhaps none is greater than Michigan vs. Ohio State.

It has everything. Colorful personalities, rabid fan bases, and even history. The two teams met for the first time in 1897, a 34–0 Wolverines victory, and the game has been played every season since 1918, a streak that ranks 10th in NCAA Division I-A for the longest uninterrupted series. Since 1922, more fans have attended the game than any other college football matchup.

But what really sets the rivalry apart is that the game almost always means something in terms of the conference and national picture—although that wasn't always true. Early on, Michigan dominated the series. The Wolverines were 13–0–2 in the first 15 meetings, including a humiliating 86–0 blowout in 1902. Ohio State finally broke through in 1919 with a 13–3 victory.

"Any time you play in this game, it's exciting," former Michigan Coach Lloyd Carr said. "When the championship is on the line, I don't think it gets much better than that."

Lately, Ohio State has held the edge and enters the 2009 season having won five straight. The last time either team won more than four straight was 1927, with the upper hand shifting back and forth through the years.

In 1922 the Wolverines spoiled Ohio Stadium's dedication game with a 19–0 victory. Harry Kipke was the star, scoring two touchdowns and kicking a field goal. In the series' first game at newly constructed Michigan Stadium in 1927, the Wolverines once again posted a shutout victory, 21–0.

Ohio State controlled the series from 1934 to 1937, shutting out the Wolverines all four times. However, Michigan responded with three consecutive victories of its own, including Heisman Trophy winner Tom Harmon's amazing 1940 performance when he ran and passed for four touchdowns and returned an interception for another in a 40–0 Wolverines win.

Michigan had a 6–0–1 record from 1945 to 1951, including the unforgettable "Snow Bowl" in 1950. The Wolverines didn't make a first down, complete a pass, or have a run of over six yards, but they won 9–3 thanks to a safety and touchdown off blocked punts.

The win secured Coach Bennie Oosterbaan's Michigan team its fourth straight Big Ten title. However, it also helped lead to Ohio State hiring Woody Hayes.

In 1954 the Buckeyes drove 99 yards for the go-ahead win in 1954, en route to the national championship, and the Buckeyes began a 15-year run in which it won 11 times.

But under the guidance of first-year coach and former Woody Hayes assistant Bo Schembechler, Michigan shocked the top-ranked Buckeyes 24–12 in Michigan Stadium and snapped Ohio State's 22-game winning streak in 1969. Hayes called that Ohio State club the best he ever coached. The Buckeyes had defeated all of their previous opponents by 27 or more points.

"Damn you, Bo," Hayes growled during a banquet honoring the 1969 Wolverines team. "You will never win a bigger game than that."

It began what's known as the "10-Year War," when Michigan vs. Ohio State decided the Big Ten title nine times.

In 1973 Michigan believed it was headed to the Rose Bowl after rallying to tie the Buckeyes 10–10. However, a committee of Big Ten athletics directors had to break the tie, and in part because of an injury suffered by Michigan quarterback Dennis Franklin during the game, they narrowly chose Ohio State to represent the league in the Rose Bowl.

The Rivalries

Desmond Howard celebrates a 1990 touchdown against Notre Dame. His Heisman moment the next season came against Ohio State when he scampered 93 yards for a punt-return touchdown. As he struck the Heisman pose in the end zone, ABC's Keith Jackson exclaimed, "Goodbye Ohio State, hello Heisman!"

Wolverines quarterback Jim Harbaugh issued "The Guarantee" in 1986. After Minnesota dashed Michigan's hopes of an undefeated season the previous week, Harbaugh guaranteed the Wolverines would beat their fiercest rival. They did, but Michigan needed a missed 45-yard field-goal try by Ohio State's Matt Franz to clinch the 26–24 victory.

From 1988 to 2000, Michigan had a 10-2-1 record against the Buckeyes and Ohio State Coach John Cooper.

"My record against Michigan speaks for itself," said Cooper, who was subsequently replaced by Jim Tressel.

The most memorable play during that era was Desmond Howard's 93-yard punt return in 1991 for a touchdown. Upon reaching the end zone, he struck his famed Heisman pose and a few weeks later won the award.

In 1997, with Lloyd Carr as head coach, the top-ranked Wolverines defeated No. 4 Ohio State 20–14 to gain a Rose Bowl berth. Defensive back Charles Woodson's 78-yard punt return was the pivotal play in the game and propelled him to a Heisman Trophy.

"Charles Woodson certainly played one of his greatest games in the very, very biggest game we have at Michigan, in a game that meant everything to us," Carr said.

Michigan went on to win a share of the national championship by defeating Washington State in the Rose Bowl.

It wasn't until 2006 that college football was able to enjoy its first No. 1 vs. No. 2 meeting between Michigan and Ohio State. However, the day before, former Michigan Coach Bo Schembechler, who graduated from Ohio State, died at age 77.

It was the second-highest scoring game in the 103-game series (the highest was 86 points in 1902, won by Michigan 86-0). Although running back Mike Hart accumulated 142 rushing yards and three touchdowns, Ohio State quarterback Troy Smith finished 29-of-41 for 316 yards with four touchdowns and one interception to essentially lock up the Heisman Trophy and pull off a dramatic 42–39 victory.

"It was definitely difficult for us," quarterback Chad Henne said. "Coach Carr loves him dearly and so do we … It's sad to see him go. We dearly miss him. We tried to fight for him today."

Michigan vs. Ohio State

[Michigan leads series 57–42–6]

Year	Winner	Score	Site
1897	Michigan	34–0	Ann Arbor
1900	Tie	0–0	Ann Arbor
1901	Michigan	21–0	Columbus
1902	Michigan	86–0	Ann Arbor
1903	Michigan	36–0	Ann Arbor
1904	Michigan	31–6	Columbus
1905	Michigan	40–0	Ann Arbor
1906	Michigan	6–0	Columbus
1907	Michigan	22–0	Ann Arbor
1908	Michigan	10–6	Columbus
1909	Michigan	33–6	Ann Arbor
1910	Tie	3–3	Columbus
1911	Michigan	19–0	Ann Arbor
1912	Michigan	14–0	Columbus
1918	Michigan	14–0	Columbus
1919	Ohio State	13–1	Ann Arbor
1920	Ohio State	14–7	Columbus
1921	Ohio State	14–0	Ann Arbor
1922	Michigan	19–0	Columbus
1923	Michigan	23–0	Ann Arbor
1924	Michigan	16–6	Columbus
1925	Michigan	10–0	Ann Arbor
1926	Michigan	17–16	Columbus
1927	Michigan	21–0	Ann Arbor
1928	Ohio State	19–7	Columbus

1929	Ohio State	7–0	Ann Arbor
1930	Michigan	13–0	Columbus
1931	Ohio State	20–7	Ann Arbor
1932	Michigan	14–0	Columbus
1933	Michigan	13–0	Ann Arbor
1934	Ohio State	34–0	Columbus
1935	Ohio State	38–0	Ann Arbor
1936	Ohio State	21–0	Columbus
1937	Ohio State	21–0	Ann Arbor
1938	Michigan	18–0	Columbus
1939	Michigan	21–14	Ann Arbor
1940	Michigan	40–0	Columbus
1941	Tie	20–20	Ann Arbor
1942	Ohio State	21–7	Columbus
1943	Michigan	45–7	Ann Arbor
1944	Ohio State	18–14	Columbus
1945	Michigan	7–3	Ann Arbor
1946	Michigan	58–6	Columbus
1947	Michigan	21–0	Ann Arbor
1948	Michigan	13–3	Columbus
1949	Tie	7–7	Ann Arbor
1950	Michigan	9–3	Columbus
1951	Michigan	7–0	Ann Arbor
1952	Ohio State	27–7	Columbus
1953	Michigan	20–0	Ann Arbor
1954	Ohio State	21–7	Columbus
1955	Ohio State	17–0	Ann Arbor
1956	Michigan	19–0	Columbus
1957	Ohio State	31–14	Ann Arbor
1958	Ohio State	20–14	Columbus
1959	Michigan	23–14	Ann Arbor
1960	Ohio State	7–0	Columbus
1961	Ohio State	50–20	Ann Arbor
1962	Ohio State	28–0	Columbus
1963	Ohio State	14–10	Ann Arbor

1964	Michigan	10–0	Columbus
1965	Ohio State	9–7	Ann Arbor
1966	Michigan	17–3	Columbus
1967	Ohio State	24–14	Ann Arbor
1968	Ohio State	50–14	Columbus
1969	Michigan	24–12	Ann Arbor
1970	Ohio State	20–9	Columbus
1971	Michigan	10–7	Ann Arbor
1972	Ohio State	14–11	Columbus
1973	Tie	10–10	Ann Arbor
1974	Ohio State	12–10	Columbus
1975	Ohio State	21–14	Ann Arbor
1976	Michigan	22–0	Columbus
1977	Michigan	14–6	Ann Arbor
1978	Michigan	14–3	Columbus
1979	Ohio State	18–15	Ann Arbor
1980	Michigan	9–3	Columbus
1981	Ohio State	14–9	Ann Arbor
1982	Ohio State	24–14	Columbus
1983	Michigan	24–21	Ann Arbor
1984	Ohio State	21–6	Columbus
1985	Michigan	27–17	Ann Arbor
1986	Michigan	26–24	Columbus
1987	Ohio State	23–20	Ann Arbor
1988	Michigan	34–31	Columbus
1989	Michigan	28–18	Ann Arbor
1990	Michigan	16–13	Columbus
1991	Michigan	31–3	Ann Arbor
1992	Tie	13–13	Columbus
1993	Michigan	28–0	Ann Arbor
1994	Ohio State	22–6	Columbus
1995	Michigan	31–23	Ann Arbor
1996	Michigan	13–9	Columbus
1997	Michigan	20–14	Ann Arbor
1998	Ohio State	31–16	Columbus

The Rivalries

1999	Michigan	24–17	Ann Arbor
2000	Michigan	38–26	Columbus
2001	Ohio State	26–20	Ann Arbor
2002	Ohio State	14–9	Columbus
2003	Michigan	35–21	Ann Arbor
2004	Ohio State	37–21	Columbus
2005	Ohio State	25–21	Ann Arbor
2006	Ohio State	42–39	Columbus
2007	Ohio State	14–3	Ann Arbor
2008	Ohio State	42–7	Columbus

Michigan vs. Notre Dame

Strange but true, Michigan taught Notre Dame how to play football, and then the schools played three times, once in 1887 and twice in 1888. Not surprisingly, Michigan won all three.

Fast-forward more than 100 years and they're arguably the two most successful programs in college football.

Michigan ranks No. 1 in all-time victories; the Fighting Irish are second.

Notre Dame has won 12 national championships; the Wolverines claim 11.

Even their fight songs stand out against the competition.

However, things have not always been copasetic between the programs. A bitter feud between Michigan Coach Fielding Yost and Notre Dame's Knute Rockne resulted in an interruption in the series from 1909 to 1942. After two wartime games, Michigan Coach Fritz Crisler decided to take the Irish off the schedule once again, and they didn't play for another 35 years.

For the most part, they've played every year since 1978, usually early in the season and the game often foreshadows the kind of year each team will have.

The Rivalries

Quarterback Rick Leach overcame a sprained ankle to lead Michigan to a 28–14 victory in the much-anticipated 1978 matchup.

In 1980 Michigan scored a touchdown in the final minute, but Notre Dame prevailed 29–27 on a last-second 51-yard field goal by Harry Oliver.

"I hated to lose that game in the worst way," Wolverines Coach Bo Schembechler said. "It was the type of game you win 20 times and lose 21 times."

Schembechler's team got its revenge the following season, beating the No. 1-ranked Irish 25–7.

Michigan spoiled Lou Holtz's Notre Dame head coaching debut in 1986 with a 24–23 victory but lost the next four meetings. Notre Dame receiver Raghib (Rocket) Ismail was the star in the 1989 matchup when the teams were ranked first and second in the polls, by returning two kickoffs for second-half touchdowns in the 24–19 Irish win.

That winless string finally came to an end with Desmond Howard's terrific touchdown catch in 1991. With the Wolverines leading 17–14, Michigan was faced with fourth down at the Notre Dame 25-yard line. Needing a foot to gain a first down, quarterback Elvis Grbac lofted a post pass that seemed out of Howard's reach, but he extended to make a diving grab in the right corner of the end zone for a 24–14 victory.

In 1994 Notre Dame took the lead 24–23 with 52 seconds remaining when Derrick Mayes caught a seven-yard touchdown pass from quarterback Ron Powlus. Michigan quarterback Todd Collins responded with a scoring drive that culminated with a 42-yard Remy Hamilton field goal with two seconds left, giving Michigan a 26–24 victory.

The most lopsided game of the series occurred in 2003, when Michigan rolled to a 38–0 victory, which it matched in 2007.

Linebacker LaMarr Woodley sprints for the end zone after recovering a fumble by Notre Dame's Brady Quinn in Michigan's 2006 trouncing of the Fighting Irish. The win was one of several beatings the Wolverines laid on the Irish in the first decade of the 21st century.

Michigan vs. Notre Dame

[Michigan leads series 20–15–1]

Year	Winner	Score	Site
1887	Michigan	8–0	South Bend
1888	Michigan	26–6	South Bend
1888	Michigan	10–4	South Bend
1898	Michigan	23–0	Ann Arbor
1899	Michigan	12–0	Ann Arbor
1900	Michigan	7–0	Ann Arbor
1902	Michigan	23–0	Toledo, Ohio
1908	Michigan	12–6	Ann Arbor
1909	Notre Dame	11–3	Ann Arbor
1942	Michigan	32–20	South Bend
1943	Notre Dame	35–12	Ann Arbor
1978	Michigan	28–14	South Bend
1979	Notre Dame	12–10	Ann Arbor
1980	Notre Dame	29–27	South Bend
1981	Michigan	25–7	Ann Arbor
1982	Notre Dame	23–17	South Bend
1985	Michigan	20–12	Ann Arbor
1986	Michigan	24–23	South Bend
1987	Notre Dame	26–7	Ann Arbor
1988	Notre Dame	19–17	South Bend
1989	Notre Dame	24–19	Ann Arbor
1990	Notre Dame	28–24	South Bend
1991	Michigan	24–14	Ann Arbor
1992	Tie	17–17	South Bend
1993	Notre Dame	27–23	Ann Arbor
1994	Michigan	26–24	South Bend
1997	Michigan	21–14	Ann Arbor
1998	Notre Dame	36–20	South Bend
1999	Michigan	26–22	Ann Arbor
2002	Notre Dame	25–23	South Bend
2003	Michigan	38–0	Ann Arbor

2004	Notre Dame	28–20	South Bend
2005	Notre Dame	17–10	Ann Arbor
2006	Michigan	47–21	South Bend
2007	Michigan	38–0	Ann Arbor
2008	Notre Dame	35–17	South Bend

Michigan vs. Michigan State

It's the rivalry that divides the state and carries over to every other sport.

Love thy neighbor? Not after kickoff.

Their football teams first crossed paths in 1898, when Michigan State was called Michigan Agricultural College. The Aggies didn't put up much of a fight in the first three meetings, losing by a combined score of 204–0.

Michigan held its in-state nuisance scoreless in 20 of the first 27 meetings, until Michigan State responded with four consecutive wins from 1934–37. Michigan won the next 10 meetings, but the Spartans dominated the series during the decades of the '50s and '60s, going 14–4–2.

Since 1953, when Michigan State began Big Ten play, the rivals have gotten something more than bragging rights. The victor lays claim to the Paul Bunyan Trophy, which was donated to the schools by Michigan Governor G. Mennen Williams.

Since 1970, Bo Schembechler's second season as Michigan's head coach, the Wolverines have dominated, with the Spartans unable to win back-to-back meetings.

Ranked No. 1 entering the 1990 matchup, Michigan went for a two-point conversion during the closing moments to win the game, but receiver Desmond Howard was tripped up and unable to make the catch. The upset by the unranked Spartans helped them gain a share of the Big Ten title with the Wolverines.

Michigan State's clock operator was in the spotlight

The Rivalries

11 years later at Spartan Stadium. With MSU trailing 24–20, the Wolverines defense appeared to have stopped the Spartans two yards shy of the goal line, when Spartans quarterback Jeff Smoker spiked the ball with 0:01 on the clock. While Michigan players and coaches screamed that the clock was stopped prematurely, the Spartans huddled up, and Smoker threw a touchdown pass to running back T.J. Duckett.

"It's a rivalry where the two schools don't like each other," former Michigan State Coach Bobby Williams said. "It's everything. It's the fans, the players, the coaches, you name it. They have that game marked; we have that game marked."

Three seasons later, Michigan got even by coming back from a 27–10 deficit with seven minutes remaining to pull out a 45–37 victory in triple overtime. Wide receiver Braylon Edwards made two leaping grabs in the end zone to help tie the game, 27–27, and freshman quarterback Chad Henne found him again for the winning score.

"I think this game speaks to the spirit of the stadium, to the tradition, and this rivalry," Lloyd Carr said afterward. "Anybody who saw this game either in this stadium or across the country on television saw one of the greatest football games, in my opinion, ever played."

The Paul Bunyan Trophy
Michigan vs. Michigan State

[Michigan leads series 67–29–5]

1953	Michigan State	14–6	East Lansing
1954	Michigan	33–7	Ann Arbor
1955	Michigan	14–7	Ann Arbor
1956	Michigan State	9–0	Ann Arbor
1957	Michigan State	35–6	Ann Arbor
1958	Tie	12–12	East Lansing
1959	Michigan State	34–8	Ann Arbor
1960	Michigan State	24–17	East Lansing

1961	Michigan State	28–0	Ann Arbor
1962	Michigan State	28–0	East Lansing
1963	Tie	7–7	Ann Arbor
1964	Michigan	17–10	East Lansing
1965	Michigan State	24–7	Ann Arbor
1966	Michigan State	20–7	East Lansing
1967	Michigan State	34–0	Ann Arbor
1968	Michigan	28–14	Ann Arbor
1969	Michigan State	23–12	East Lansing
1970	Michigan	34–20	Ann Arbor
1971	Michigan	24–13	East Lansing
1972	Michigan	10–0	Ann Arbor
1973	Michigan	31–0	East Lansing
1974	Michigan	21–7	Ann Arbor
1975	Michigan	16–6	East Lansing
1976	Michigan	42–10	Ann Arbor
1977	Michigan	24–14	East Lansing
1978	Michigan State	24–15	Ann Arbor
1979	Michigan	21–7	East Lansing
1980	Michigan	27–23	Ann Arbor
1981	Michigan	38–20	East Lansing
1982	Michigan	31–17	Ann Arbor
1983	Michigan	42–0	East Lansing
1984	Michigan State	19–7	Ann Arbor
1985	Michigan	31–0	East Lansing
1986	Michigan	27–6	Ann Arbor
1987	Michigan State	17–11	East Lansing
1988	Michigan	17–3	Ann Arbor
1989	Michigan	10–7	East Lansing
1990	Michigan State	28–27	Ann Arbor
1991	Michigan	45–28	East Lansing
1992	Michigan	35–10	Ann Arbor
1993	Michigan State	17–7	East Lansing
1994	Michigan	40–20	Ann Arbor
1995	Michigan State	28–25	East Lansing

The Rivalries

Chris Perry gets upended by Minnesota's Ukee Dozier in the 2001 battle for the Little Brown Jug. The oldest trophy in college football, it's been a part of the Michigan-Minnesota rivalry since 1903.

1996	Michigan	45–29	Ann Arbor
1997	Michigan	23–7	East Lansing
1998	Michigan	29–17	Ann Arbor
1999	Michigan State	34–31	East Lansing
2000	Michigan	14–0	Ann Arbor
2001	Michigan State	26–24	East Lansing
2002	Michigan	49–3	Ann Arbor
2003	Michigan	27–20	East Lansing
2004	Michigan	45–37 (3OT)	Ann Arbor
2005	Michigan	34–31 (OT)	East Lansing
2006	Michigan	31–13	Ann Arbor
2007	Michigan	38–24	East Lansing
2008	Michigan State	35–21	Ann Arbor

Michigan vs. Minnesota

Although the series hasn't been the most competitive, the Little Brown Jug is the oldest trophy game in college football.

Michigan team manager Tommy Roberts originally purchased the jug, which can hold approximately five gallons of water, from a Minneapolis store in 1903 for 30 cents because Coach Fielding Yost feared tainted water (which back then wasn't as far-fetched as it sounds).

The Golden Gophers entered the game unbeaten, and the Wolverines were riding a 28-game winning streak. The game ended prematurely in a 6–6 tie after spectators rushed the field, and storm clouds were also in the area. In Michigan's haste to leave, the jug was left behind.

Oscar Munson found it and gave it to the school's athletics director, L.J. Cooke, and the jug was subsequently inscribed with "Michigan Jug—Captured by Oscar, October 31, 1903."

When Yost wrote asking for the jug's return, Cooke responded, "If you want it, you'll have to come up and win it."

The Wolverines had to wait until 1909, but they did

The Rivalries

just that with a 15–6 victory.

In 1930 the jug was stolen from the Michigan athletic department and wasn't found for four years, until an Ann Arbor gas station attendant discovered it behind some bushes. Now stored in a metal case, the jug is painted in the colors of both schools and features the score of each game.

The Little Brown Jug
Michigan vs. Minnesota

(Michigan leads series 70-24-3)

Date	Winner	Score	Site
1903	Tie	6–6	Minneapolis
1909	Michigan	15–6	Minneapolis
1910	Michigan	6–0	Ann Arbor
1919	Minnesota	34–7	Ann Arbor
1920	Michigan	3–0	Minneapolis
1921	Michigan	38–0	Ann Arbor
1922	Michigan	16–7	Minneapolis
1923	Michigan	10–0	Ann Arbor
1924	Michigan	13–0	Minneapolis
1925	Michigan	35–0	Ann Arbor
1926	Michigan	20–0	Ann Arbor
	Michigan	7–6	Minneapolis
1927	Minnesota	13–7	Ann Arbor
1929	Michigan	7–6	Minneapolis
1930	Michigan	7–0	Ann Arbor
1931	Michigan	6–0	Ann Arbor
1932	Michigan	3–0	Minneapolis
1933	Tie	0–0	Ann Arbor
1934	Minnesota	34–0	Minneapolis
1935	Minnesota	40–0	Ann Arbor
1936	Minnesota	26–0	Minneapolis
1937	Minnesota	39–6	Ann Arbor
1938	Minnesota	7–6	Minneapolis
1939	Minnesota	20–7	Ann Arbor

Brandon Graham chases down Minnesota's Adam Weber in 2008. The Wolverines retained the Little Brown Jug, which they have not lost since 2005 and have owned for every other season since 1987.

1940	Minnesota	7–6	Minneapolis
1941	Minnesota	7–0	Ann Arbor
1942	Minnesota	16–14	Minneapolis
1943	Michigan	49–6	Ann Arbor
1944	Michigan	28–13	Minneapolis
1945	Michigan	26–0	Ann Arbor
1946	Michigan	21–0	Minneapolis
1947	Michigan	13–6	Ann Arbor
1948	Michigan	27–14	Minneapolis
1949	Michigan	14–7	Ann Arbor
1950	Tie	7–7	Minneapolis
1951	Michigan	54–27	Ann Arbor
1952	Michigan	21–0	Ann Arbor
1953	Minnesota	22–0	Minneapolis
1954	Michigan	34–0	Ann Arbor
1955	Michigan	14–13	Minneapolis
1956	Minnesota	20–7	Ann Arbor
1957	Michigan	24–7	Minneapolis
1958	Michigan	20–19	Ann Arbor
1959	Michigan	14–6	Minneapolis
1960	Minnesota	10–0	Ann Arbor
1961	Minnesota	23–20	Minneapolis
1962	Minnesota	17–0	Ann Arbor
1963	Minnesota	6–0	Minneapolis
1964	Michigan	19–12	Ann Arbor
1965	Minnesota	14–13	Minneapolis
1966	Michigan	49–0	Ann Arbor
1967	Minnesota	20–15	Minneapolis
1968	Michigan	33–20	Ann Arbor
1969	Michigan	35–9	Minneapolis
1970	Michigan	39–13	Ann Arbor
1971	Michigan	35–7	Minneapolis
1972	Michigan	42–0	Ann Arbor
1973	Michigan	34–7	Minneapolis
1974	Michigan	49–0	Ann Arbor

1975	Michigan	28–21	Minneapolis
1976	Michigan	45–0	Ann Arbor
1977	Minnesota	16–0	Minneapolis
1978	Michigan	42–10	Ann Arbor
1979	Michigan	31–21	Ann Arbor
1980	Michigan	37–14	Minneapolis
1981	Michigan	34–13	Minneapolis
1982	Michigan	52–14	Ann Arbor
1983	Michigan	58–10	Minneapolis
1984	Michigan	31–7	Ann Arbor
1985	Michigan	48–7	Minneapolis
1986	Minnesota	20–17	Ann Arbor
1987	Michigan	30–20	Minneapolis
1988	Michigan	22–7	Ann Arbor
1989	Michigan	49–15	Minneapolis
1990	Michigan	35–18	Ann Arbor
1991	Michigan	52–6	Minneapolis
1992	Michigan	63–13	Ann Arbor
1993	Michigan	58–7	Minneapolis
1994	Michigan	38–22	Ann Arbor
1995	Michigan	52–17	Ann Arbor
1996	Michigan	44–10	Minneapolis
1997	Michigan	24–3	Ann Arbor
1998	Michigan	15–10	Minneapolis
2001	Michigan	31–10	Ann Arbor
2002	Michigan	41–24	Minneapolis
2003	Michigan	38–35	Minneapolis
2004	Michigan	27–24	Ann Arbor
2005	Minnesota	23–20	Ann Arbor
2006	Michigan	28–14	Minneapolis
2007	Michigan	34–10	Ann Arbor
2008	Michigan	29–6	Minneapolis

The Rivalries

TRADITIONS

THE COLORS

The school's official colors, maize and blue, have been around longer than the football program. A committee of students in the literary department selected the colors in 1867. The colors worn by Michigan's athletic teams were unofficially selected as deep blue and bright yellow by the Athletic Association in the early 1900s. The uniforms have undergone changes over the years, but the football team began wearing blue jerseys in 1927 and added white "away" jerseys in 1949. Player names were added to the jerseys beginning in 1980.

THE HELMET

Legendary Coach Fritz Crisler was responsible for the most recognizable helmet in college football. When Crisler took over as head coach in 1938, he replaced the team's then-black helmets with the winged design featuring the school's maize and blue colors. Crisler added the winged design "to dress it up a little," he claimed. But the new look was not just for styling. Crisler felt it would aid his quarterbacks in finding receivers downfield. Incidentally, the Wolverines doubled their passing yards and cut their interceptions nearly in half the first year they wore the redesigned helmets.

WOLVERINES

How Michigan acquired the nickname "Wolverines" is largely unknown. The ferocious carnivore is not indigenous to the state, but Michiganders have carried the moniker at least since the border dispute with Ohio known as the "Toledo War" in 1803. Researchers have speculated that its origin dates back to the days of the fur trade, when Sault Ste. Marie served as a hub for wolverine pelts in the 1700s. In 1927 a pair of wolverines named Bennie and Biff were paraded around

Michigan Stadium in cages on game days, but their nasty dispositions led to their retirement after just one season.

THE BAND

The biggest unit representing the school at football games is not the team. The University of Michigan Marching Band typically consists of 225 people and has been part of the school's tradition longer than the team. It was originally formed in 1844, began performing at football games in 1899, and was nicknamed "The Transcontinental Band" after performing at Yankee Stadium and the Rose Bowl during the 1950 season. The marching band was also the first from the collegiate ranks to perform at the Super Bowl, in 1973.

The Michigan Marching Band claims to have originated the "Script Ohio," unveiled October 15, 1932, in Columbus, Ohio, to honor its hosts.

The inaugural Sudler Trophy, awarded annually to the nation's top college marching band, was bestowed upon the Michigan Marching Band in 1983.

"THE VICTORS"

Louis Elbel attended Michigan's 12–11 conference championship victory over Chicago in 1898 and left Marshall Field feeling that the school needed a proper victory song. The Michigan Marching Band played "Hot Time in the Old Town," and Elbel, a music student, felt it didn't measure up to the moment. The melody for "The Victors" popped into his head as he walked home that day. He composed the song on the piano the following evening and changed the song into a march while taking a train to Ann Arbor. At the urging of his brother, Elbel had band arranger E.R. Schremser prepare song sheets for 23 instruments. John Philip Sousa and his band were the first to play the song, and the marching band adopted the song to celebrate athletic victories in May 1899. Here are the lyrics:

Traditions

Hail! To the victors valiant
Hail! To the conqu'ring heroes
Hail! Hail! To Michigan
The leaders and the best
Hail! To the victors valiant
Hail! To the conqu'ring heroes
Hail! Hail! To Michigan
The champions of the West!

MICHIGAN STADIUM

The "Big House" has been the home of Michigan football since 1927. Originally seating 72,000 spectators, the stadium was built with 440 tons of reinforcing steel and 31,000 square feet of wire mesh on land that had once been home to a barn, a strawberry patch, and an underground spring. Coach Fielding Yost had the foresight during the planning stages to allow for expansion. Michigan defeated Ohio Wesleyan 33–0 in the first game at Michigan Stadium on October 1, 1927, but the stadium was actually dedicated on October 22, 1927, with a 21–0 victory over Ohio State. The facility was filled to capacity with 84,401 in attendance for the event.

Over the years, seating capacity grew to its current 107,501 (with ongoing renovations scheduled to be completed in 2010). Michigan set an NCAA single-game attendance record in 2003 when 112,118 fans jammed the stadium to watch the 35–21 victory against Ohio State.

GAME DAY

The Michigan Marching Band leads the way from campus to the stadium entrance before each home game, with a thousand or more fans in its wake. The golf course across from the stadium is premium tailgating real estate. Fans climb up over a hundred rows of seats in Michigan Stadium, the nation's largest football stadium, to take their places and await the arrival of their

A capacity crowd of 97,000 packs Michigan Stadium for the 1949 contest against Michigan State. The Big House is home to the largest crowds to ever see football games, including more than 112,000 for the 2003 game with Ohio State.

team. As game time approaches, the players burst from the tunnel and run onto the field under the Michigan football banner. Players and cheerleaders alike jump up to touch it as they stream underneath.

BOB UFER

As much as Fielding Yost, Bo Schembechler, Benny Friedman, Desmond Howard, Tom Harmon, or even Tom Brady, Bob Ufer is a revered Michigan icon. The voice of Michigan football from 1945 through 1981, Ufer was the most blatant "homer" in broadcasting annals, and he made no apologies for it. For televised Michigan games, fans across the state would mute their TVs and listen to Ufer's call.

Among many colorful "Uferisms" are his description of a back "running like a penguin with a hot herring in his cummerbund." He referred to Woody Hayes and Ohio State as "Doctor StrangeHayes and his scarlet and gray legions." It was Ufer who coined the term "Mee-chigan." Not to mention "God bless your cotton-pickin' maize and blue hearts."

Ufer, a world-class middle-distance runner as a Michigan student in the early 1940s, broadcast 362 games from 1945 until he died of cancer in 1981.

Bob Ufer honked a horn from General George Patton's Jeep after big Michigan plays. The horn would sound three times for a touchdown, twice for a field goal or safety, and once for an extra point.

THE GREATEST TEAMS

1901–1905 (55–1–1)

Fielding H. "Hurry Up" Yost coached Michigan through the first quarter of the 20th century. During his first five seasons, his immortal "point-a-minute" teams put up 2,821 points to the opposition's 42. From 1901 through 1904, Michigan did not lose a game and claimed a share of the national title all four years. Yost chose his 1902 "Heston backfield" as the best of his coaching tenure. With Willie Heston at left half, joined by halfbacks Albert Herrnstein and Everett Sweeley, fullback Neil Snow, and Harrison Weeks at quarterback, the 1902 Wolverines outscored their opponents 644–12 on the way to an 11–0 record. The previous year, Yost's first in Ann Arbor, Michigan finished 11–0 with a 550–0 total score. On New Year's Day, 1902, Yost took his team out to California to play in the inaugural Tournament of Roses Game (now called the Rose Bowl) and beat his old employer, Stanford, 49–0. The game was so one-sided that 14 years passed before there was another one.

1923 (8–0)

Michigan captured the sixth national title of the Yost era in 1923, posting a perfect 8–0 record. The Wolverines outscored the opposition 150–12, including five shutouts. Halfback Harry Kipke and center Jack Blott were All-Americans. Both would go on to coach Michigan to championship: Kipke as head coach, Blott as line coach.

1933 (7–0–1)

Coach Harry Kipke brought a national title to his alma mater in 1933 behind All-American center Charles Bernard, whom pro coaches called the great-

Tom Harmon, Michigan's first Heisman Trophy winner, kicks an extra point in front of mostly empty stands at Chicago's Stagg Field in 1939. The Wolverines destroyed the Maroons 85–0.

est college player in the country that year, and tackle Frances "Whitey" Wistert. Quarterback Stanley Fay served as team captain. Only a tie with Minnesota, which would go on to win the national championship the following year, marred an otherwise perfect record. The 1933 Wolverine defense never allowed more than six points and held five of eight opponents scoreless.

1940 (7–1)

The Wolverines finished third in the national rankings, their only blemish being a 7–6 loss to Minnesota, which went on to win the national championship. Michigan won the first of its four Heisman Trophies, honoring halfback Tom Harmon. Fullback Bob Westfall and end Edward Frutig joined Harmon as All-Americans. Only three opponents managed to score on the 1940 Michigan team, captained by quarterback Forest Evashevski.

1947 (10–0)

Few if any teams ever played offense with the precision and verve of Fritz Crisler's "Mad Magicians" of 1947. Their execution of the buck lateral and spinner cycle out of the single-wing formation left opponents frustrated, often leading them to tackling two or three Michigan backs, none of whom had the ball. The Wolverines also had two All-American halfbacks with Bob Chappuis, the Heisman Trophy runner-up, and Chalmers "Bump" Elliott. Led by tackle Alvin Wistert, end Len Ford, and linebackers Dan Dworsky and Rick Kempthorn, the defense had five shutouts and gave up a total of 53 points. Gene Derricotte was the nation's premier punt returner. The Associated Press held a special post bowl poll—a first—after Michigan's 49–0 pounding of South California in the Rose Bowl. The vote bumped Michigan ahead of Notre Dame but wasn't binding.

Greatest Teams

1948 (9–0)

Fritz Crisler retired from coaching and left the team with Bennie Oosterbaan. Behind quarterback Pete Elliott, end Dick Rifenburg, and tackle Alvin Wistert, all All-Americans, the Wolverines extended their winning streak to 23 games, dating back to the middle of the 1946 season. Defensively the Wolverines yielded 44 points and tallied five shutouts. The conference's no-repeat rule precluded a postseason trip, but Michigan repeated as national champions. Oosterbaan's national title was the last by a first-year major-college head coach for 53 years.

1964 (9–1)

With Bump Elliott, one of the famous "Mad Magicians" of 1947, as head coach, Michigan reached the Rose Bowl and routed Oregon State, 34–7, to finish 9–1 and ranked No. 4 in both polls—one foot short of a national championship. On October 17 against Purdue, All-American quarterback Bob Timberlake ran through the Boilermaker defense for a 54-yard touchdown run, cutting a 21–14 deficit to 21–20 with less than five minutes remaining. But Timberlake, the Big Ten's MVP that season, was stopped just short on the two-point conversion.

1970–74 (50–4–1)

Bo Schembechler's teams of the early 1970s flirted with perfection, winning 50 of 55 games over five seasons. The star-studded units featured All-Americans at halfback (Billy Taylor), on the offensive line (Dan Dierdorf, Reggie McKenzie, and Paul Seymour), on the defensive line (David Gallagher and Henry Hill), at linebacker (Marty Huff and Mike Taylor), and in the secondary (Thom Darden, Randy Logan, and Dave Brown). The 1971 club took an 11–0 record to the Rose Bowl only to drop a one-point decision to Stanford.

Greatest Teams

1976 (10–2)

Michigan spent most of the season at No. 1, but the Wolverines were 8–0 on November 6, when a 16–14 loss at Purdue dropped them from the top spot. Rob Lytle amassed 1,469 rushing yards at 6.65 yards per carry on his way to Big Ten MVP honors. In addition to sophomore quarterback Rick Leach's passing, All-America linebacker Calvin O'Neal broke his own school record with 153 tackles after posting 151 the previous season.

1997 (12–0)

The first national championship in half a century came Michigan's way in 1997. Cornerback Charles Woodson became the first primarily defensive player ever to win the Heisman Trophy. He intercepted eight passes and also contributed to the offense and special teams. The offense also featured quarterback Brian Griese, running back Chris Howard, and receiver Tai Streets. Tight end Jerame Tuman and defensive end Glen Steele were All-Americans.

Charles Woodson completed his Heisman Trophy resume with a 78-yard punt return against Ohio State. He added an interception to help seal the win and convince voters he was the best player in college football that year.

Greatest Teams

THE GREATEST BOWL GAMES

1902 Rose Bowl
Michigan 49, Stanford 0

The Tournament of Roses had been celebrated on New Year's Day in Pasadena for more than a decade with a parade and various sporting events before a football game was added to the festivities. Michigan, "The champion of the West," was invited to play Stanford, the Pacific champion, in that inaugural game. The crowd of 8,000 on hand at Tournament Park witnessed Michigan run for 527 yards to Stanford's 67 in the 49–0 rout. Halfback Willie Heston picked up 170 of Michigan's yards, with fullback Neil Snow scoring five touchdowns. The game was called with more than eight minutes left to go as Stanford captain Ralph Fisher was delegated to concede the victory to the visitors. Michigan Coach Fielding Yost had been let go as Stanford coach after the previous season because of a rule calling for Stanford grads exclusively to coach Stanford's teams. The outcome was so lopsided that the Tournament of Roses committee replaced the football game with things like chariot races, ostrich races, and polo for the next 14 years before football returned in 1916.

1948 Rose Bowl
Michigan 49, Southern California 0

Michigan's second bowl game, the 1948 Rose Bowl, ended just like the first—in a 49–0 triumph. This time the victim was Southern California. Led by Heisman Trophy runner-up Bob Chappuis and conference MVP Bump Elliott, the Wolverines outgained the Trojans 491 yards to 133. Michigan scored in every quarter, took a 21–0 advantage into the locker room at halftime, and tacked on seven more points in the third quarter

Halfback Bob Chappuis was wrapped up by a Southern California tackler on this play but not before he picked up seven yards and a first down in the 1948 Rose Bowl. With 491 yards of total offense, the Wolverines whipped the Trojans.

and 21 more in the fourth. Notre Dame was ranked No. 1 at the time and had beaten USC 38–7 to conclude the regular season, but the Associated Press held a special nonbinding poll after the bowl games, with voters ousting Notre Dame from the top spot for Michigan.

1951 Rose Bowl
Michigan 14, California 6

Michigan brought a 5–3–1 record to Pasadena to face fifth-ranked California. Needless to say, the Golden Bears were favored to win. Cal outgained Michigan 192–65, racked up a 10–2 edge in first downs in the first half, and took a 6–0 lead by intermission. In the second half, Coach Bennie Oosterbaan's Wolverines picked up 226 total yards and 15 first downs compared to 52 yards and two first downs for California. Fullback Don Dufek ran for two Michigan touchdowns in the fourth quarter for the 14–6 victory.

1965 Rose Bowl
Michigan 34, Oregon State 7

Michigan finished the 1964 regular season with an 8–1 record, the Big Ten title, and a fourth-place national ranking. Oregon State came into Pasadena 8–2 and ranked eighth. After a scoreless first period, the Beavers reached the end zone first on a 5-yard touchdown pass from Paul Brothers to Doug McDougall. Later in the second quarter, tailback Mel Anthony scored on an 84-yard run, and the rout was on. A 43-yard touchdown by Carl Ward put Michigan up 12–7 at the half. Game MVP Anthony scored twice more in the third quarter, and quarterback Bob Timberlake tacked on a 24-yard touchdown run down the sideline in the fourth. Michigan improved to 4–0 in the postseason.

1979 Rose Bowl
Southern California 17, Michigan 10

Although Bo Schembechler's fifth straight loss in the Rose Bowl was hardly cause for celebration, this was almost certainly the most controversial. The Trojans' winning touchdown was scored by running back Charles White, who was stripped of the ball by Ron Simpkins while crossing the goal line. Although Mark Braman recovered at the 1, many watching the game felt that while White may have reached the end zone, the ball did not.

1981 Rose Bowl
Michigan 23, Washington 6

Michigan lost two early season games by a combined total of five points, then rattled off eight straight wins, including three consecutive shutouts, and traveled to Pasadena having not surrendered a touchdown during the previous 18 quarters. Following the Rose Bowl victory against Washington, which managed just two field goals, the streak stood at 22 quarters. Wolverines tailback Butch Woolfolk ran for 182 yards, including a 6-yard touchdown run that put Michigan up 7–6 at halftime. Quarterback John Wangler and wide receiver Anthony Carter connected for a third-quarter touchdown. Michigan kicker Ali Haji-Sheikh added a 25-yard field goal, and Don Bracken set a Rose Bowl record with a 73-yard punt.

1986 Fiesta Bowl
Michigan 27, Nebraska 23

Michigan ended the regular season 9–1–1 and boasted the nation's top scoring defense. Nebraska had won nine straight, sandwiched between losses in the opener and the finale. The two conference runners-up met in the Fiesta Bowl. A 42-yard field goal by Michigan's Pat Moons, set up by a 21-yard Jamie Morris run, was the extent of the scoring in the first

Bo Schembechler hoists the hardware after his Wolverines topped Southern California in the 1989 Rose Bowl.
Schembechler left the school at the top: his last two
teams played in the Rose Bowl, splitting a pair of games
with the Trojans.

quarter. Nebraska scored twice before halftime, on a short pass from McCathorn Clayton to Doug DuBose and a three-yard DuBose run, for a 14–3 score. The Wolverines stormed back with 24 unanswered points in the third quarter, including a pair of short touchdown runs by quarterback Jim Harbaugh. Michigan forced six Cornhusker fumbles, recovering three, and Dave Arnold blocked a punt to set up a short Moons field goal. With the win, Michigan finished the season ranked second in both polls.

1988 Hall of Fame Bowl
Michigan 28, Alabama 24

With Bo Schembechler recuperating from heart surgery, offensive coordinator Gary Moeller stepped in against Alabama. The Wolverines took control in the second quarter with touchdown runs of 25 and 14 yards by Jamie Morris for a 14–3 halftime lead. In the third quarter, Morris notched a 77-yard touchdown run, extending the margin to 21–3. But the Crimson Tide took the lead on 21 unanswered points due to a 16-yard pass from Jeff Dunn to Howard Cross and two Bobby Humphrey touchdown runs. With the clock winding down and Michigan facing fourth-and-three, quarterback Demetrius Brown hit flanker John Kolesar on a 20-yard touchdown pass for the 28–24 win. Morris ran for a Hall of Fame Bowl record and Michigan bowl-game record 234 yards.

1989 Rose Bowl
Michigan 22, Southern California 14

Bo Schembechler took No. 11 Michigan to face No. 5 Southern California, led by Heisman Trophy runner-up Rodney Peete. The quarterback scored twice on short runs in the second quarter for a 14–3 halftime team, but that was it for the Trojans. A 23-yard Brown-to-Walker pass and a 61-yard Leroy Hoard run set up a pair of one-yard scoring plunges by Hoard in the fourth quarter. Linebacker John Milligan clinched the victory with an interception with 50 seconds remaining. Leroy Hoard accumulated 142 rushing yards on 19 carries. Michigan finished No. 4 in the final Associated Press poll.

1998 Rose Bowl
Michigan 21, Washington State 16

Michigan added emphasis to its most recent national title with a 21–16 Rose Bowl victory over Pac-10 champion Washington State. A 15-yard scoring pass from Ryan Leaf to Kevin McKenzie put the Cougars on top 7–0 to end the first quarter. In the second, Michigan QB Brian Griese and wide receiver Tai Streets connected on the first of two long touchdown passes, from 53 yards out, to knot the score at 7 entering intermission. In the third quarter, Leaf engineered a 99-yard drive that culminated in a 14-yard reverse by wide receiver Michael Tims to reclaim the lead for the Cougars. Michigan's James Hall blocked the PAT attempt, and the score remained 13–7. Then came Griese-to-Streets II—a 58-yard scoring bomb that put the Wolverines up to stay, 14–13. In the fourth quarter, Griese found tight end Jerame Tuman from 23 yards out to extend the lead to 21–13. Washington State added a field goal to pull within striking distance at 21–16, but Michigan held the ball for the next seven minutes, converting three third downs in the process, and time ran out on the Cougars. Griese received game MVP honors on the strength of an 18-for-30, 251-yard, three-touchdown passing performance. The 12–0 Wolverines were national champions for the 11th time.

2000 Orange Bowl
Michigan 35, Alabama 34, overtime

The Maize and Blue had to overcome 14-point deficits twice to win the first overtime game in Michigan history. After a scoreless first quarter, the Crimson

Anthony Thomas plows into the end zone for a touchdown in the 2000 Orange Bowl, driving an Alabama defender back. In a battle of two of the nation's best running backs, Thomas' Wolverines were one point better than Shaun Alexander's Crimson Tide.

Tide took a 14–0 lead in the second on a pair of Shaun Alexander touchdown runs, but the Wolverines answered with a 27-yard scoring pass from Tom Brady to David Terrell in the second quarter and a 57-yard Brady-to-Terrell strike in the third. Alabama took another two-touchdown lead in the fourth quarter on a 50-yard Alexander run and a 62-yard Freddie Milons punt return, only to see Michigan pull even again. Brady hit tight end Shawn Thompson on a 25-yard scoring strike on Michigan's first play in overtime, and Hayden Epstein made what turned out to be the game-winning extra point. After Andrew Zow connected with Antonio Carter for a 21-yard score, the PAT failed.

2003 Outback Bowl
Michigan 38, Florida 30

Michigan quarterback John Navarre completed 21 of 36 passes for 319 yards, and Florida's Rex Grossman went 21-of-41 for 323 yards, but Chris Perry stole the show. Michigan's junior running back ripped Florida's defense for 193 yards, 85 rushing and 108 receiving, and scored four touchdowns.

2005 Rose Bowl
Texas 38, Michigan 37

Although Michigan didn't come out on top, its first-ever meeting with Texas was memorable, with the Longhorns pulling out the victory on the final play, a 37-yard field goal by Dusty Mangum as time expired. Although sophomore quarterback Vince Young accounted for 372 yards total offense and all five Longhorn touchdowns, with 180 passing yards and 192 rushing, Michigan quarterback Chad Henne was the first true freshman to start a Rose Bowl and passed for 227 yards. Setting Rose Bowl records were Henne (four touchdown passes), wide receiver Braylon Edwards (three touchdown receptions), and wide receiver/kick returner Steve Breaston (315 all-purpose yards).

THE GREATEST GAMES

1950: Michigan 9, Ohio State 3

It was more "survival of the fittest" than a game. Under the most trying of conditions, the Wolverines upset the Buckeyes in a game forever known as the "Snow Bowl." A two-day blizzard, including nine inches of snow the morning of the game, struck Columbus, Ohio, that weekend. Ice and snow covered the field and stands, but, amazingly, more than 50,000 spectators still showed up. Michigan, which punted 24 times, won despite not gaining a first down or completing a pass. Tony Momsen blocked a Vic Janowicz punt and recovered it in the end zone for a touchdown, and another block resulted in a safety.

1969: Michigan 24, Ohio State 12

First-year Michigan Coach Bo Schembechler guided the Wolverines to a stunning upset of the No. 1 Buckeyes, who had won 22 straight games and seemed destined to repeat as national champions. Still fuming over a 36-point loss in Columbus the previous season in which Woody Hayes ran up the score, the fired-up Wolverines forced seven turnovers and held the Buckeyes scoreless in the second half. Michigan fullback Garvie Craw scored two rushing touchdowns.

1995: Michigan 31, Ohio State 23

Running back Tshimanga Biakabutuka spoke five languages fluently, but his feet did all the talking against Ohio State. Biakabutuka rushed for 313 yards as the Wolverines upset the No. 2 Buckeyes. Biakabutuka gained 22 yards on his first carry and kept going, upstaging Heisman Trophy winner Eddie George in the process.

The Greatest Games

1997: Michigan 20, Ohio State 14

The victory resulted in a perfect regular season, another year of bragging rights, a trip to the Rose Bowl, and a Heisman Trophy-clinching performance. Junior defensive back Charles Woodson won over a majority of Heisman voters with a 78-yard punt return for a touchdown and a crucial interception. Linebacker Ian Gold batted down a fourth-down pass attempt to secure the win. The No. 1 Wolverines went on to win their first national championship in 49 years, beating Washington State in the Rose Bowl.

2001: Michigan State 26, Michigan 24

It came down to the last second, even if Michigan fans will forever believe the Spartans undeservingly got an extra play. The Wolverines thought they had Michigan State stopped short of the end zone, but the clock read 0:01 after Spartans quarterback Jeff Smoker spiked the ball. He subsequently threw a touchdown pass to running back T.J. Duckett for the victory. Michigan State's final drive was prolonged by two Michigan penalties, including a personal-foul call on a fourth-down pass.

2003: Michigan 38, Minnesota 35

Even the Wolverines had a hard time believing that they managed to successfully erase a 21-point, fourth-quarter deficit at the Metrodome. "We still don't know what happened," defensive end Larry Stevens said after Michigan scored 31 points in the final quarter to complete the biggest comeback in school history. Quarterback John Navarre passed for 353 yards, all but 50 after halftime. He threw two fourth-quarter touchdown passes and caught another from receiver Steve Breaston. Running back Chris Perry caught 11 passes for 122 yards and rushed for another 84 yards. Freshman kicker Garrett Rivas made a 33-yard field goal with 47 seconds remaining to complete the scoring.

Quarterback Brian Griese acknowledges the cheering fans at Michigan Stadium after the Wolverines knocked off Ohio State in 1997 to seal their trip to the Rose Bowl. The Wolverines toppled Washington State on New Year's Day to seal their national title.

Thanks, Acknowledgments, and Sources

Thank you to my family for your love, support, and patience. The same goes for my extended family around the country and world. You all know who you are and how important you are to me (even when I ignore your emails, phone calls, and instant messages while doing things like writing books).

Thank you Tom Bast for green-lighting this project and everyone at Triumph Books who worked on it.

Thank you, fans. Without you, this project never would have happened.

The sources for this book are essentially too numerous to list, but most of the accumulated information simply came from years of being a sportswriter, along with the numerous official team sources. That means more media guides, Internet sites, press conferences, interviews, transcripts, and press releases than you can imagine—and numerous bowls, conferences, services, and teams. Some additional sources deserve special mention:

University of Michigan 2004 Media Guide
University of Michigan 2008 Media Guide
2008 Michigan Spring Football Guide
mgoblue.com
ESPN.com
The Association Press
The Official 2008 Division I and Division I-AA Football Records Book
The College Football Hall of Fame website
The Pro Football Hall of Fame website
ESPN College Football Encyclopedia: The Complete History of the Game, by
   Michael MacCambridge, 2005
2008 SEC Football Media Guide
NCAA.com
NFL.com
Sugar Bowl Classic: A History, by Marty Mule, 2008
Rose Bowl website

About the Author

Christopher Walsh has been an award-winning sportswriter since 1990 and currently covers the University of Alabama football program for the *Tuscaloosa News*. He's been twice nominated for a Pulitzer Prize, won three Football Writers Association of America awards, and received the 2006 Herby Kirby Memorial Award, the Alabama Sports Writers Association's highest honor. Originally from Minnesota and a graduate of the University of New Hampshire, he currently resides in Tuscaloosa.

His previous books include:

100 Things Crimson Tide Fans Need to Know & Do Before They Die, 2008.

Who's No. 1? 100-Plus Years of Controversial Champions in College Football, 2007.

Where Football is King: A History of the SEC, 2006.

No Time Outs: What It's Really Like to be a Sportswriter Today, 2006.

Crimson Storm Surge: Alabama Football, Then and Now, 2005.

Return to Glory: The Story of Alabama's 2008 Season, 2009 (contributing writer).

The "Huddle Up" series will remain a work in progress. To make comments, suggestions, or share an idea with the author, go to http://whosno1.blogspot.com/. Check out other 2009 editions: Texas, Alabama, Notre Dame, Ohio State, Oklahoma, Tennessee, and the New York Giants.

Dedication

For Mary

Triumph Books
542 South Dearborn Street
Suite 750
Chicago, Illinois 60605
(312) 939-3330
Fax (312) 663-3557
www.triumphbooks.com

Printed in U.S.A.
ISBN: 978-1-60078-181-0

Design by Mojo Media Inc.

Photos courtesy of AP Images except where otherwise noted.